Queer Blood and Fire

Queer Blood *and* Fire

The Experiences of Gay and Lesbian Salvation Army Officers

BY
Brad Watson

RESOURCE *Publications* · Eugene, Oregon

QUEER BLOOD AND FIRE
The Experiences of Gay and Lesbian Salvation Army Officers

Copyright © 2025 Brad Watson. All rights reserved. Except for brief quotations in critical publications or reviews, no part of this book may be reproduced in any manner without prior written permission from the publisher. Write: Permissions, Wipf and Stock Publishers, 199 W. 8th Ave., Suite 3, Eugene, OR 97401.

Resource Publications
An Imprint of Wipf and Stock Publishers
199 W. 8th Ave., Suite 3
Eugene, OR 97401

www.wipfandstock.com

PAPERBACK ISBN: 979-8-3852-6306-6
HARDCOVER ISBN: 979-8-3852-6307-3
EBOOK ISBN: 979-8-3852-6308-0

VERSION NUMBER 11/21/25

This book is dedicated to the Salvation Army officers who offered a sacred trust in sharing their stories through both the survey and interviews. I trust that I have honoured them faithfully. It is also dedicated to all the queer Salvationists around the world who serve, often under hardship and sometimes direct attack, yet graciously continue to minister to the needs of their communities as faithful disciples of Jesus.

Thanks are recorded to my parents, Ritchie and Gail, my partner Jason, and my children Zoe and Dominic. Your support has been precious. Also, thanks to my doctoral supervisors Reverend Professor Glen O'Brien, University of Divinity–Melbourne, and Professor Doug Ezzy, University of Tasmania–Hobart. Your guidance and expertise were second to none.

Contents

List of Tables | viii

Introduction | 1

Section 1—History

Chapter 1: History and Social Context of The Salvation Army and the LGBTQ+ Community | 21

Chapter 2: Growing Up and Joining Up: The Salvation Army's Teaching on LGBTQ+ People to LGBTQ+ People | 51

Section 2—Harm

Chapter 3: Moral Injury | 75

Chapter 4: Religious Trauma | 95

Chapter 5: Sexual Orientation and Gender Identity Change Efforts | 112

Chapter 6: Discrimination, Internalized Homophobia, and Suicide | 126

Section 3—Hope

Chapter 7: Authenticity | 145

Chapter 8: Opportunity | 162

Chapter 9: Writing a Hopeful Queer Future for The Salvation Army | 183

Chapter 10: Writing a Hopeful Queer Theology for The Salvation Army | 198

Appendix 1—Survey | 227

Appendix 2—Interview Questions | 241

Bibliography | 245

List of Tables

Table 1—*Self-identification of Sexuality* | 8
Table 2—*Officer Status* | 9
Table 3—*College Location* | 10
Table 4—*Age of Participants* | 10
Table 5—*Years of Service as Officers* | 11
Table 6—*Survey Participants' Officer Training College* | 66
Table 7—*Interview Participants' Officer Training College* | 67
Table 8—*Summary of Moral Injury Intervention Resources* | 91
Table 9—*Congregational Attitudes to LGBTQ+ People* | 107
Table 10—*Types of SOGICE Practised in TSA* | 117

Introduction

THE BOOK IS ABOUT the lived experience of officers of The Salvation Army (TSA) in Australia who identify as having diverse sexuality. An officer is a Salvation Army member "who has been trained, commissioned and ordained to service and leadership in response to God's call. An officer is a recognized minister of religion."[1]

The Salvation Army rightfully enjoys a celebrated place in the hearts and minds of many people. This book challenges that celebrated history and records harms done to a particular minority group through theology and practice. It demonstrates that the anti-discriminatory and person-centered approaches espoused and practiced in the organization's social and community programs are not equally applied to its own people. Remarkably, significant positive stories of authentic integrated living, unique ministry opportunities and theological reflection also emerge. Lessons for the church around diversity in creation, enlivened grace, justice through solidarity and advocacy, inclusive ministry, and community are all articulated.

The book is in three sections. The first is a review of the history of TSA and its relationship with the LGBTQ+ community. This is done through both literature review and reflection on the lived experience of the research participants as their lives intersect with particular moments in the historical narrative. A line is traced from the earliest days of TSA to current times considering the critical moments of omission in the metanarrative of the organization that reflect an epistemic injustice through silencing or neglect of the LGBTQ+ perspective or impact on that community. This epistemic injustice has most commonly been experienced

1. The Salvation Army, *The Salvation Army Year Book 2024*, 29.

through a testimonial injustice operative via identity prejudice, whereby people identifying as LGBTQ+ have a deflated credibility due to a prejudice against their person.[2] Significant events, government submissions, and key turning points (positive and negative) in the relationship between TSA and the LGBTQ+ community are noted.

A second line is traced through the theological teaching of TSA on LGBTQ+ relationships and same-sex erotic activity. This is done primarily through a review of materials used to disciple Salvationists at critical times in their discipleship journey, such as when they become soldiers within the movement. A solder is a "converted person at least 14 years of age who has, with the approval of the Corps (church) pastoral care council, been enrolled as a member of The Salvation Army after signing the soldier's covenant."[3] These materials are chosen as they are the ones that are used across the movement in discipleship and all participants in the research would have undertaken these "recruits' classes" at some time. Teaching in the area of LGBTQ+ people and relationships undertaken in the theological schools of TSA are also reviewed, although more briefly through the memories of the research participants. There is a general absence of commentary on same sex relationships prior to 1980 in either the written materials reviewed or the theological teachings as recalled by the participants. From 1980 through to the early 2010s there was an increased negative and at times venomous teaching reported. Following some critical incidents in 2012, there is silence again. The thirty-year window between the early 1980s and early 2010s is a critical timeframe as it is when many of the research participants grew up and/or joined the movement. Many also trained for officership during that period.

The second section of the book concentrates on those harms experienced by officers who identify as LGBTQ+ during their service in TSA. Chapter 3 discusses the evidence for moral injury among the participants, both self-generated and other-generated. Alongside the participants' stories, literature covering the progression of moral injury studies from its earliest days in military settings, such as Shay (1991), Litz (2009), and Brock & Lettini (2012), to more contemporary, Australian, and extra-military research by Frame (2015), Carey and Hodgson (2018), and others, are reviewed.[4] Moral injury considers the impact of being party to human

---

2. Fricker, *Epistemic Injustice*.
3. The Salvation Army, *The Salvation Army Year Book 2024*, 30.
4. Shay, "Learning About Combat Stress from Homer's Iliad"; Litz et al., "Moral Injury and Moral Repair in War Veterans," 695-706; Brock and Lettini, *Soul Repair*;

suffering that confronts one's core beliefs and values.[5] Self-generated moral injury is that caused through omission or commission of behaviors that violate one's one morals, values and beliefs. Other-generated moral injury occurs when the behavior of others violates or betrays one's morals, values, or beliefs. The symptomology for each is different, but both have some resemblance to post-traumatic stress disorder (PTSD) and in early consideration of moral injury it was considered a sub-set of PTSD.[6] In the moral injury chapter, there is discussion of the difference between the two (moral injury and PTSD) and the need for more work in this area as diagnosis of moral injury requires appropriate clinical testing.

Chapter 4 discusses the experience of religious trauma by the research participants. In many cases this has been through the experience of religious abuse. There is evidence of minority stress theory and microaggressions at play, which are both described in the chapter. The participants discuss the effect of religious trauma on their spiritual practices because of the way that events, rites, or disciplines have been used against them.

Sexual orientation and gender identity change efforts (SOGICE) are then discussed. While it was anticipated that there would be evidence of SOGICE experiences among the research participants, what was surprising was the scale and recency of these experiences. 46 percent of participants in the survey reported such experiences and they were discussed by many of the interview subjects. Some instances were recorded in the last decade, including at least one attempted exorcism. The breadth of SOGICE experiences was also extensive, from prayer ministries and video or book material, through to conferences and visits to overseas SOGICE practitioners funded by TSA.

Chapter 6 considers the nexus between workplace discrimination, internalized homophobia, and suicidal ideation. The clear progression for some participants from discrimination to mental health concerns was evident. Four of the interview participants discussed suicidal ideation, some on multiple occasions, and two discussed their need for hospitalization following mental health breakdowns. These experiences provide a view of the possibility of significant and potentially lethal harm through the experiences of the research participants during their service in TSA.

Frame, *Moral Injury*; Carey and Hodgson, "Chaplaincy, Spiritual Care and Moral Injury."

5. Litz et al., "Moral injury and moral repair in war veterans."

6. Frame, *Moral Injury*, 2.

The final section of the book considers the positive stories from the survey and interview participants. These are reflected in their pursuit of authenticity, opportunities for ministry, and a theological reflection that integrates sexuality and Christianity. The majority of the participants were 'out' and living as people seeking to live wholly and authentically as followers of Jesus who are also LGBTQ+. They articulate how this has been salvific for themselves and provided unique opportunities for ministry that have only occurred because they are both ministers of religion and queer.

The theology that has been expressed by the research participants is summarized at the conclusion. It is a story of acknowledging their place in the diverse creation of God, the strength and justice that comes through solidarity and support of others, and their contribution to ministry as gifted and Spirit-led disciples. More than anything, it is a reflection on grace, and of grace. This is grace in the face of adversity, hostility, and discrimination. It is found in the work of God around them and for them, the salvation experiences they have had, and the grace to live authentic lives that show the love of God to others. Their expression of holiness is centered in supporting, grace-filled community that reflects the ever-expansive and inclusive gospel.

Context

The Salvation Army is an international Christian movement that currently operates in 134 countries as a registered church and service provider with more than 100,950 employees.[7] It functions as a church that self-identifies as "an evangelical part of the universal Christian church" and also as a provider of social service programs. It has an officer force of 26,374 officers and around two million church members.[8]

The organization has long claimed to serve suffering humanity without discrimination, as noted in its international mission statement. Both internal and externally facing documents assert this claim, or expand upon it, as in the Inclusion Statement of The Salvation Army in Australia.[9] This claim, however, only applies in reality to members of the community seeking assistance from TSA. Officers and soldiers are

---

7. The Salvation Army, *The Salvation Army Year Book 2024*, 40.
8. The Salvation Army, *The Salvation Army Year Book 2024*, 40.
9. The Salvation Army. "Inclusion."

bound to rigid behavioral expectations, especially with regard to sexual behavior and relationships. Specifically, the expectation is that sexual behavior is only appropriate in a marriage relationship and that marriage is only sanctioned between one man and one woman. This continues to marginalize faithful Salvationists who are same-sex attracted and maintain committed relationships that are often examples of mutuality, respect, and faithfulness.

As The Salvation Army's international context is so broad, the scope of this research was confined to officers in Australia. In Australia, the international TSA rules around relationships are enforced, but in many states grass-roots attitudes are more inclusive. This research notes that there are state-by-state differences and an officer is more likely to feel safe in the workplace or congregation in Victoria or Tasmania, and less likely in Queensland.

Both current and former officers were surveyed and interviewed. This enabled consideration of whether sexuality was a factor in their resignation from officership. Comparisons are made between the locations for officer training and there is a noted difference in how pastoral care, sexual ethics, and SOGICE were considered and covered in the Sydney officer college, when compared to the Melbourne officer college. Officers trained in Sydney were more likely to be exposed to SOGICE through their officer training and introduced conceptually to SOGICE during class time. In some cases, SOGICE was then directly funded by TSA, with instances of financially supported SOGICE reported in New South Wales. Officers training in Melbourne were more likely to be exposed to SOGICE in corps or in placements, and some reported bullying by colleague cadets.[10]

The Author and the research

I was commissioned as a Salvation Army officer in November 1999, having trained in the Melbourne (Parkville) Salvation Army college. I have served in Australia in corps (church) appointments, youth work, communications, community services, and emergency services. I have

---

10. A 'corps' is a Salvation Army unit, akin to a parish in another denomination, where opportunities for gathered worship, service and evangelism are offered to members. It is usually led by a 'corps officer' (akin to a parish minister) and populated by soldiers and other members of TSA. A 'cadet' is a soldier of The Salvation Army in formal training and formation toward commissioning as an officer.

also served in a number of overseas countries as a humanitarian disaster responder under the banner of The Salvation Army.

I identify as gay, and this provides the context for my interest in this research. My engagement with the research question was shaped by my own experience, my own study, and my involvement with activities and groups engaged with improving the situation for other Salvationists who identify as LGBTQ+. This positioned me within the research as a reflexive insider, which presented both challenges and opportunities, but mostly benefits. I did not have to do the work of translating context in considering the stories that had been shared with me. I had the advantage of the perspective of someone who is both queer and an officer in Australia, enabling understandings that are only available as a reflexive insider with longitudinal experience of the subject matter.

To promote objectivity whilst capturing my own experiences, and to protect my own anonymity and privacy alongside the other participants, I completed the survey as a participant and then typed up a transcript as if I were an interview subject. My experience was then incorporated as if I were any other participant and amalgamated with the collective data of the surveys and the coded responses of the interviews.

The Research

This project was an interdisciplinary study that engaged with the disciplines of church history, religious studies, and practical theology. It was influenced by pastoral studies and sociology. Each discipline was utilized in conversation with each other and through a queer lens. The subject matter lent itself to such an approach. In order to place the lived experience of the participants in context, the historical work was required. An exploration of the impacts of their experience required a review of how the leadership, structures, policies, and practices of TSA each contributed to particular outcomes, including the psychological impacts experienced. To properly articulate their experience in a way that would help advance the conversation around equality in TSA, the work of practical theology was required.

Twenty-four surveys were completed by participants and used in the study. These were completed online in an anonymous format that required consent to participate through commencing the survey voluntarily following the provision of information about the research, and then a second consent at submission. In total forty-four surveys were commenced. Six were excluded as the surveys were completed by people who self-described as "straight." Fourteen were deleted as the second consent to participate was not completed via conscious submission at the end of the survey, leaving the twenty-four completed surveys.

Eleven people also participated in a long-form in-depth interview and their stories are included in the book. To volunteer, these people needed to directly contact the researcher following their survey. The interviews then occurred online following receipt of written consent by the participants. Using Zoom enabled a recording of the interview and subsequent transcription for accuracy. All recordings were deleted after the transcriptions were completed and confirmed. Fourteen people initially volunteered, of which two did not complete their consent forms, and one person subsequently withdrew consent. They were each therefore excluded from the report. All material related to those individuals has been deleted. Transcripts of the interviews were sent to participants who had provided consent and opportunity was given to edit, change, or delete anything they desired. Only following confirmation of their transcripts has material been included in the project. One person wrote a letter rather than participating in an interview.

All participants have been given pseudonyms in the book. All locations and dates that could identify people have been removed. There are three participants that have been given two pseudonyms to ensure that connecting parts of their story cannot be conflated in ways that may identify them. For additional protection, in chapters 2 and 5, there are sections where no stories are attributed to any persons, with pseudonyms or otherwise. The pseudonyms used throughout the book are names taken from New Testament followers of Jesus. This is done to reflect the ongoing faithful discipleship of the majority of those that participated in the research.

Twenty-four participants may appear to be a low number. In Australia there are currently 1525 Salvation Army officers, 624 active and 901 retired.[11] If the proportion of officers who are non-heterosexual or gender diverse is approximately 3 percent, then there are around fifty Australian officers who probably are LGBTQ+.[12] Twenty-four participants represent

11. The Salvation Army, *The Salvation Army Year Book 2024*, 69.

12. This figure (3 percent) is based on a national, representative survey that indicates 5.5 percent of all Australians, *2.9 percent of Christians*, and 8.4 percent of those with no religion identify their sexuality as lesbian, gay, bisexual, or 'other'. LGB+ Christians

just under half of that number and is not statistically insignificant even when considering those former officers who participated.

The participants self-identified mostly as gay or lesbian, with three pansexuals and two that identified as 'questioning':

Table 1: Self-Identification of Sexuality

Self-identification of sexuality	Number
Gay/Lesbian (same sex/ same gender attracted)	19
Pansexual (sex and gender unimportant in choice of partner)	3
Questioning	2
Total	24

The absence of bisexuals is noted, as is the absence of transgender participants. It is possible that some bisexual officers identify their sexuality according to the gender of the person that they are in relationship with, which for many Salvationists would be heterosexual by default (despite some same-sex attraction). Some traditionally would have considered themselves as "heterosexual with homosexual struggles" when they are possibly actually bisexual. Some of these people would have been excluded from the survey data by choosing to self-identify as "heterosexual/straight" in the survey.

The absence of transgender and nonbinary participants is not surprising. While there are several transgender and nonbinary Salvationists in Australia, it is doubted that any of them would see themselves in officership, partially because transgender and nonbinary officers have never been visible. Also, if officers were questioning their gender, it is doubtful that there would be sufficient safety to explore that within officership.

The participants' standing as officers was noted as either currently active in service, retired or as past officers who have left TSA for other employment, as follows:

---

appear to be distributed through all large Christian denominations. From: Ezzy et al., "LGBTQ+ Christians in Australia," Abstract.

INTRODUCTION

Table 2: Officer Status

Officer status	Number
A current active officer, cadet, or ministry candidate	14
A retired officer	1
A past officer who has left for other employment	9
Total	24

This is a positive spread of experience, weighted slightly toward active, current officers. It is a moment in time snapshot of their standing as officers and it is noted that some "active" officer participants may have resigned since the time of their survey or interview. I, for one, have left officership since the completion of the project.

The officers who trained reflect a spread of decades and training locations. The locations are indicative of the era in which people trained (for example, the East Melbourne college predated the Parkville college, which predated the Ringwood college). They also distinguish those who trained in the former Australian Eastern Territory from those who trained in the former Australia Southern Territory.[13] Eight trained in the former Australia Eastern Territory, nine in the former Australia Southern Territory, five in the Australia (reunited) Territory and one overseas.

---

13. The Salvation Army in Australia has had a number of different administrative structures. From 1881 the work in Australia was administered from headquarters in Melbourne. From 1921, Australia was split into two administrations with headquarters in Melbourne for the "Southern Territory" (Victoria, Tasmania, South Australia, Western Australia, and the Northern Territory) and Sydney for the "Eastern Territory" (Australian Capital Territory (when established), New South Wales, and Queensland). On December 1, 2018, TSA reverted to one Australian territory, headquartered in Melbourne.

Table 3: College Location

College location	Number
East Melbourne (Officer Training School)	1
Parkville (Salvation Army Training College)	7
Ringwood (Catherine Booth College/ Eva Burrows College)	6
Petersham (Officer Training School)	1
Bexley North (Salvation Army Training College/ Booth College)	7
Overseas	1
Candidate for training or cadet in training	1
Total	**24**

While they reflect a spread of age groups, the vast majority were aged between thirty and fifty years old. This tells us little, as many people do not train to be officers until they are in their thirties, and the upper age brackets would have lower representation following resignations.

Table 4: Age of Participants

Age	Number
18–30	1
30–50	12
50–65	7
65+	4
Total	**24**

The years of service were also spread, but the vast majority had less than twenty years of officer service. The average length of service for those who were interviewed was thirteen years. Especially when considering those participants who had resigned, this demonstrates that many others had undertaken committed, lengthy service.

Table 5: Years of Service as Officers

Years of service	Number
0–10	13
11–20	5
21–30	3
31–40	2
41–50	0
51–60	1
Total	24

Acronyms and definitions

Acronyms are explained on their first use and terms internal to TSA are explained on their first occurrence, either in text or in footnotes. The acronym LGBTQ+ is most commonly used and refers to people who identify as lesbian, gay, bisexual, transgender, queer or questioning. The plus encompasses those that are asexual, pansexual, and other gender and sexually diverse people, such as brother-boys and sister-girls.[14] While oftentimes the letter 'I' is also included in community acronyms, it is omitted here as this research did not include intersex participants. Conversely, the letter 'T' *is* retained, despite the absence of transgender participants, to keep a commonly recognized acronym for the reader. Where a shorter or varied acronym is used to describe the non-heterosexual community, for example LGB (lesbian, gay, bisexual), this is because it is either a quotation from an author using a different acronym, or it specifically refers to just those elements of the LGBTQ+ community.

"Queer" is also used occasionally as an inclusive and collective term for the LGBTQ+ community. This is a contested term due to the derogatory way it has been historically used. However, in the spirit of reclaiming

---

14. Aboriginal communities use the terms 'brother-boy' and 'sister-girl' to describe transgender people and their relationships in order to validate and strengthen their gender identities and relationships. Non-trans but non-gender-conforming Aboriginal people may also use these terms.

such terms and embracing their positive connotations, the term is used here with apologies to those who may struggle with it.

Methodology

The research endeavored to capture and understand the lived experience of LGBTQ+ Salvation Army officers. It used a qualitative methodology that aimed to observe experiences and phenomena, generate theory from said phenomena, and ultimately describe these experiences.

Qualitative research is inductive in that it is generative of theory.[15] There is a deductive element when a theory is being tested, but its general orientation is the interpretation of themes that are generated during the research process.[16] While this research presupposed that some harm or hardship may have been experienced by LGBTQ+ officers, and literature was surveyed in preparation for exploring related theories, the surveys and interviews also generated many positive stories and theological reflection. An openness to new and unexpected phenomena enabled the development of a more complete picture of the experiences of these officers. This picture included positive articulations of community and solidarity, affirmation of both sexuality and faith, relationship with God as a part of God's diverse and very good creation, and grace expressed through each area of their lives including their faithful relationships.

As a researcher I was conscious of my own positionality. Rather than hoping a methodology would eliminate all biases, or alternatively establish an assumed position, the research interrogates each subject and position reflexively.[17]

The generic methodology used in this research followed a certain pattern:[18]

- The research was developed through the researcher asking questions about the theoretical framework within which the research would be conducted, what the substantive issue to be researched should be, and what would be the desired outcome of the research.[19]

---

15. Strauss and Corbin, *Basics of Qualitative Research*, 8.
16. Fossey et al. "Understanding and Evaluating Qualitative Research," 717.
17. Neitz, "Insiders, Outsiders, Advocates and Apostates and the Religions They Study," 130.
18. Bryman, *Social Research Methods*, 268–70.
19. Liamputtong and Ezzy, *Qualitative Research Methods*, 2nd ed., 13.

- In selecting the subject group, the goal was to operate as a phenomenologist—studying the situation and everyday world from the viewpoint of the subject group.[20] Confining the scope of the subject group to one country, and therefore one Salvation Army territory, allowed for consistency of cultural setting, legislative frameworks affecting the organization, internal theology, organizational inclusion policies, officer management processes, and working environments.

- Relevant data was collected using methods appropriate to the research question. This research used surveys and in-depth interviews, supplemented by literature review.

- The data was interpreted with the aim of determining what the articulated experiences mean for the people who experienced them and comprehensively describe them.[21] Coding of the data into categories enabled the material to be sorted into the chapters that have evolved.

- This interpretive work was grounded in conceptual or theoretical frameworks with a broad view of both the past and the future, and also cultural factors that are at play in TSA in Australia.[22]

- Theological themes were observed throughout the interviews in particular. These were synthesized for discussion at the end of the book. They evolve from the intersection of the participants' experiences of faith and sexuality, and their positive articulation of theological matters that have developed from considered engagement with those experiences, as well as Scripture, reason, and tradition.

This research needed to consider the sensitivity of the subject material. Human sexuality is a private affair, especially in many religious circles. Because sensitive topics may pose threats to the research participants, trust was critical, and special consideration of organizational politics and ethics needed to be included.[23] Supports were offered to the participants through referral to external agencies specializing in LGBTQ+ services as well as employee assistance programs. Participants could exit participation at any stage and withdraw consent for their material to be used up until a few months after their transcript was completed and confirmed. Trust was

20. Liamputtong and Ezzy, *Qualitative Research Methods*, 18.
21. Liamputtong and Ezzy, *Qualitative Research Methods*, 19.
22. Liamputtong and Ezzy, *Qualitative Research Methods*, 28.
23. Lee, *Doing Research on Sensitive Topics*, 2.

developed in the assurances of security provided to participants and the communications provided prior to, and during, the interviews.

There was potential that it would be difficult to recruit participants due to the sensitivity of the research. This was ultimately done through advertising in TSA's national officer personnel newsletter and on social media pages dedicated to progressive Salvation Army practice. One closed social media group for LGBTQ+ Salvationists was also used. In each case, the owners of the online pages and newsletters provided written approval for the research to be promoted. Of note, the use of the officer personnel newsletter created some organizational curiosity in the research and drew some negative responses toward me as the researcher.

Surveys:

The survey was conducted using a Qualtrix platform under a license offered for this research by TSA's Policy, Research, and Social Justice Department in Melbourne. Confidentiality and distance to TSA's research team was assured throughout the online survey and data analysis, as only the author and one supervisor had password-protected access to the data.

Some questions were duplicative of those conducted in TSA's annual employee engagement survey. This enabled comparison with the general workforce of TSA in areas such as their experience of leadership and workplace discrimination. Some questions were duplicative of those utilized in research by Ezzy, Fielder and McLeay.[24] This enabled comparison with other Australian Christian denominations.

Interviews:

The qualitative research interview seeks to comprehend the world from the subject's point of view. The interviewer wants to understand the meaning of their experiences, to uncover their lived experience as they explain it and prior to theoretical explanation.[25] It allows for participants to elaborate on answers, give examples, and describe experiences. It then allows the researcher to reconstruct particular events and draw on lived experiences and eye-witness accounts.

---

24. Ezzy et al., "LGBTQ+ Christians in Australia."
25. Kvale and Brinkman, *InterViews*, 2nd ed., 1.

The interviews conducted in this research allowed for relationship and rapport to be built, even within the hour or so spent together. Topics were explored at depth and the researcher had the freedom, despite the pre-planned questions, to carefully pursue leads that arose in conversation. Having a planned structure to begin with, however, helped standardize the wording and sequence of thoughts and allowed for easier comparison of the interviews that were conducted.[26]

The assumption of vulnerability and the need for protection underlined and informed ethical considerations. In the interviews, the researcher could not overlook the possibility that participants could become empowered as the opportunity to amplify their voice and articulate their experiences through the research became apparent; how this would be acknowledged was somewhat difficult when an aim must be to protect anonymity. Ultimately, there was significant risk that the research could have endangered the participants. Preserving data security, confidentiality, and anonymity was paramount.

Interviews that record oral history and lived experience are particularly important in the LGBTQ+ community because, in some periods of history, there are silences in the written accounts. This research notes the silence of LGBTQ+ perspectives in TSA history, and silence on the impacts, unintended or intended, of the teaching and history of TSA on that community. Conducting these interviews as a research method with this cohort was vital in recovering the personal experiences, perspectives, and life journeys of this group. They bring to life both anecdotal and historical matter and break official silences so that a fuller understanding of situations could emerge.[27] Their perspectives on being authentic, serving faithfully, and being expressions of grace in the world called for particular attention.

Once the surveys were completed, interpreting the data appropriately was required prior to any theories being properly established and findings written. This was done using NVivo software which enabled coding and sorting of the material. The coding used was based on thematic analysis, as repeated words, themes, situations, or concepts emerged from reading the material. As I had membership in this ethnographic setting, I have tried to account for any tacit knowledge that was included or led to the development of the chapter themes.

26. Kvale and Brinkman, *InterViews*, 106.
27. Riseman and Robinson, *Pride in Defence*, 10-11.

It was important to ground the research in the data, the observations made and the literature that related to each topic. While categories were developed to bring the data to life, this was not to establish truth, but rather to conceptualize what had taken place in the lives of the participants and group these experiences together.

Special note regarding research in my own organization:

Conducting qualitative research within your own organization requires special care. The researcher's role/s vis-à-vis the organization will affect their approach to the research. For example, do they approach as outsider or insider, facilitator, or expert. There are plenty of advantages to being an "insider," for example: intimate knowledge of the organization. However, as an insider, the researcher cannot walk away from any unwelcome outcomes and may be seen as less independent or less objective.[28] A combination of observation and participation can give distinct experiences and empirical information that may not otherwise be available.[29] The key is to be conscious of how your position as an insider may affect your observations.

The complexity of the insider/outsider construct is particularly felt in religious organizations. The boundaries that determine insiders (and outsiders) are of central importance to religious groups, providing definition and relationship to their adherents. Positively, they enable the religious researcher to locate and contextualize subjects and to articulate their own standpoint vis-à-vis the religious group.[30] Also, where the researcher is an insider, they would have a lived appreciation of the sacred within that organization, including the cultural agents that created belonging and boundaries—indeed they may have a bond with the subjects of the research through such sacramental experiences.[31] This notion of the sacred can impact the approach to the research; is this a study of (or in) a religious group or is it a piece of theological study? The distinction between the two can be cloudy for the insider especially, despite both approaches trying to unravel some aspects of the mythmaking, identity, and culture of the organization.

28. Kayrooz and Trevitt, *Research in Organisations and Communities*, 12.
29. Fielder and Ezzy, *Lesbian, Gay, Bisexual, and Transgender Christians*, 170.
30. Knott, "Inside, Outside and the Space In-Between," 41-2.
31. Knott, "Inside, Outside and the Space In-Between," 45.

Neitz observes that the complexity of the insider/outsider issues are exacerbated by the position of the researcher in relation to the *position in society* of the religious group being researched. This could include how they (as a group) are positioned in the culture and construct of their society and whether they are a powerful religious tradition on the rise or embedded in the state, or a beleaguered or small religious group.[32] She has developed a helpful location matrix that divides researchers into four "cells" according to adherence and the situation of the religion (while helpful, she also accepts that it doesn't recognize the real complexities of the researcher situation).[33] In the case of this research, I may have held a senior role in the religious organization I was researching at the time, but they (The Salvation Army), in turn, have a complex relationship with the Australian community: broadly supported for their large social work and social enterprises, but diminishing as an evangelistic force and often on the outer for perceived religious positions, particularly with regards to LGBTQ+ matters. The following chapters will explore this relationship and religious position through the history and teaching of TSA in relations to people who identify as LGBTQ+.

Limitations

There is a limitation on the ability to provide solutions to religious and spiritual trauma. This is the realm of other fields of expertise, particularly psychology. I join Hollier in affirming that finding ways for LGBTQ+ people to heal from religious and spiritual trauma requires more research and appreciate the work of McConnaughey in this regard.[34] While she concentrates on broader experiences of trauma, including sexual assault, her lessons can be applied.[35]

Finally, more work needs to be done to consider the various intersectionalities at play in the lives of people such as those participating in this research. They are not just LGBTQ+ and Christian. Some are women, some are Indigenous, some have disabilities or chronic illnesses, some are from migrant backgrounds. The story that is told depends on

---

32. Neitz, "Insiders, Outsiders, Advocates and Apostates and the Religions They Study," 129.

33. Neitz, "Insiders, Outsiders, Advocates and Apostates and the Religions They Study," 137.

34. Hollier, *Religious Trauma, Queer Identities*, 201.

35. McConnaughey, *Trauma in the Pews*.

the perspective that is taken and the multiple overlaying identities and circumstances involved. There needs to be constant questioning of which voices or perspectives are missing at any given table.[36]

Contribution

When Joel Hollier completed his doctoral work, he acknowledged that more needed to be done to examine the experiences of LGBTQ+ clergy.[37] This needed to be done in a way that accounted for denominational leadership, theological education, and pastoral professional development. This book is one piece of work that contributes to the field in such a way.

It is the only study to date that investigates the lived experience of non-heterosexual Salvation Army officers. It is one of the few within the Wesleyan context overall, and the only one in Australia. While Wood, Halliday, Solevåg, Tyson, and Herben have been noted for their contributions to institutional or theological thinking around LGBTQ+ issues for TSA, none (other than Halliday's personal testimony) have been from the perspective of a group of queer Salvationists.

This is one of the first studies to also consider the experience of moral injury among queer Christians.[38] While there is an inability to fully diagnose such a condition without clinical tools applied on an individual level, there is sufficient evidence of symptomology and conditions that would contribute to the experience of such injury.

---

36. Pack, "The Future Church is LGBTQIA+ Inclusive," 25 January 2024.

37. Hollier, *Religious Trauma, Queer Identities*, 223.

38. For broader discussion about the risk of moral injury among LGBTQ+ people stemming from SOGICE, and the need for more research, see: Jones et al., "Religious Trauma and Moral Injury from LGBTQA+ Conversion Practices."

Section 1—**History**

Chapter 1: History and Social Context of The Salvation Army and the LGBTQ+ Community

THE SALVATION ARMY (TSA) has not had a positive history with the LGBTQ+ community. The experiences of LGBTQ+ officers within TSA are directly affected by this history, and impacted by the culture, story, legacy, and teachings of the past. This chapter provides an overview of the relevant events, statements, and intersections with social movements for TSA, in order to provide a historic framework that underpins the stories that research participants have shared during the surveys and the interviews. It draws on both historical studies, and the historical reflections of the participants. The Salvation Army's teachings on issues related to the LGBTQ+ community are included in chapter two.

TSA has historically been actively and implicitly involved in suppression of the LGBTQ+ community and support of criminalization of homosexual activity. Examples of this are seen through the inadvertent consequences of actions such as the "Maiden Tribute in Modern Babylon" campaign, exacerbated by links to British colonialism, overt opposition to decriminalization efforts, submissions to government supporting anti-LGBTQ+ policies, and support of Sexual Orientation and Gender Identity Change Efforts (SOGICE).[1]

In part, TSA's opposition to the LGBTQ+ community is a product of its place in history. The denomination is borne from Victorian-era morality and colonialism—a product of its time and place. In recent years

---

1. SOGICE have been variably named "Conversion Therapies," "Conversion Practices," "Ex Gay Therapies," and "Reparative Therapies," all of which are misnomers. SOGICE are discussed in chapter five.

this negative history has been exacerbated by engagement with SOGICE and conservative church resources, most often from the United States, use of particular translations of Scripture, and responses to related matters in the public sphere.

A turning point in Australia was the infamous Joy FM interview of 2012 in Melbourne. Discussed later in the chapter, this was an interview between Joy FM hosts and a TSA officer that could have been interpreted to say gay people deserved death and was a public relations disaster. This may be the best/worst public relations event for TSA in living memory, as it caused great harm to people and the public profile of TSA, but has also proven to be a significant catalyst for change that is now underway. I will also argue, however, that such change is being met by ongoing hostility and resistance.

'Homosexuality' and Victorian England

The Salvation Army is very much a product of Victorian England. This is an era and place in Western European history that holds somewhat of a reputation for excessive sexual repression, austerity, and prudery. The social convention was that discussions around topics such as sex, sexuality, and bodily functions were taboo,[2] and yet in some circles, the Victorians could not stop talking about diverse sexualities and sexual practices.

The trajectory that drove church and society towards any sexual repression was not linear. And realistically, it was not just an age of moral rectitude, but also hypocrisy. Pornography and prostitution flourished. There was an unstable and inconsistent approach to sex and sexuality among the general population. Public puritanism of the middle classes drove sex underground. When it came to same-sex activity, even by the eighteenth century, when there was particular savagery beginning towards patrons of Molly Houses (what contemporarily we might call "gay bars"), some churchmen colluded in protecting some homosocial environments.[3]

Prior to the late nineteenth century homosexuality was not illegal in the UK, only the act of "sodomy." From the Middle Ages, sex between men started to be described by parts of the church as a moral sin. Medieval theologians invented the term "sodomy" in the eleventh century

---

2. Garton, *Histories of Sexuality*, 101-123.
3. Gibson et al., *Sex and the Church in the Long Eighteenth Century*, 195-230.

as the "sin of denying God" and linked it to the story of Sodom in the Old Testament.[4] This distinction between homosexuality and sodomy is important, and is reflected in a law originally meant to imply any non-procreative sex and initially used as a political tool by Henry VIII (1533), creating a new crime that the state was concerned with policing and punishing partly as an attempt to (re)assert the state, especially the King, over the Church.[5] Similarly, "sodomy" as a term in Tudor times meant any "unnatural" act including masturbation and nocturnal emission.[6] This law was used to prosecute both same-sex and opposite-sex offences, often non-consensual. In latter times, to be convicted, you needed to be caught in the act and prosecution required at least two eyewitnesses and evidence of both penetration and ejaculation, leading to some horrific forensic examinations.[7] Nonetheless, from the seventeenth century onward, there was increased focus on male-to-male sexual activity and capital punishment by fire or hanging occurred in the eighteenth and nineteenth centuries.[8] Cocks examines the crime of sodomy, as well as lesser charges such as assault with sodomitical intent, and argues that the mid-nineteenth century was the high point of sodomy prosecutions in England. He contends that changes in policing attitudes, along with religious support, was the root cause of this increase.[9]

It is worth noting that earlier Western societies in general, and the church specifically, did not hold homosexuality to be immoral. Rather, practicalities such as infant mortality meant there was some hostility to any non-procreative sexual activity.[10] Boswell has demonstrated that it was increasingly from the twelfth century that there was a progressive intolerance growing in European Christianity, not only toward homosexuality but also Muslims, witches, Jews, and women.[11] While some jurisdictions, such as Castille (France) and parts of modern Italy,

---

4. Jordan, *The Invention of Sodomy in Christian Theology*, 1.

5. Jordan, *The Invention of Sodomy in Christian Theology*, 29. Also popularly retold in: Lemmy and Miller, *Bad Gays*, 61.

6. Gibson et al., *Sex and the Church in the Long Eighteenth Century*, 195ff.

7. The evidentiary requirement of emission of sperm was solidified in 1781 according to Cocks, but was then removed in 1828—Cocks, *Nameless Offences*, 32-24.

8. Foucault, *The History of Sexuality—Volume 1*, 101. Blackmore also details these executions in his historical novelisation of the events surrounding Rev John Church and the Vere Street Coterie 1809-1810; Blackmore, *Radical Love*.

9. Cocks, *Nameless Offences*, 7.

10. Fielder and Ezzy, *Lesbian, Gay, Bisexual and Transgender Christians*, 6.

11. Boswell, *Christianity, Social Tolerance and Homosexuality*, 324.

adopted early laws proscribing sodomy, these were rare and not based on Christian influence.[12] There is only limited negative Christian commentary regarding homosexual behavior at this time. For example, Aquinas discussed "unisexual lust" as an "unnatural crime,"[13] but his argument that it was unnatural simply because it was unnatural was both circuitous and unhelpful. Culturally and religiously, where there was condemnation of male-to-male sexual activity (it was almost always *male* activity) this was a "response more to the pressures of popular antipathy rather than the weight of Christian tradition" or any formed theology on the matter.[14] I note that some more recent medievalists and queer theorists criticize Boswell's analysis, saying it is anachronistic to speak of "gay people" in pre-modern times, while also critiquing his ignorance of women. However, as Kuefler says, most historians still "confirm the broadest outlines if not the details."[15]

Gradually this intellectual shift in society led to laws that outlawed homosexuality and introduced capital punishment in some jurisdictions. As a result, the claim that homosexuality is "unnatural and immoral" became the defining claim of *more recent* Western opposition to homosexual behavior.[16] This shift from neutral to hostile attitudes to homosexual acts may, in part, have come about through the medicalization of sexuality and the religious conceptualization of homosexuality as a sin, and as a result of sociological reconsideration of the period rather than biblical or theological discussion. Medicalization is where something non-medical becomes subject to the influence of medical professionals, which Foucault says marginalized homosexuality as an illegitimate identity. He also found that the practice of confession within Christianity progressively moved homoerotic thoughts, feelings, and anything else relating to fornication (sex outside marriage) as a "sin" to be absolved.[17]

It was into this (latter) environment that TSA was born.

It is not just that TSA was born into Victorian England and its thinking that is of importance. The Salvation Army's growth was initially aligned directly with the British colonial project. Those countries where

---

12. Boswell, *Christianity, Social Tolerance and Homosexuality*, 329.
13. Aquinas, *Summa Theologiae*, I-II, q. 94, art. 3, reply obj 4.
14. Boswell, *Christianity, Social Tolerance and Homosexuality*, 329.
15. Kuefler, "Homoeroticism in Antiquity and the Middle Ages," 1246-1266.
16. Fielder and Ezzy, *Lesbian, Gay, Bisexual and Transgender Christians*, 6.
17. Foucault, *The History of Sexuality*.

TSA was able to quickly establish missions were British colonies,[18] and the language of colonization can be found in many of The Salvation Army's founding documents, including the William Booth manifesto, *In Darkest England and The Way Out*.[19] Invariably, up until recent history, in each of these countries TSA has supported the retention and enforcement of the anti-LGBTQ+ laws and penal codes that the British introduced. Later in the chapter we will discuss a specific example from New Zealand.

These laws, to which we will now turn our attention via the Maiden Tribute campaign, have transformed the cultures of many countries. One example is the Kingdom of Buganda, now part of Uganda. There, young aristocrats were sent to the king as "pages"; to be used not just as servants, but also for anal intercourse. When European missionaries arrived, some of the pages converted and started to refuse intercourse with the king—after being taught by the Europeans that it was sinful. In 1885-6 King Mwanga executed thirty-four pages for refusing his advances, twenty-two of whom were later canonized as martyrs by the Catholic Church.[20] This started an attitudinal change in Uganda that meant even in 2023 the Ugandan Parliament passed further legislation outlawing homosexual activity, including affirming the death penalty for "aggravated homosexuality."[21] TSA is embedded in Ugandan society with 134 Corps and Outposts,[22] and the numerical strength of Salvationists in countries such as Uganda now has reverse influence on the Western TSA by promoting anti-LGBTQ+ attitudes back toward Western nations.

The Maiden Tribute in Modern Babylon Campaign and 'Gross Indecency'

The Salvation Army's more specific dark history with the LGBTQ+ community starts in 1885. (Although, the law of averages means that an LGBTQ+ person likely stood in the listening crowd at Mile End, London, during the movement's inception in July 1865). This was the time of the

18. The Salvation Army, *The Salvation Army Year Book 2023*, 38-9, Table of "Countries where The Salvation Army is at work" with years of commencement.

19. Booth, *In Darkest England and the Way Out*.

20. Rao, "Re-Membering Mwanga," 1–19; also, Potts and Short, *Ever Since Adam and Eve*, 74.

21. Budoo-Scholtz, *Ugandan President Signs Repressive Anti-LGBT Law*, Human Rights Watch, 30 May 2023.

22. The Salvation Army, *The Salvation Army Year Book 2023*, 273.

"Maiden Tribute in Modern Babylon" campaign, which started with some incredible women and positive intent. Florence Soper-Booth of TSA, suffragette Josephine Butler, and converted brothel owner Rebecca Jarrett partnered with Bramwell Booth (also TSA) and William Stead of the Pall Mall Gazette to "procure" a 13-year-old girl from her parents for the purported purposes of prostitution. They published their story in Stead's paper demonstrating both the link of poverty to harm and the ease of child-trafficking in the United Kingdom (UK). Their work ultimately led to the Parliament of the UK raising the age of consent to sixteen years through the 1885 Criminal Law Amendment Act.

However, Stead was also an opponent of homosexuality and anti-gay sentiment had been brewing across England throughout the nineteenth century. He was reported to be a larger-than-life crusader wishing to use his platform to mobilize the public to outcry against sexual immorality and "sexual criminality."[23]

As the Criminal Law Amendment Act was considered in parliament in the early hours of August 6, and the debate dragged through the night, controversial MP Henry Labouchere introduced another clause that would make all "gross indecency" between two men illegal. While some have suggested that Stead prompted Labouchere directly to move this amendment, the true motivation remains a mystery, and their connection cannot be confirmed, especially given the amendment was only lately introduced and debated on the floor of parliament for a mere four minutes. It is just as likely that this was one of Labouchere's habitual attempts at parliamentary obstructionism, or a result of his own homophobia.[24]

Under the Labouchere Amendment, a male who attempted to procure an act of "gross indecency" with another male (of any sexual disposition) was guilty of a crime. Just what "gross indecency" meant was never well defined, perhaps because Victorian morality demurred from describing such activity. In practice it meant just about anything short of anal intercourse—which was by then covered by the *Offences Against the Person Act 1861*, an update of the 1828 Act which replaced the laws of Henry VIII, but which still required evidence that penetration had taken place. Under this new Labouchere Amendment, Oscar Wilde, Alan Turing, and countless others were convicted and punished for committing homosexual acts.[25] And through this Amendment, the

---

23. Walkowitz, *City of Dreadful Delight*, 95.
24. Fize, "The Homosexual Exception?" paragraph 8.
25. Parliament of the United Kingdom, "1885 Labouchere Amendment," accessed

celebrated social-justice campaign of TSA coincidently and inadvertently became its first negative salvo against the LGBTQ+ community, albeit as an unintended consequence.

Some have suggested that this was the first law to specifically target homosexual men as a group of people, rather than targeting a non-procreative act. However, the notion that it created a law against a class of person rather than simply codifying what was already assumed to be law is challenged. Cocks notes that homosexual offences, in general, comprised a notably "routine aspect of criminal justice."[26] Indeed, it can be argued that the two year imprisonment imposed for gross indecency was a more lenient approach to homosexuals than the death penalty for sodomy.[27]

Either way, it was then adopted in penal codes across the Empire and spread wherever English law was used as a basis. Today it remains in some ex-colonial penal codes, such as in section 165 of the Kenyan Penal Code where it is almost the exact wording as the Labouchere Amendment. Section 377A of the Singapore Penal Code was another example of the Labouchere wording and was not repealed until January 2023, but at the same time that parliament legislated to protect the traditional definition of marriage as a union between a man and a woman.[28] Variations of the Labouchere wording are still found in the penal codes of Malaysia, Myanmar, Pakistan, Bangladesh, and Sri Lanka.

Demedicalization, SOGICE, and the Revised Standard Version and New International Versions of the Bible

From the later part of the nineteenth century to the late 1960s, homosexuality was of keen interest to the medical fraternity and treated as a medical phenomenon. Rather than informing this conversation theologically, churches often silently followed the culture. What started primarily as investigations into the reasons that some people were sexually attracted to their own gender led to treatments to see if this could be changed. From the 1940s, electro-shock treatments were used, as were vomit-inducing

---

22 May 2023.

26. Cocks, *Nameless Offences*, 20.

27. Bristow, "Remapping the Sites of Modern Gay History" 116-142.

28. Goh Han Yan, "Parliament Repeals Section 377A, Endorses Amendments Protecting Definition of Marriage," *Straits Times* (Singapore), 29 November 2022.

treatments.[29] In Australia, treatments included a penile plethysmograph (an instrument used to measure changes in blood flow to parts of the body) that was attached to the penis to measure increases and decreases in size. A device that could emit an electric shock was also attached. Every time a member of the same sex appeared before the "patient" a shock was administered so long as that image was visible. From the 1940s to the 1960s frontal lobotomies were also performed on homosexuals in some countries.[30] In Australia, protestors famously dumped sheeps' brains on the surgery floor of Doctor Harry Bailey in Sydney, who had been conducting brain operations on men to "cure" homosexuality.[31] This is where some of the research participants enter the story:

> *I think it was still a mental illness under the DSM,[32] so there was a lot of stuff saying it wasn't healthy. A lot of material . . . I mean at that stage I remember reading about experiments they were doing where they were putting electric shocks on people, and you know, showing them pictures and then trying to do that . . . I didn't get a different version that this wasn't something that was an illness or something wrong, something that shouldn't be part of me. So, that's the way I saw it. So, it became a fight, like a spiritual battle to get rid of this thing.—Matthew (Interview participant)*

From the 1940s onwards a shift commenced in the medical and psychological community. Alfred Kinsey's seminal 1948 work shone light on the number of people who may have had homosexual attraction and homosexual experience. His team found this could be true for around 10 percent of the male population (they studied women later).[33] His research was criticized for its sampling (surveying institutionalized men) and the number was later revised down to 4 percent of the male population experiencing *exclusively* homosexual attraction and/or experience.[34]

Evelyn Hooker then conducted the first scientific study of gay men in a non-therapeutic setting with a decent sample size and control group.

---

29. Often the patient would be shown homoerotic images while drugs were administered to induce vomiting, thus creating a psychological association between homoerotic activity and illness.

30. Milar, "The Myth Buster," 24.

31. Bongoirno, *Dreamers and Schemers*, 281.

32. Diagnostic and Statistical Manual of Mental Disorders.

33. Kinsey et al, *Sexual Behaviour in the Human Male*.

34. Gebhard, "Incidence of Overt Homosexuality in the United States and Western Europe."

This was in 1957, and she found that there were no differences in pathology between gay and straight men, and thus homosexuality should not be construed to be a mental disorder.[35] While published in the 1950s, it was somewhat ignored until 1970, partly because she was female.[36] However, subsequent researchers replicated her results and precipitated a move away from medicalized paradigms.[37] Each helped to pave the way for the American Psychiatric Association in 1973 to remove homosexuality from the list of mental disorders contained in the DSM.

This determination by the American Psychiatric Association was not universally accepted, most notably by Evangelicalism, a movement of the church with which TSA self-identifies.[38] Reaction included public campaigns by figures such as Anita Bryant, a popular singer who had two US top ten hits,[39] and author Tim LaHaye, author of the *Left Behind* series of apocalyptic novels, which were popular among evangelicals. In 1978 he was asked by Tyndale House (publishers of *The Living Bible*) to write a book, after the Anita Bryan campaigns, which he titled *The Unhappy Gays*. He claimed he wanted to address the "homosexual epidemic,"[40] but used very few (mostly discounted) resources and no biblical exegesis. He also claimed that SOGICE were possible, proposed strange theories behind homosexuality, claimed that parents would rather their children were "dead" than "gay," and claimed that homosexuals made it their business to recruit others to homosexuality.[41] He posited that even though psychologists say that SOGICE is not possible, the church should simply ignore them.

This was conflated by popular translations of the Bible entering the market at the same time. It was the 1946 Revised Standard Version (RSV) that first mistranslated 1 Corinthians 6:9-11 to introduce the word "homosexuality" into the biblical text.[42] It was a move that replaced behaviors

---

35. Hooker, "The Adjustment of the Male Overt Homosexual," 18-31.
36. Milar, "The Myth Buster," 24.
37. Hollier, *Religious Trauma, Queer Identities*, 23.
38. The Salvation Army's international mission statement describes the denomination as "an evangelical part of the universal Christian Church." The Salvation Army, *The Salvation Army Year Book 2023*, title page.
39. Billboard, "Anita Bryant," *Billboard.com*, 2023.
40. LaHaye, *The Unhappy Gays*, 8.
41. LaHaye, *The Unhappy Gays*, 157, 94.
42. Baldock, *Forging A Sacred Weapon*. This is also the subject of a recent documentary titled, "1946: The mistranslation that shifted culture", released 2022; and also: The Reformation Project, "An Evening with Rev. David: The Story Behind a Historic

such as pederasty and abuse with a condemnation of homosexuals as a group.⁴³ However, this mistranslation also found its way into the New International Version (NIV)—published in the same year as *The Unhappy Gays*—and into Tyndale's *The Living Bible*. The NIV would soon become a popular translation in many churches, including TSA in Australia where the provided Bibles for congregations were almost universally NIV. As a result, churches began to change their official statements and dogma. Chapter two will discuss the specific teachings and membership materials of TSA that reflect this move.

Efforts to consolidate the traditional view of marriage and opposition to LGBTQ+ inclusion in the church were emboldened during the AIDS crisis of the 1980s and 1990s. Out of this era grew influential groups such as Focus on the Family (first founded 1977), who in turn had explicit ties to the infamous ex-gay movement NARTH (National Association for Research and Therapy of Homosexuality).⁴⁴ TSA often used Focus on the Family resources and, in turn, Focus on the Family would quote TSA research to support its work.⁴⁵ Focus on the Family continue to promote SOGICE on its website under the section "Get Help."⁴⁶ SOGICE were at their peak in the 1980s and 1990s. TSA supported these programs and the surveys and interviews in this research give evidence of use of such materials in corps and training facilities.

Each of these conflating factors has led one commentator, Baldock, to state that the 1970s, 1980s, and 1990s were the worst time in history for LGBTQ+ people to grow up in the Christian Church.⁴⁷ All of our survey and interview subjects, except for only one or two older participants, grew up during these years. Some remember specific occasions where TSA militated against LGBTQ+ people. One of the most prominent was on October 2, 1989, when the Sydney Congress Hall Band and other uniformed Salvationists joined the Fred Nile march

---

Letter About Biblical Translation", YouTube, 8 November 2019, where the discovery of the mistranslation and conversations with the translation committee of the RSV are discussed using Microfiche of their letters held at Yale University.

43. Baldock, *Walking the Bridgeless Canyon*, 236-8.

44. Hollier, *Religious Trauma, Queer Identities*, 30.

45. An example of this mutual support in the area of sexuality is: Earle, *A Grassroots Guide to Protecting Your Community from Pornography*, 6 where pornography is linked to human trafficking.

46. "Sexuality," Focus on the Family, accessed 5 July 2023.

47. In conversation with the author, 2021.

against the Sydney Gay and Lesbian Mardi Gras.[48] This led to a public street clash with LGBTQ+ protestors who came out in force (outnumbering the Nile group five to one).[49]

In Australia, it was only to worsen as a rise in the populist right clashed with societal moves toward marriage equality, transgender recognition, and calls for bans on SOGICE.[50]

Decriminalization era and other government interactions

The Salvation Army in the South Pacific become closely tied to efforts against the decriminalization of homosexuality in the 1980s. The most public and influential instance was the outspoken campaign in 1985 against the Homosexual Law Reform Bill in New Zealand. Specifically, TSA leadership of the New Zealand Territory aided the facilitators of a petition to stop the decriminalization of homosexual activities in consenting males over the age of 16 in that country.

A key leader at the time was Territorial Social Secretary, Colonel Melvin Taylor. The Social Secretary was the leader of all social and community services of TSA in New Zealand. He later described the campaign as "homophobia in action," regretting the hurt caused by TSA at the time. Christina Tyson noted that there was no doubt that thirty years later the New Zealand LGBTQ+ community still associate TSA with that action and the "toxic vitriol" expressed by Salvationists at the time.[51]

In more recent times, the New Zealand Territory has moved to apologize for its action (2006) and also tried to move the conversation forward positively. This included a bi-lateral conversation and joint

---

48. Reverend the Honourable Frederick (Fred) Nile (b 1934) was an Australian Congregational minister and later Uniting Church minister (1964-2003) until he resigned claiming the church no longer literally interpreted the Bible. He then served as the President of the Fellowship of Congregational Churches, those that had declined to join the Uniting Church in 1977. He served as a New South Wales state politician (member of the Legislative Council) from 1981-2023. A controversial figure, he is most famous for his role in the Billy Graham movement, leading an ultra-conservative Christian group named "Festival of Light," passionate opposition the LGBTQ+ community, attempts to ban hijab and niqab in NSW, and likening school ethics classes to Nazism.

49. McCrossin, "Rainbow People Welcome," 9 April 2024. The Australian Broadcasting Corporation (ABC) and Special Broadcasting Service (SBS) television coverage of the event is still available online, and includes (at the end) a Salvationist in full uniform.

50. Barns, *The Rise of the Right*, 7.

51. Tyson, "Rejecting Rejection," 26 Oct 2017.

statement with lobby group Rainbow Wellington on the 25th anniversary of the petition and law reform bill.[52] The Territory also commissioned a survey of its own membership in 2014, under the guidance of then Territorial Commander, Commissioner Robert Donaldson. The central question of the survey was: "Which of the following would best describe your current attitudes toward same-sex relationship?" Of the answers available, "I hold unswervingly to the historic understanding of the church, that sexual relationships are appropriate only for a man and a woman in a marriage relationship," was chosen by a marginal majority—TSA officers 51 percent and TSA soldiers 58 percent. Of the other available answers, "I live with a degree of uncertainty: I long for clear teaching on this matter but suspect the answer is far from simple," was next most popular—officers 37.5 percent, soldiers 27.6 percent; and thirdly, "I am convinced that committed, monogamous, same-sex relationships are fully capable of honoring God," was only chosen by a minority—officers 11.36 percent, soldiers 14.85 percent.[53]

It is noted that this attitude in New Zealand, where many churches petitioned together, bears some contrast to the churches' attitudes toward decriminalization in the United Kingdom. As early as the 1950s, the Church of England had supported homosexual law reform and accommodated homosexuals in a way that provided community and status, albeit in a "stained-glass closet," to quote Jones.[54] Notably, however, The Salvation Army was not among supporters of decriminalization in the UK, nor did it support later attempts to repeal the famous Section 28 legislation that prohibited local authorities from promoting homosexuality, saying it would be harmful to both children and the family unit. TSA argued it would add pressure to young people to experiment sexually and may result in bullying of children that fail to conform.[55]

In Australia, from the 1970s, Australian organizations such as Gay Liberation and the Campaign Against Moral Persecution (CAMP) campaigned for LGB equality. Campaigns specifically around decriminalization began from that decade but continued across the Australian

---

52. Roberts, "Rainbow Wellington and The Salvation Army Reach a Rapprochement," 2012.

53. "Same-Sex Attitude Survey," The Salvation Army New Zealand, Fiji, Tonga & Samoa Territory, 2014.

54. Jones, "The Stained-Glass Closet."

55. The Salvation Army, Letter to the First Minister of Scotland entitled "Re: The Proposed Repeal of Section 2A (28) Local Government Act 1988", 10th February 2000.

states through the 1980s and into the 1990s in Tasmania where the debate was particularly acrimonious. For LGBTQ+ Tasmanians, it was a long battle, with some origin in the 1970s through a Launceston based doctor, Dr Bob Brown (later a federal Australian Greens Senator). Later, campaigners took their case to the United Nations Human Rights Committee which ruled against the extant Tasmanian laws in early 1994. Even then, it took until 1997 for the minority, conservative, Tony Rundle-led state government to enact homosexual law reform, the last Australian state to do so.[56]

Even in Tasmania, however, it should be noted that not all in the church stood against decriminalization. Rodney Croome, a long-time activist in Tasmania who rose to prominence when arrested in Hobart for championing gay rights, speaks of how the gay and lesbian counselling service in that city was protected by a church during this period. The Congregational Church in Davey Street provided rooms for the service to use and a "front" to protect users of the service who arrived to seek support.

Alongside law reform, there was HIV/AIDS campaigns that generated much activism, meaning that Australia had one of the world's best health responses to the epidemic.[57] At each step, the evolving activism has been met by equally passionate opposition, often in the form of the evangelical churches both in public debate and government engagement. Willet notes that more often they were minority religious groups such as Presbyterians and Pentecostals (minority at the time), rather than Anglicans and Catholics, and mostly based in rural and provincial areas, but they provided a rallying point for conservativism and conservative politicians in particular.[58]

Explicit homophobia became increasingly common in public discourse through the AIDS crisis of the 1980s and into the years of the Howard government (1996-2007). Under Howard, a Methodist-turned-Anglican who was politically and ideologically conservative, several subtle (and not so subtle) policy settings eroded the possibility of LGBTQ+ equality. An example was making marital status a criterion for eligibility to accessing reproductive technologies. This was in response to *McBain vs Victoria* (2000) where a Melbourne gynecologist sought

---

56. Bongiorno, *Dreamers and Schemers*, 352.

57. This history is summarised in: Riseman, "Australia's History of LGBTI Politics and Rights."

58. Willett, "Australia: Seven Jurisdictions, One Long Struggle," 220-221.

clarification before the court as to whether legislated state limitations on same sex couples accessing IVF services were consistent with the federal Sex Discrimination Act 1984. The judge found that they were not and gave the federal law precedence—leading the Howard Government to change the federal law.[59]

More direct government discrimination was found in the legal redefinition of marriage to clarify that it must be between a man and a woman. These changes were presented by the Howard Government as pragmatic responses to economic or social pressures, but may be considered conservative social engineering.[60] It was as recently as 2003 that future Prime Minister Tony Abbott, on the ABC Insiders program, stated that the Howard government was keen to support "traditional Christian marriage" and a year later that Howard, while saying that he couldn't countenance a change in the laws to allow for same-sex marriage, did change the law to explicitly rule it out.[61]

Public homophobia was introduced to parliamentary debate during the Howard years. In March 2002 Senator Michael Heffernan used a near empty chamber and parliamentary privilege to accuse gay High Court judge Michael Kirby of using his commonwealth car to cruise Darlinghurst (Sydney) for "rent boys." In the ensuing days, the Australian Senate censured both Heffernan and Prime Minister Howard for their role in the affair. The motion from Senator John Faulkner was amended by Senator Dr Bob Brown (mentioned earlier in relation to gay-rights campaigns in Tasmania) to include the Prime Minister, and narrowly passed the Senate thirty-one votes to thirty.[62]

The mood of the Senate then shifted to further conservatism with the arrival of new crossbenchers. The Family First Party won a critical seat in the upper house in 2004 upon which the Howard Government was dependent for a voting majority. The Family First party were unashamedly right-wing conservatives referencing somewhat fundamentalist Christian values as expressed in the wealthier Pentecostal churches they were founded from (for example, Paradise Assemblies of God, Adelaide). They openly opposed same-sex marriages and adoption by same-sex couples. Contemporary commentators, including Laurie Oakes and Glen Milne, warned of the dangers of a coalition government dependent on

59. Maddox, *God Under Howard*, 78.
60. Maddox, *God Under Howard*, 73.
61. Maddox, *God Under Howard*, 98.
62. The Parliament of Australia, *Hansard*, 19 March 2002.

Family First, the latter saying, "Many will be suspicious of any legislative deals that come at the cost of allowing religion to intrude into Australian politics for the first time."[63]

TSA engaged with the Howard (and subsequent) governments, initially through the Office of the National Secretariat and in later years through the Head of Government Relations. These individuals are empowered to make representations to parliamentarians, although formal submissions to government also require clearance by Territorial Leadership.

The Salvation Army's stated position on homosexuality was taken out of circulation in 2012 in response to the Joy FM interview (discussed shortly). It was still made clear in Australia, however, through government submissions in the late 2010s. First was the 2016 submission to the Senate Select Committee on the Exposure Draft of the Marriage Amendment (Same-Sex Marriage) Bill, prior to the government's same-sex marriage postal survey of 2017.[64] Within this submission, a complementarian theology is evident, at points discussing "traditional" gender roles based on gender difference. It asserted that "for important theological, philosophical, historical, social, legal, cultural, and anthropological reasons, the institution of marriage ought not to be redefined," and that restraint from doing so did not represent arbitrary discrimination. It also argued that marriage embodied the potential for procreation as part of the natural order, seemingly forgetting those heterosexual couples who cannot, or choose not to, procreate.[65]

Notably, TSA did not run an active public campaign during the same-sex marriage postal survey. Positively, there was no intentional direction to TSA membership during this time, allowing for a conscience vote. The Uniting Church in Australia and TSA were two of only a few denominations that did not run "no" campaigns.

63. Loughnane, Gartrell and Bartlett, interviews with Oakes, *Sunday*, Channel 9, 10 October 2004; Milne, "Emboldened Howard set to reshape nation," *Sunday Telegraph* (Sydney), 10 October 2004.
64. The Australian Marriage Law Postal Survey was a national survey to gauge support for legalising same-sex marriage in Australia in 2017, conducted by the Australian Government. 79.5 percent of Australians eligible to vote responded, of which 61.6 percent responded "yes" and 38.4 percent responded "no." The subsequent Marriage Amendment Act passed parliament on 7 December 2017 and received Royal Assent on 8 December 2017 to come into effect the following day.
65. The Salvation Army, *Marriage and the Recognition of Same Sex Unions*, Submission to the Senate Select Committee on the Exposure Draft of the Marriage Amendment (Same-Sex Marriage) Bill, 2016.

After the new legislation passed, TSA did however make further representations to government on the matter. In 2018, a subsequent submission argued for government to protect The Salvation Army's right to deny use of TSA social-trust properties for same-sex marriages and to protect it from litigation at the hands of its own clergy should they wish to conduct a same-sex marriage. The submission states, "It is conceivable that a well-intentioned member of the clergy may seek to officiate a same-sex wedding in breach of Salvation Army Orders & Regulations, or other ecclesiastical law processes. In such a case, The Salvation Army simply seeks the ability to regulate its clergy to act only in accordance with its own beliefs and practices."[66]

The period leading up to the same-sex marriage postal survey was particularly harmful for the LGBTQ+ community in Australia. Vitriolic homophobic speech was used freely in defense of the "no" vote. It sparked significant debate in many churches, including TSA, who pretended a neutral stance towards its congregations whilst still making the aforementioned government submissions. This was felt by the participants in this research:

> . . . it was the time of the gay marriage plebiscite (sic). The Salvation Army taking its position . . . there was a lot of change in the organization as well, and I guess I just reached a crisis point of going, "I can't live authentically as I am within this system."—Martha (Interview)

> It was the first time I took some of my trans kids to Youth Camp. They'd been to Kids Camp, and it was perfectly fine at Kids Camp . . . They were embraced, and supported, and no-one needed to know, and it was all wonderful. [Then at] their first Youth Camp an external preacher was brought in. and he preached about same-sex marriage, and how it was tearing the church apart . . . I had a group of them come to me after one of the group sessions in tears.—Salome (Interview)

> It was 2016-7 and the vote was everywhere. It was in the press everywhere, so he [the Corps Youth Pastor] ran another little series on "it's the beginning of the end."—Elizabeth (Interview)

There are two more government policy interactions of note in recent history. One is The Salvation Army's interaction with the Safe Schools

---

66. The Salvation Army, "The Salvation Army's Response to the Expert Panel on Religious Freedom," Religious Freedom Submissions, 2018.

program. This program originated around 2010 in Victoria to ensure that schools were safe places for all students, including those who identify as LGBTQ+. It was born out of needs identified by school communities, based on an understanding that LGBTQ+ students were at higher risk of bullying, discrimination, and suicide. Late in 2016, The Salvation Army's Victorian Social Policy Unit issued a statement in support of the Safe Schools program. Unfortunately, less than two weeks later the territorial office overrode this support, claiming it did so because of the inconsistencies in how it was rolled out in different states and that anti-bullying programs need to consider all high-risk student groups.[67]

Media reports, however, claimed that the backflip was the result of an internal backlash from the organization's membership about the program's support to LBGTQ+ students.[68] In this case, it was not only the appearance that internal pressure had forced a backflip that did the damage. The support and then the retraction came sometime after Safe Schools was actually a media issue, but only a fortnight after the well-documented suicide of thirteen-year-old Tyrone Unsworth, a Queensland victim of homophobic bullying. At a time when sympathies in the broader community were seemingly high, TSA was publicly unsympathetic.

The other recent key interaction is with the proposal in some states and territories of Australia to address SOGICE. Most recently, on January 30, 2021, three Salvation Army congregation leaders from Victoria were among signatories to an Australian Christian Lobby (ACL) advertisement protesting Victorian legislation to ban "conversion therapies."[69] While these three women spoke without authority or permission, it was again a situation where the public saw "The Salvation Army" printed three times in major newspapers, in an anti-LGTBIQ+ context. It also publicly aligned TSA with an arch-conservative lobby group, the ACL.

---

67. The Salvation Army, "The Salvation Army Announces National Position on Safe Schools," The Salvation Army, 30 November 2016.

68. Street, "Why I Won't Be Supporting The Salvation Army This Christmas," *The Sydney Morning Herald*, 7 December 2016; Urban, "Salvation Army Retreat on Safe Schools Program," *The Australian*, 5 December 2016.

69. Australian Christian Lobby, "Dear Premier, We Are Not Criminals", Facebook, 1 February 2021.
The Australian Christian Lobby (ACL) are a conservative, right-wing Christian advocacy and political lobbying organisation. They are mostly known for anti-gay, anti-transgender, and anti-abortion campaigns, and for their religious discrimination advocacy.

The 2012 Joy FM interview

I have said that the infamous 2012 Joy FM interview was the best/worst thing to happen to TSA in this area. Publicly, it was one of the most damaging public relations incidents of the last twenty years. Internally, it became a significant catalyst for introspective review and change. This radio interview in Melbourne was between Dean Beck, "Salt and Pepper," and The Salvation Army's Major Andrew Craib on June 21, 2012. "Salt and Pepper" quoted from The Salvation Army's *Salvation Story* doctrine book where some Bible texts are referenced in support of The Salvation Army's teaching on sexuality.[70] One is from Romans chapter 1 and "Salt and Pepper" asked Craib if TSA taught this text as meaning gay and lesbian people deserved death. Instead of denying that interpretation, Craib affirmed that TSA believed the Bible.[71] Sadly, his response also failed to point out that the book that the interviewers used (published 1996) was, by the date of the interview, already out of print and superseded by another book, *The Handbook of Doctrine* (published 2010). The latter edition made no comment on the matter of sexuality—it dealt only with more foundational Christian beliefs without much social commentary.

TSA immediately issued a retraction and apology under the direction of Australia Eastern Territorial Commander, Commissioner James Condon.[72] This apology stated that the comments in the interview did not align with The Salvation Army's beliefs or values, that it continued to be non-discriminatory in its employment and service delivery, and asked the LGBTQ+ community to "forgive (it) for failing to properly represent the message of unconditional love that has always been, and is, the defining characteristic of our organization."[73] It also stated that TSA welcomes everyone into their worship services without discrimination, which is not entirely truthful. Other apologies and "clarifications" were published by TSA in Canada, the US, and the UK.

Regardless, the damage was done. At least annually, usually around the times of the Red Shield Appeal (May) or Christmas Appeal (Nov-Dec), detractors against TSA will re-circulate information

---

70. The Salvation Army, *Salvation Story*, 28-29.

71. For a number of years this interview was still available on the Joy FM website. Now, while a Facebook reference to the interview can be found in archives, the actual interview has been taken down.

72. "Clarification Regarding Interview Comments on Homosexuality," The Salvation Army Australia, June 23, 2012.

73. "Clarification . . . .," The Salvation Army Australia.

about the interview. This leads to an annual need for TSA to restate a non-discriminatory position. One positive is that the damaging international position statement on human sexuality was immediately withdrawn and the first international non-discrimination statement by TSA was published that year.[74]

It was also one of many occasions when the participants in the research found themselves having to defend the organization:

> *I remember being horrified in XXX all those years ago. And again, feeling . . . I knew that he'd gone too far, and I knew he'd been misunderstood too. But I remember the . . . apology because I was [a leader] when it happened . . . I found it the other day. It's actually on the ABC website, the words that I wrote, saying, "This is not who we are, not what we mean to portray." I was defensive of the organization too, saying it's a misinterpretation of what was said.*—Matthew

> *I spent some time in public relations for the Salvos and twice had community groups pull back from supporting us because of the perceived discrimination against LGBTIQ+ people by the organization.*—Joseph

The internal reaction was significant. Over the subsequent years a shift occurred in how LGBTQ+ issues, theology, and care were discussed in many corps, in headquarters settings, and in The Salvation Army's training colleges. While there is no direct evidence of a link between the 2012 interview and these specific changes, there is a noticeable shift around that date that points to a reconsideration in this area by many Australian Salvationists.

The external reaction is still relatively raw over a decade on, and is often exacerbated by overseas media and social media. The source of much of this is commentary out of the United States. Because of the globalized world in which we live, reactions in the United States are visible in Australia. Because of the structure of TSA internationally, there is financial dependence on the US Territories of TSA to support the movement globally, meaning they wield power and influence. It is therefore worth a brief excurses to show that the US has proven to be the area of the most controversy when it comes to LGBTQ+ issues, adding to the conflicted environment in which LGBTQ+ officers in Australia operate.

---

74. "Non-discrimination," The Salvation Army International—Non-discrimination, December 2012.

In 1998 TSA turned down $3.5 million US in funding from the City of San Francisco because it chose not to comply with the city's domestic spouse ordinances. These regulations required any business or charity that contracted with the city and provided spousal health insurance to married couples to also provide the same benefits to the same-sex and other unmarried domestic partners of employees. TSA simply stated that it could not comply, instead choosing to scale back services to the aged and homeless.[75]

In 2001 the US National office of TSA challenged the Bush Administration to exempt charities receiving federal funding from local anti-discrimination laws. This application was denied.[76] Then, in 2004 The Salvation Army threatened to forgo over $70 million in funding of homeless programs in New York over the recurring issue of providing health benefits to same-sex spouses.[77]

Employment practices of TSA were in the spotlight when social services case worker Danielle Morantez claimed that she had been fired by TSA after coming out as bisexual. She also raised concerns about discriminatory comments in the organization's employee handbook.[78] TSA unapologetically stated, through spokesman Major George Hood, that "a relationship between same-sex individuals is a personal choice that people have the right to make . . . but from a church viewpoint, we see that going against the will of God."[79]

TSA was charged in 2017 by the New York City Commission on Human Rights with discriminatory intake policies against transgender clients.[80] This came *after* The Salvation Army in the US published a You-

---

75. Lynch and Fernandez, "Salvation Army Cuts S.F. Programs / Charity Spurns City's Domestic Partner Law," *San Francisco Chronicle*, June 4 1998.

76. Bruni and Becker, "Charity Is Told It Must Abide by Antidiscrimination Laws," *The New York Times*, 11 July 2001.

77. Windsor, "Salvation Army Uses Homeless to Fight Gay Benefits," Chicago-Pride.com, 24 May 2004.

78. Morantez and Becker, "Fired by the Salvation Army for Being Bisexual," *Truth Wins Out*, 25 July 2012.

79. Bowean and Eng, "Salvation Army Denies Being Anti-Gay," chicagotribune.com, 1 December 2012.

80. Hoy, "NYC Commission on Human Rights Charges Four Substance Abuse Centers with Discriminatory Intake Policies for Transgender Patients," New York City Commission on Human Rights, 13 July 2017.

Tube testimonial from a transgender woman in Las Vegas speaking about the support of the organization.[81]

In 2019 TSA in the US had significant battles surrounding public perception of its attitude to the LGBTQ+ community. The first came during the lead up to the NFL's Thanksgiving Day Game, often used as the launch of The Salvation Army's Christmas Kettle Campaign (fundraiser). Singer Ellie Goulding initially refused to sing at the half-time interval over The Salvation Army's treatment of LGBTQ+ people.[82] While the performance went ahead after negotiations between the organization and the performer, public sentiment continued to sour as, soon after, Chick-Fil-A, a major restaurant chain that provided significant donations to TSA, announced it would be "changing its philanthropic structure" so that customers knew their values. This meant very public withdrawal of support to "anti-gay" groups such as the Christian Athletes Association and TSA.[83]

TSA launched a defense. This was in the form of an op-ed written for USA Today by National Commander, Commissioner David Hudson. This piece is extremely defensive in tone, quoting multiple statistics demonstrating non-discriminatory service delivery to the LGBTQ+ community. Instead of utilizing such an opportunity to take a reconciliatory approach, the Commissioner went on to affirm a non-inclusive faith stance saying, "no one wants to see programs for those living in poverty eliminated simply because some disagree with the theology of those who provide them," "it's true that The Salvation Army's pastoral leaders, who subscribe to the international tenets of the church on which we are founded, do themselves adhere to a traditional Biblical definition of marriage," and "our faith is the very foundation of our officers' commitment to serve anyone, including those who might not share that faith"—implying that gay and lesbian people do not share Christian faith.[84]

---

81. The Salvation Army, "Lost Vegas—The Salvation Army Provides Hope without Discrimination," YouTube, 26 February 2016.

82. Grow, "Ellie Goulding, Salvation Army Clash Over Gay Rights and Halftime Performance," *Rolling Stone*, 14 November 2019.

83. Del Valle, "Chick-Fil-A's Many Controversies, Explained," *Vox*, 19 November 19; Kosakowski, "Chick-Fil-A Foundation Announces 2020 Priorities to Address Education, Homelessness, Hunger," *The Chicken Wire*, Chick-Fil-A, 18 November 2019.

84. Hudson, "Salvation Army Commander: Yes, We Are Faith-Based Charity but We Serve and Love Everyone," *USA Today*, Gannett Satellite Information Network, 22 November 2019.

Current movements for change

There are a number of internal movements for change that now influence TSA in Australia. These have been augmented by organizational statements and programs. Briefly, I will cover the 2014 Tri-territorial Theological Forum, the "Let's Talk About . . . " program that includes human sexuality, efforts for Rainbow Tick Accreditation, Inclusion Statements, and the 2022 International Symposium on Human Sexuality.

The 2014 Theological Forum was significant because it was the first time that LGBTQ+ affirming documents were published in the name of TSA. These included formal supportive arguments for reconsidered theology, inclusion, and lived testimonies from gay people in the movement. One of the most telling was a brave presentation, in the historic context, from Kris Halliday, a gay Australian officer who shared his testimony.[85] This is the first known published testimony of an openly gay officer discussing their calling to TSA officership.

In the early 2010s The Salvation Army's International Headquarters had developed a community conversation facilitation tool, *Building Deeper Relationships Using Faith-Based Facilitation*. This was originally funded and produced as a tool for community development workers undertaking community consultations. It was later adapted for use in discussing a range of contentious issues from Voluntary Assisted Dying through to Human Sexuality under the new title "Let's Talk About . . . ".[86]

In Australia, the tool was not used until 2022. Training occurred in Sydney to skill around seventy people in using the generic tool. Then a select group of around twenty were trained to use the tool in facilitating conversations around human sexuality, and more specifically, same-sex relationships. These conversations are intended for TSA congregations around Australia and the first occurred in late 2022. It is too early to determine the degree of success but early evidence, including my experience as a facilitator, has shown that, while uptake of the facilitated conversations has been minimal, most participants are engaging respectfully in the process and the conversations.

They are being met, however, with healthy skepticism from those participating in this research:

---

85. Halliday, "A Reflection on Calling," Thought Matters Conference 2014.

86. The Salvation Army, "Faith-Based Facilitation," The Salvation Army International, accessed 15 July 2023.

> *I like the idea of them, and my optimism lies in folk learning a language to speak in healthy ways about topics that have often been heated and divisive. I think it's a step in the right direction, but I do wonder if the long-term goal and the long-term outcomes will be the same.—Survey Respondent*

> *Some of these, like the faith-based facilitation, have taken too long to roll out. And there's not enough explanation to people in our corps about what they are about.—Survey Respondent*

> *FBF has hardly rolled out yet. We hosted an FBF session at my corps last year, and it was a positive start, allowed people to start conversation and resulted in a non-binary young person starting to re-engage in the corps.—Survey Respondent*

> *The Let's Talk gear feels like tokenism and nothing more.—Survey Respondent*

> *I hope it is a cause for optimism but I fear a conservative backlash.—Survey Respondent*

> *Such initiatives seem to so far be about dialogue only (Let's Talk), an unsafe process for some LGBTIQ+ people. . . As for officers, there is not much of benefit in these, due in part to international regulations. All that said, there is far little to show for the above-mentioned initiatives—Survey Respondent*

> *It is encouraging, but the setbacks are difficult to deal with. They discourage and upset me.—Survey Respondent*

On 14 June 2021, the TSA board in Australia approved a new Inclusion Statement. This statement intended to publicly declare that TSA is inclusive in all areas of service. Rolled out nationally, it is meant to be displayed at all TSA sites and is intended to inform policy and practice. It was also accompanied by a branding package that included icons for people to attach to their emails signifying support of minority communities. It states:

> The Salvation Army Australia acknowledges the Traditional Owners of the land on which we meet and work and pay our respect to Elders past, present and future. We value and include people of all cultures, languages, abilities, sexual orientations, gender identities, gender expressions and intersex status. We are committed to providing programs that are fully inclusive. We are committed to the safety and wellbeing of people of all ages, particularly children.

The statement has two inherent weaknesses. The first is that is fails to acknowledge conflicted theologies and the restrictions against same-sex relationships tied to the soldier and officer forms of membership. The other is that there is no visible intent to enforce use or compliance with the statement. As the research participants observe:

> *Sadly, they are just a way for the army to say it doesn't discriminate—Survey Respondent*

> *Cautious optimism, contained due to lack of concrete policy or overt promise to support LGBTIQ+ Salvationists or corps members and 'free reign' those who hold anti-LGBTIQ+ views seem to have. Similarly, change of senior, and territorial leader brings renewed risk and uncertainty. There is a constant looking over one's shoulder despite these signs of progress.—Survey Respondent*

> *Most weeks there will be a number of issues that come up because the atmosphere at the current time—since the territory in Australia released our inclusion statement and inclusion icons—has become very hostile . . . The other one was another leader who reacted very negatively to our diversity and inclusion plan for the territory and the words were, "What else are they going to want?"—Joseph (Interview)*

> *[I said to him]: "That's harmful. I don't mind that you don't see things the same way as me. I don't mind that the inclusion statement disgusts you. You cannot be harmful".—Elizabeth (Interview)*

> *We've got inclusion in the Army now, but we've got to get equality. Equality means I can marry someone if I choose to . . . Equality means that I can choose that road. One day, God help us. We'll get there, but maybe not in my lifetime, you know.—Matthew (Interview)*

While TSA in Australia is moving seemingly quicker than the international movement as a whole, there are some international advancements. Same-sex relationships have been discussed at International Leaders' Forums, including specific sessions in the International Conference of Leaders in Vancouver in September 2022.

Ahead of this gathering the General released two statements, however, that firmly planted The Salvation Army's position on LGBTQ+ equality as unlikely to change. The first was a letter to coincide with the release of a new set of resources for Salvation Army soldiers. This letter of 1 July 2022 states:

> Of particular note is the complex topic of Human Sexuality. In this I note that our discussions have not led to any desire to move away from our current articulated view. Although it is likely that some Salvationists hoped for change, given the complex nature of this matter around the world it is agreed that further theological thought and reflection is required.[87]

This letter was met with much pain from LGBTQ+ Salvationists. They thought it untruthful to say that there is no desire to move from the current articulated view, and also understated to say that it is only "likely" some Salvationists hoped for change. A second similar statement from General Peddle, was made during the opening remarks to the conference itself. He said:

> I confirm our position [on human sexuality] as unchanged and not under review. I note this is little comfort to those who disagree and to some who have found little grace at the Army when they have needed it most. Our ambivalence, judgements, and condemnation have not pointed anyone to Jesus. It cannot be about an endorsement of, but rather a willingness to "walk with" . . . The worldview suggests we are intolerant, no longer on the right side of history, antiquated in our beliefs, and that the moral law of the gospel is no longer acceptable. Legislators are often not Christian, know little of the Bible, and care less for its teaching. The result is that in years to come we will find ourselves often at odds with the world.[88]

Positioning this conversation as a battle of competing worldviews immediately alienated LGBTQ+ people already within TSA. While acknowledging the harm caused by ambivalence and judgement, the General's statements actually perpetuated such harm through suggesting that there is only one view of the "moral law of the gospel" and that even faithful, monogamous, Christians in same-sex relationships will not find endorsement or support.

The General called for an International Symposium on Human Sexuality at the start of August 2022. This symposium had ninety-nine delegates drawn from each Salvation Army territory to discuss a range

87. Peddle, *Letter to Salvationists*.

88. The Salvation Army, "ICL 2022, Limitless God," *The Salvation Army International*, 26 September 2022.

of matters relating to human sexuality. While there were some claims to diversity of sexual orientation among the group, these are unfounded and it appears almost no LGBTQ+ people were present (estimates from those present suggest there was one solitary gay officer). At least one nomination was explicitly rejected on the grounds that the "overtly visible sexuality" of the individual (a gay man) may be confronting.[89] The General was again clearly duplicitous: "My challenge to our Salvation Army is to be clear regarding 'our position' but then fully responsible to listen, understand, and serve everyone—no restrictions and no discrimination."[90]

Reports from the symposium are mixed, with leaders claiming safe and respectful conversations while some delegates do not agree. The rhetoric spoke of those at the margins of society and that LGBTQ+ people are "lost people to be found," failing to acknowledge they are often at the center of congregational life. Basic understanding of human sexuality was absent at times, with the convenor claiming some still believed sexual orientation was chosen.[91] No concrete recommendations were forthcoming around LGBTQ+ matters, other than pursuing more "Let's Talk . . ." conversations at local level.

Lastly, Rainbow Tick Accreditation has instigated conversation and change in TSA in Australia. Originally attained by the St Kilda Crisis Services of TSA—the first faith-based organization to do so—Rainbow Tick Accreditation is intended to demonstrate to the LGBTQ+ community that a service is safe, respectful, and will factor their specific needs into service delivery. It is now a Victorian Government requirement for funding in some areas, notably Family Violence services. As a result, the Social Mission department of TSA went on a journey of accreditation across 2021 and 2022.

The significance of this journey is the impact on the greater organization. As a result of the "Australia One" process which nationalized the operations of TSA in Australia from December 2018 onward, it was no longer possible to attain accreditation for single services or streams of service in Victoria without having to address policy and procedures at a national level. Eventually, the review process agreed in early 2022 that

---

89. Anon, Whatsapp message to the author, May 2023.

90. Peddle, "Foreword from the General," in *International Symposium on Human Sexuality 2022*, 5.

91. Forrest, "A personal reflection on the International Symposium on Human Sexuality," 24.

TSA met the standards for accreditation at thirty-four Social Mission sites in Victoria as well as Territorial Headquarters.

Unfortunately, while the auditors were satisfied, Rainbow Health Australia—the owners of Rainbow Tick—were still not willing to award accreditation on cultural safety grounds. Simply put, giving a tick to TSA would be misleading to the LGBTQ+ community if they went to sites other than The Salvation Army's Social Mission sites in the state of Victoria. It took until early 2023 for negotiations to lead to the accreditation being awarded.

Positively, as part of this process, two new appointments have been made to advance diversity and inclusion, one in the governance space and the other in the social program operations space. The initial incumbents in both roles lasted less than one year, both making claims around an experience of an unsafe workplace. Also, at the same time, internal politics meant that Territorial leaders asked for the celebration and communication of the Rainbow Tick accreditation to be muted. Heads of Department needed Chief Secretary (CEO) approval prior to speaking on the matter.[92]

Ongoing hostility

At times it can feel that each positive step forward is met with brutal hostility. This is not new, but is perceived by research participants to be worsening.

Sometimes it is in the form of official publications that make statements which, to some, would be innocuous. Historically, to lead to an example, it was common for two female officers to be appointed together to lead a TSA Corps. The leaders of TSA were so heteronormative in thinking that when these pairings of women resulted from choice by the two women concerned, it was never considered that such a pairing could be a lesbian relationship. The 1990 Australian play and 1994 screenplay by David Stevens, "The Sum of Us," included the story of Gran and Aunt Mary who were "real strict Salvation Army" while also engaged in consensual sexual activity for over forty years. However, such a positive re-telling of diversity within officer ranks has been met with derision from within TSA. When reviewing the movie as part of a series on The Salvation Army in the movies, Hentzchel wrote that it

---

92. Winsome Merrett, Chief Secretary, meeting with author, 19 May 2023.

"misrepresented ideologies" and "defiled Salvationists" by implying that the bond was a lesbian relationship, and added that the movie ridiculed Salvationists and their symbols (e.g., the uniform) through the implication of such behavior.[93]

Each of these recent shifts listed above should be cause for hope for the LGBTQ+ people within TSA. Unfortunately, however, they have been accompanied by increased hostility, resistance, and at times abusive communications. While increasing numbers of TSA officers and leaders are finding themselves proximate to LGBTQ+ Salvationists, and are realizing their previous theological and pastoral responses may be inadequate, other responses are causing hurt and harm. Hollier summarizes this well: "The divided church is a reality they live and breathe, as their reality of gender and sexuality becomes increasingly hostile territory."[94]

This divided church is seen clearly in society at large. Fielder and Ezzy observe that the continued rejection of LGBTQ+ sexualities and gender variations is connected to a broader loss of power and privilege by the Church in Australia and the undermining of the hegemonic heteronormativity of conservative Christianity.[95] This loss was cemented by the advent of marriage equality, which was perceived by many in conservative Christianity as an existential threat.[96]

The research participants speak directly to this division and how it impacts their ministry:

> *For me, the stuff that flies around on social media is challenging. It's like there's bullets flying everywhere and I'm just caught in the cross fire.... I went to my first officers' fellowship and that was probably the most uncomfortable week I'd ever had. I probably would have preferred to not be there. We joked, XXX and I, when I looked at my Fit Bit stats for that week, my heart rate was about 15 beats a minute higher than it is at any other time, except sustained for the whole week. So, I was just in a constant state of stress.—Simon (Interview)*

> *The hate mail... "You've turned your back on God"—I hadn't even got to "why" yet and I'm getting letters from retired officers*

---

93. Hentzschel, "The Army on the Big Screen Part 2," 26.
94. Hollier, *Religious Trauma, Queer Identities*, 38.
95. Fielder and Ezzy, "Religious Freedom for Whom?"
96. McLeay et al., "The Shifting Christian Right Discourse on Religious Freedom in Australia," 209.

HISTORY AND SOCIAL CONTEXT 49

telling me God will judge me and I've lost my salvation, you know.—Mary (Interview)

I had area officers who liked to make their understanding of theology known to people, including making statements along the lines of or LGBTIQ + people are abominations and going to hell.[97] And then, of course, I had to work with them!—Salome (Interview)

I have not publicly come out as I do not feel it is currently safe to do so in The Salvation Army.—Mark (Interview)

I have no faith in the 'Army' anymore, it no longer feels like a safe organisation/church to be a part of. Like many of my LGBTQIA+ officer colleagues, I always feel like the shoe is about to drop and we'll be ousted. And like many others I've spoken with, I am working on an exit plan.—Survey Respondent

We're in a very hostile environment, with a great number of very vocal anti-LGBT people within The Salvation Army, so if you say the wrong thing or you post the wrong thing on Facebook, if you put up a picture that could be construed as something that it's not, or maybe something that it is . . . . There are attacks and distractions so you are . . . so it feels like a constant repression.—John (Interview)

I have been told by one female officer that she "loves me enough to want to save me from hell" and the same officer claimed to me that the "real injury was to her as someone ostracised for holding 'orthodox' beliefs" (her words).—Joseph (Interview)

The ways in which this hostility is manifest are too numerous to mention. As this research was made known and promoted, I received messages from Salvationists about hurt to straight officers that is being ignored, calls for me to repent, and advice that there should be no such thing as an LGBTQ+ officers because all gay people are either diseased, criminals, or pedophiles.[98]

There are allies in the mix. Research indicates that women, educated people, and those with LGTBQ+ relatives or friends, are most likely to be supportive. On the other hand, men with strong religious affiliations are less likely to be supportive.[99] These allies are mostly quiet in their

---

97. Area Officers in TSA Australia are Salvation Army leaders responsible for the leadership of collaborative mission within a geographic area.

98. Emails and letters sent to the researcher, February 2023.

99. Fingerhut, "Straight Allies," 2230-2248.

support, however there are a few online and group environments that are producing more vocal supporters. These include "Salvos for a more inclusive church" (Facebook), "The Progressive Salvationist" (Facebook), and "Included"—a webpage of podcasts, seminars, research, and testimonies. "Rainbow Wear" is producing merchandise including TSA shields in rainbow colors. There is also a closed group online specifically to support LGBTQ+ Salvationists.

The experience of many of the research participants is that they are confronting hurtful conservative voices regularly. It seems that these voices often, with good intent, portray some existential or ontological threat via the potential affirmation of LGBTQ+ people in the faith community. This threat leads to a stereotypical "flight or fight" response, which seems to most often be: "fight," even when those that perceive threat are part of the "establishment." Recent Australian research by McLeay et al., describes this existential stress as a "pre-reflective sense of alienation, betrayal, abandonment, displacement, and even rage, among a group," and recognizes that for some in conservative churches this can lead to "meaning vertigo"—where their sense of social meaning is threatened and those known "rules" that govern the "sect" are no longer certain.[100] David Gushee reflects on reactions to such threats and says, "Evangelicalism promotes itself as better than fundamentalism but typically offers a fundamentalist approach to those it believes are heretical. The polemic is bitter and strong."[101]

In the face of this, many LGBTQ+ officers continue to serve. Many continue to find hope and love. Many continue to see their lives contribute to the transformation of lives and communities. We will hear these amazing stories as further chapters unfold.

Conclusion

This chapter has provided an initial "lay of the land." The shared history between the LGBTQ+ community and TSA has not been positive. We have come a long way from the days of TSA actively supporting opposition to decriminalization, promoting SOGICE, and firing officers upon the first whiff of potential homosexuality. But amid this, the hostility and hurt continues.

---

100. McLeay et al. "The Shifting Christian Right Discourse on Religious Freedom in Australia," 198.

101. Small, "Dr. David Gushee on Christian humanism after evangelicalism," Spiritual Misfits Podcast, 1 October 2022.

Chapter 2: Growing Up & Joining Up: The Salvation Army's teaching on LGBTQ+ people to LGBTQ+ people

THE PARTICIPANTS IN THIS research mostly grew up in The Salvation Army (TSA) church. At some point all participants became members of the church and then officers. Building on the understanding of the history of TSA and the LGBTQ+ community in chapter 1, this chapter discusses the specific teachings and messages given to LGBTQ+ officers within the movement on *their* sexuality. It will argue that there have been two major shifts over the years that coincide with key moments in history outlined in chapter one.

The first shift was in the 1970s and 1980s that produced a negative and harmful introduction of certain materials and engagement with SOGICE. This coincided with conservative evangelicalism's reaction to demedicalization of homosexuality, the decriminalization debates, and the rise of SOGICE discussed in chapter 1. The second was a more positive shift towards inclusion from around 2012 onwards. It will be argued that there was a significant propulsion towards this from both internal reflection after the 2012 Joy FM interview (discussed in chapter 1) and external pressures to funding and service accreditation. There was also a higher quality of education for TSA officers generated through the University era of officer training from this time, producing better biblical and theological insights.

The first section of the chapter considers the teachings and messages that the participants received as they grew up. This will be considered alongside findings of studies outside TSA. The second section focusses on what was taught in TSA, using the materials and resources for preparing people for soldiership as a window into the organization's taught theology. This section compares this literature review with the survey and interview responses. The final section discusses the experiences of LGBTQ+ officers during their training to become officers, using primarily interview material.

Like any Christian movement, there is a certain amount of movement in the teaching of TSA over time. This is dependent on a number of factors, including the prevailing issues of the day, theological revelation and debate, and internal and external influences. When it comes to teachings on sexuality within the denomination, it is recognized that this can still vary from pulpit to pulpit, leader to leader, year to year.

None of this occurs in a vacuum. While chapter 1 discussed the "lay of the land" for TSA as a denomination, this chapter commences with the grounding for our research participants—their experience growing up.

Growing Up

According to the Private Lives Study of 2005, of the 72.8 percent of the LGBTQ+ population that were brought up in a Christian home in Australia only 14.8 percent were currently practicing their religion.[1] Certainly a decline has occurred in church participation and religious practice in general in Australia, with disaffiliation from Christian denominations and a significant growth in people identifying as observing no religion reported in successive censuses. Affiliation with Christian denominations declined from 88.2 percent of the general population in 1966 to 52.1 percent in 2016, with immigration introducing more diverse religious practice and an increased secularization of the broader community.[2] Even against this wider landscape, the disaffiliation of LGBTQ+ people has occurred at a marked and comparatively higher rate.

One reason behind the decline would be the pain caused through continued alignment with environments that had caused trauma. This trauma results from a tortuous history of practice and teaching that has resulted in deep wounds that will be discussed in future chapters.[3] This leads to a cognitive dissonance between faith and sexuality for many

---

1. Couch et al., "The Religious Affiliation of Gay, Lesbian, Bisexual, Transgender and Intersex Australians," *People and Place* 16, no. 1 (2008).
2. Bouma and Halafoff, "Australia's Changing Religious Profile," 131.
3. Hollier, *Religious Trauma, Queer Identities*, 5.

individuals, a fear regarding the nature of sexuality, and variant ways of handling it—ranging from denial, to celibacy, to promiscuity. As a result, LGBTQ+ youth from religious backgrounds are more likely to feel worse about their lives and are more likely to think about, or succeed in, self-harm than those from non-religious families.[4]

For some, it would be because healthier forms of community are found outside religious environments. The decision to leave may be due to the belief that people outside of Christianity show more love, morality, and affirmation. This is certainly the case for many LGBTQ+ people who have found their "family" in the LGBTQ+ community. In this sense they are drawn toward something positive outside the church, rather than driven from the church, although in some cases it would be both. The expressions of community that result are often analogous to those expressed in biblical stories such as the parable of the banquet, where all-comers are invited and celebrated, and enliven the grace that is demonstrative of holy love.

A third reason is the association of faith communities with families of origin. Where Christians grow up in a church it is most often because they are introduced to this church by family. Recent research in New South Wales has indicated that, while some young people found their families supportive, families are rarely mentioned by LGBTQ+ youths as a key source of support. That research, by the Office of the Advocate for Children and Young People, found that LGBTQ+ youths were less likely to confide anything to a family member (45 percent compared to 62 percent of non-LGBTQ young people).[5]

A fourth reason would be exposure to SOGICE.

Yet the participants in this research remained, or re-joined, and went on to become TSA officers. In our final chapters some of the reasons will be further discussed, including where they find enduring hope or where they have found solidarity and support with others. In many cases it is evident that they survived in the church partially because they were not "out" to their church or their family prior to entering ministry. One interview subject came out to their family, but then joined TSA and tried to live as a heterosexual for a time.

For most of the research participants, the growing up years were not a comfortable time. The school setting would prove to be as hard as

---

4. Hillier et al., "I Couldn't Do Both at the Same Time," 82,

5. Office of the Advocate for Children & Young People, *The Voices of LGBTQIA+ Young People in NSW*, 9.

the church setting for many and reinforced the negative self-worth of these individuals:

> *In the school setting as well, it was very clear that that wasn't a safe place. And it was pretty clear that, if you wanted to stay safe, that it wasn't going to be a safe place. Um . . . and so I just repressed. Repressed, repressed, repressed.—Simon (Interview)*

> *From about grade six it became, you know, "you're a poofter," "you're a fag," "you're a dirty homo," and generally came with either some sort of negative connotation—"don't go in there, the homo's in there," you know, "why is the poofter allowed in the change rooms?"—John (Interview)*

> *At school it wasn't positive either. It was the AIDS crisis of the eighties and nineties. We were all being told that this was a gay disease and that gay people would die. If we weren't being told this, we were being bullied by anyone that might have suspected we were different.—Joseph (Interview)*

Some even grew up in an era where gay bashing was a perceived to be sport:

> *I grew up in Sydney, where people would go and bash gay people. That was their sport on the weekend—to go bash gay people. My brothers were very vocal about gay men.—Salome (Interview)*

These comments show that school was unpleasant and threatening for many of our interview participants. But also growing up in the church meant further exposure to youth activities that were often unsafe. The participants in the research reflected on this:

> *You're told in youth groups that if you're Christian you can't be gay, so I'm definitely Christian, so I definitely can't be gay then.—Mary (Interview)*

> *I might have been seventeen or eighteen and there was this guy who I just always thought was just wonderful . . . and you know he was about three years older than me and I was very keen on young XXX, but also remember thinking I wasn't supposed to feel this way about a guy. And I remember [asking for prayer during the worship service] and talking to the CO [Corps Officer] about it. I can't remember what he said, but I do remember that he followed me up about a week later, or not long after . . . And I remember telling him that it was "all good," and that it was settled. Of course, that was a lie.—James (Interview)*

> *I was told homosexuality was an abomination. That's the word I remember reading in books that I read. Because I had these feelings, so I wanted to understand... At the earliest ages, as I said, I felt intrigued by guys, not girls.*—Matthew (Interview)

Being told that they cannot be themselves or that they were abominations was not uncommon. These kinds of comments were reflected by most of the interview participants, especially those over the age of forty. Some interview participants sadly noted that this sort of attitude is still presenting itself to young people in TSA Corps today:

> *The area officers got changed, and as soon as the new area officer came in, the comment was made in a group... the kids who were coming were trans kids... I had openly gay people coming to the [Corps] and bringing their kids along, and I knew all that was challenging for them [the area officers]. And then that destructive comment came up.*—Salome (Interview)

> *The challenge was put forward that the social centers weren't referring people through to the church. And this particular person piped up and said, "I'm sorry, but I would never do that again. I did it once with one of my young people. It happened to be a young gay gentleman and I would never put them through that torment again."*—Salome (Interview)

> *I know many people who are LGBTQ+ but I cannot with a clear conscious tell them that they are welcome as a part of The Salvation Army.*—Mark (Letter)

Prior to ministry, the research participants also had secular employment. The welcome and inclusion that they received very clearly varied according to the decade in which they grew up and the industry that they were working in. Compare one participant from the 1980s to another from the early 2010s:

> *I was eighteen, and I'd started work with a government department then. There were a couple of gay guys that were employed around there and they were really, really under the—in the firing line as far as prejudices and really bad attitudes go, and that's when I sort of started to think, "Oh, that's me that they're talking about."*—Andrew (Interview)

> *I was already out in my workplace, so I was already out with these non-church-based people. It was totally, like, a non-issue.*

> *I worked in science. Everyone's like curious, and like pretty much anything goes.*—Elizabeth (Interview)

These comments show a shift over time in the secular workplace. But they also highlight how a concurrent shift has not occurred in many religious workplaces.

There were a few positive experiences. One interview participant spoke of the "gay couple down the road" who befriended his parents. Another spoke of open conversations in their household of what had happened between men in "the War." One spoke of the extra lengths that her mother went to, to learn about her sexual orientation and discuss it with wise guides. And there was one sad instance, where a research participant had lost their father at a young age, leading their mother to ask the local Corps Officer to have the "birds and bees" talk with them:

> *I remember he gave me this book that was published by some, you know, organisation or Christian group. And I the first thing I went looking for was homosexuality in it. I sort of looked in the index and it was just said it was—what were the words—not that it was an abomination or aberration but that it was unnatural.*—Simeon (Interview)

Joining Up

Somehow, after navigating their youth in these environments, the research participants became soldiers in TSA. This is considered full membership in TSA and is a pre-requisite to officership. Becoming a soldier typically involves a series of preparation classes before signing the soldier covenant publicly during a worship service at the local Corps. As this is often the main means of soldiers' indoctrination, it is the resource material used for solider preparation that has been surveyed as part of this research. In a number of cases, it is also this material that interview subjects mention as part of their journey.

Over time we see two critical historic shifts in the teaching on sexuality delivered through this material. The first occurs from the early 1980s. This reflects the broader shift in society where psychological associations started to remove homosexuality from diagnostic manuals (circa 1973) and churches began to respond by promoting SOGICE. This shift led TSA to start to make statements about human sexuality and include passages in their written materials about homosexuality that did not exist before.

The second shift occurred not long after the Joy FM interview discussed in chapter one. Here The Salvation Army's *Handbook of Doctrine* was mis-quoted, but nonetheless the ramifications included a withdrawal of many of the most offending statements from circulation. Since then, soldiership training in Australia has also shifted and the denomination has come full circle in that human sexuality is barely, if at all, discussed with those preparing for membership. An exception is in the 2020 "Called to be a Soldier" release from International Headquarters, which, while mostly positive and non-exclusive in the language of its chapter on sexuality, explicitly repeats that "The Salvation Army affirms that marriage is the voluntary and loving union for life of one man and one woman," and "It is the only appropriate context for sexual intimacy."[6]

It must be clearly stated that these shifts are merely observable patterns. Lest we create a situation of *post hoc ergo propter hoc* fallacy, where we assume that because Y follows X, then Y was caused by X, we note that many other influences could have been at play and that there are few records that could demonstrate direct causality.

Pre 1980

Before the 1980s the teaching on sexuality in soldiership preparation was scant. Here I review the most common soldiership preparation materials used, the *Manual of Salvationism* (1968) and *Preparation for Soldiership* (1977).

Manual of Salvationism (1968, 1974)

There are very few sections on sexuality, except in terms of marriage and pornography. In the section on marriage, there is no comment about who the parties of a wedding may be, although legally and culturally it would be expected they were one male and one female, and both heterosexuals.[7] Obscene books and papers are prohibited as they represent "a day of loose morals." Finally, "ungodly companions" of any type are to be avoided. The Scripture verse applied is 1 Peter 2:11—"Dear friends, I urge

6. The Salvation Army, *Called to be a Soldier*, 48.
7. Agnew, *Manual of Salvationism*, 58.

you, as foreigners and exiles, to abstain from sinful desires, which wage war against your soul."[8]

Ultimately, there is no specific reference to sexuality nor, explicitly, homosexuality.

> I did membership classes quite young (fourteen, I think) and we used a booked called the Manual of Salvationism. This didn't include much about sexuality, which was probably a good thing, but not long after that I was asked to help with some other "recruits" and introduced to the Chick Yuill book "Battle Orders" which really did condemn anyone that had any sort of "homosexual behaviors." This condemnation just kept going. We had Corps Cadets classes and whenever sexuality came up in those groups, it was always "love the sinner but hate the sin."[9]—Joseph (Interview)

Preparation for Soldiership (1977)

This book only contains vague direction to avoid the vices of the world and to follow the "athlete's example" of living a life with "no impurity." The verse applied is Galatians 5:17. *"For the desires of the flesh are against the Spirit, and the desires of the Spirit are against the flesh, for these are opposed to each other, to keep you from doing the things you want to do."* Again, there is no discussion of sexuality or explicit mention of homosexuality. In fact, a statement elsewhere in the material demonstrates that homosexuality was not a cultural consideration within the denomination when it says, "Jennifer thought it would be gay to go to the firm's dance."[10]

Post 1980

After 1980 homosexuality enters the discourse and becomes a topic for teaching those that would belong to TSA. Over the next thirty years, it would become increasingly pointed in the manner in which the topic was discussed, culminating in a very disturbing passage in *Salvationism 101* in 2009. Here I look at *The Salvationist Lifestyle* (1989), *Battle Orders* (1989), and *Salvationism 101* (2009).

---

8. Agnew, *Manual of Salvationism*, 70-72.

9. Corps Cadets was a common discipleship group for teenagers in The Salvation Army.

10. The Salvation Army, *Preparation for Soldiership*, 28.

The Salvationist Lifestyle (1989)

The Salvationist Lifestyle departed from other preparation materials in style. The author John Waldron pulled together writings on the soldiers' covenant that were extant in various other sources, from the earliest days of The Salvation Army through to the time he brought the book together.

In keeping with the thesis of this section, I observe that there is no discussion about human sexuality or homosexuality in any of the early materials quoted. A 1980 piece by Shaw Clifton is where the departure occurs. The then Captain (and later General) Clifton referenced the 1972 Lord Longford report on pornography (UK). He cites an example whereby he claims that pornography in an all-boys school leads to situations whereby "a crowd of people will want sex in any form."[11]

While this is a strange and obscure example, it is the first time that homosexuality is mentioned outside of TSA Orders and Regulations for Soldiers (which were only updated two years earlier, notably) and the first derogatory mention in soldier preparation materials.

Battle Orders: Salvation Army Soldiership (1989)

Battle Orders was a commonly used resource in the English-speaking world. It was used in almost all Australian Salvation Army Corps in the 1990s and early 2000s. It is the first soldiership preparation material to openly and emphatically condemn homosexual behavior and it is the material most-likely used in training many of today's current officer cohort. A number of the interview participants directly reference this material.

At the time, the writer Chick Yuill made the claim that "homosexuality is one of the most difficult subjects facing us today." He divides this "difficult subject" into two thoughts, saying there are two separate issues at hand: one about "homosexual practices" and the other regarding our "attitude to homosexuals." On the first question, he lists the usual six verses known in the LGBTQ+ community as the "clobber verses" to make a biblical claim that homosexual practices are condemned because they are "unnatural," "linked with the evils which disrupt the harmony and wellbeing of society," that "widespread homosexuality will militate against marriage and family life which are the foundations of

---

11. Clifton, "An Ugly Intruder Called Sin," in *The Salvationist Lifestyle*, 86.

a healthy society," and "those who indulge in such practices cannot be part of the Kingdom of God."[12]

Yuill goes on to say there is no place in the Christian's life for the hatred and prejudice against homosexuals that is "so prevalent among some people." He says, "No one is to be condemned because of their sexual orientation," but quickly adds that "every means of help—spiritual, medical, social, and psychiatric—should be offered."[13] This is a clear nod to the emerging SOGICE of the time, as is the direction to participants to pray and thank God for the gift of sexuality while also asking that God grant the courage to "uphold Christian standards in a confused world" and express their sexuality in accordance with God's will.[14]

> *The teaching then was very strong about us being an abomination and to the detriment of society and all the things that we read about in Chick Yuill's book.—John (Interview)*

In recent years, Yuill has apologized for the material and the hurt that it has caused. He has spoken about how personal interactions with LGBTQ+ people have changed his views, alongside more research and consideration.[15] This has meant a lot to the LGBTQ+ Salvationist community:

> *It was a talk by a guy named Chick Yuill who had, at one stage, written the membership materials for the Salvos. For him to say he'd changed his mind theologically and pastorally was massive.—Joseph (Interview).*

> *One of the most powerful things, was listening to Chick Yuill give an apology. I honestly couldn't believe it. I just had tears, because I remember reading that material, and it became part of my story of why I could not be a gay Christian, and to hear him say, "I got it wrong." To say that—that was just so powerful.—Matthew (Interview)*

---

12. Yuill, *Battle Orders*, 54.
13. Yuill, *Battle Orders*, 55.
14. Yuill, *Battle Orders*, 55.
15. Gibson, host, "Included 2021: Changed Minds with Chick Yuill," 24 July 2021, Included Conference Presentation.

Salvationism 101: Soldier Training (2009)

Salvationism 101 marks the low point of derogatory and difficult material presented to potential Salvation Army soldiers regarding homosexuality. It was written by Canadian officers living in Australia and became very popular with a significant group of highly conservative recruits that were part of the denomination at the time. Sadly, it also became the preparation material of choice in the inner cities of Melbourne and Adelaide. As it is dated after the preparation training most of the research participants experienced, there is no evidence regarding its impact in my interviews. One can only speculate on the harm caused.

Most notably the book says, "The Salvation Army has always had a conviction about the ills of society, like poverty, human trafficking, abortion, alcohol, drugs, gambling, homosexuality, pornography, prostitution, and tobacco. We've discussed these evils in terms of a new seven deadly sins—not sins that you are guilty of committing but of which you are the victim. These Seven Deadly Sins are extreme poverty, children in chains (slavery), orphans in the streets (homeless and fatherless), sex in the city (human trafficking and prostitution), AIDS and plagues, exigencies of war (child soldiers), and religious persecution."[16]

It is contemporarily astounding that homosexuality is aligned with human trafficking and that it is positioned as something of which one is a "victim." At the time, however The Salvation Army in Australia had a positional statement that read:

> Scripture forbids sexual intimacy between members of the same sex. The Salvation Army believes, therefore, that Christians whose sexual orientation is primarily or exclusively same-sex are called upon to embrace celibacy as a way of life. There is no scriptural support for same-sex unions as equal to, or as an alternative to, heterosexual marriage.[17]

It is not surprising, then, that The Salvation Army in Australia allowed the publication and distribution of this material for soldiership preparation.

Hill tells an interesting story about the localized revision of this positional statement in Australia and New Zealand. As a member of TSA's

---

16. Strickland and Court, *Salvationism 101*, 58.
17. The Salvation Army, "Human Sexuality."

Moral and Social Issues Council (MASIC) when this was discussed,[18] he notes that the issue was only addressed at the behest of a Territorial Commander who wanted a position statement that would "strengthen his hand" against a gay candidate for officer training. He describes the discussion at MASIC whereby one supportive officer could not see the difference between faithful heterosexual and homosexual couples, while another member opined that the latter would "burn in hell."[19]

Post 2012

2012-2013 marks a significant period of bad public relations for The Salvation Army in Australia. This was centered around two events: the June 2012 interview on Joy FM Melbourne where a Salvation Army officer was interpreted as saying that "gay people deserved to die," discussed in chapter 1, and the 2013 Royal Commission into Institutional Responses to Child Sexual Abuse.

Following the 2012 interview the TSA positional statements on human sexuality were removed from circulation. This occurred across most of the world and they are no longer available online. They have never been replaced or re-written. It is fascinating that while TSA has moved away from overtly homophobic statements, the surveys and interviews clearly show that it struggles to affirm LGBTQ+ people. There are still harms being caused, and partly it is now due to institutional ambivalence rather than direct oppression.

It is also following that moment in time (circa 2012) that we see a significant shift in the conversation around homosexuality and TSA in Australia. More progressive movements started rising up within the organization (e.g., *Salvos for a More Inclusive Church*) and changes occurred in the resource materials used for teaching within Corps. The irony that one of the worst moments in the movement's public history may have been a catalyst for change and reform is not lost. The momentum behind this shift has been enhanced through better biblical exegesis and theological teaching in TSA colleges, but also societal pressure, accreditation requirements for TSA social services, and threats to withdraw funding

---

18. MASIC—This council is brought together to discuss and provide guidelines and positional statements on the moral and social issues of the day.

19. Hill, *Saved to Save and Saved to Serve*, 327.

from TSA social services (which are needed to fund headquarters and support operations, which in turn support TSA corps/churches).

In this section, I look at the two soldier preparation materials published in Australia since that time, *Call to Arms* (2014) and *Exploring Soldiership* (2020).

Call to Arms: Soldiership Training for The Salvation Army (2014)[20]

The discussion of human sexuality in solder preparation seems to have come full circle at this point. There is again nothing explicit about human sexuality except for references to The Salvation Army's positional statements and guidelines, and the Orders and Regulations documents. As noted, by 2014, the positional statement on human sexuality had been discontinued but there were still guidelines for Salvationists on marriage "affirming the New Testament standard of marriage, that is, the voluntary and loving union for life of one man and one woman to the exclusion of all others."[21]

It is worth noting that as at April 2021, the Call to Arms website was still available. However, the internet links to the positional statements and guidelines were "broken." A check in August 2023 found that it had been taken down and entirely replaced by the Exploring Soldiership material.

Exploring Soldiership (2020)[22]

In this latest book there is no reference to sexuality at all. There is a reference to the Handbook of Doctrine 2010, which no longer has mention of sexuality and concentrates more on core statements of faith, but has been superseded again by the 2020 Handbook mentioned earlier in this chapter. There is now not even reference to Orders and Regulations for Soldiers, even in the extension materials, despite this still being considered the international regulation for membership.

---

20. Walker, *Call to Arms*.
21. The Salvation Army, *Salvation Army Ceremonies*, 17.
22. The Salvation Army, *Exploring Soldiership*.

Other Doctrinal Materials & Orders and Regulations

What has mostly been taught to potential soldiers of TSA regarding sexuality has changed over time. Behind those teachings and resources, sits the Handbooks of Doctrine which extrapolates on the faith statements of The Salvation Army. Given that one of these books was the basis for the JOY FM interview, we conclude this second section with a quick reference to the latest two Handbooks and then Orders and Regulations for Soldiers.

The first is *Salvation Story* (1998). It holds some significance within TSA as it was the first "handbook" published since 1969, meaning also that it was the first to be released since demedicalization and decriminalization of homosexuality. There is little in this book about sexuality. However, in Australia, much has been made of the use of Romans 1 as a prooftext within this book following the famous Joy FM interview. Contextually this passage, known as one of the six "clobber passages" in the LGBTQ+ community, is used in the book as part of a discussion on "the problem of evil." It is used after a paragraph that commences "Evil that arises from the wickedness of human beings can be seen as a risk of our creation as free, personal beings."[23]

The *Handbook of Doctrine* (2010) has only two mentions of the word sex and nothing on sexuality. One mention is where it is stated that the image of God is found in all people regardless of a number of characteristics, including sex. The other is in a footnote, referencing a book title.[24] Celibacy isn't even mentioned in the section on spiritual gifts.[25]

Orders and Regulations

For a long time, the biggest hurdle to inclusion of LGBTQ+ people in TSA was perhaps in *Orders and Regulations for Soldiers*. This book has had multiple iterations. For most of my research participants, the impacting edition would be the 1987 edition, revised in 1994. This edition states (consistent with the timelines and concurrent attitudes noted above):

> The term "misconduct of a sexually deviant kind" includes homosexual acts (if between women, termed lesbian practices). It

---

23. The Salvation Army, *Salvation Story*, 28-29.
24. The Salvation Army, *Handbook of Doctrine*, 268-9.
25. The Salvation Army, *Handbook of Doctrine*, 268

> is necessary here to distinguish between homosexual tendencies and homosexual practices. All that has been written in this chapter refers to heterosexual relationships, i.e., between men and women. The homosexual person is attracted to persons of the same sex. So long as this does not express itself in homosexual acts, it is not blameworthy and should not be allowed to create guilt. Such persons need understanding and help, not condemnation. Some can never achieve a heterosexual relationship, but it must be remembered that some men and women who have actually committed homosexual acts are still capable of heterosexual relationships. Given a close walk with the Saviour, and the strict discipline of thought and obedience which all Christian life requires, there is no reason why the homosexually disposed believer should not be a victorious Salvationist, rendering service in appropriate areas of Army activity as appointed by the officer. Homosexual practices un-renounced render a person unacceptable as a Salvation Army soldier, just as acts of immorality between heterosexual persons do.[26]

Homosexuality is therefore considered "deviant" and a "tendency" or "disposition" that is "immoral" if acted upon. There is room in this passage for SOGICE and also the humiliating notion that all LGBTQ+ people need "help."

Earlier in this chapter we noted the 2020 edition of this book. There is no longer such a discussion and, as part of an otherwise healthy discussion on human sexuality, the only negative commentary for LGBTQ+ Salvationists is the affirmation of marriage as between one man and one woman. This shift, along with the modifications of language and sentiment in soldier preparation materials, allows us to observe change over time.

Hill, quoted earlier, gives a clear summary of the state of play today. While he notes that The Salvation Army's positional statements and approaches to training have reflected changing societal and theological attitudes, he describes the current situation as a "half-way house" distinguishing between "orientation" and "activity," noting that it is "of course, still discriminatory."[27] He rightly notes that the endemic homophobia in many territories where TSA is numerically strongest, as well as the spectacle of other communions (e.g. the Anglican communion) dividing on

---

26. The Salvation Army, *Chosen to be a Soldier*, 49-50.
27. Hill, *Saved to Save and Saved to Serve*, 328.

the same issue, creates enough fear in The Salvation Army's international leadership for any change to be unlikely in the short term.

Officer Training

The final section of this chapter looks at the experience of officer training. During this phase of the research participants' lives, they are subject to Bible teaching, and theological, spiritual, and pastoral formation.

The experiences articulated depend entirely on the college that the participant attended and the decade of their training. It is seen, as above, that there are shifts that occur after 1980 and then again after the early 2010s. There is also a significant difference in the approach taken between colleges in Bexley North (NSW) and Parkville (Vic), which were the key colleges in that intervening period. Finally, there is a significant difference between the support given by college staff, especially after 2012, and the hostility experienced from other cadet trainees.

The survey participants were drawn from the following colleges:

Table 6: Survey Participants' Officer Training Colleges

East Melbourne	1	4.2%
Parkville	7	29.2%
Ringwood	6	25.0%
Petersham	1	4.2%
Bexley North	7	29.2%
I trained overseas	1	4.2%

One participant was still in the application process to commence training or in the process of undertaking training, so is not counted in the above figures.[28] The participants who trained in East Melbourne and Petersham did not make specific references to their training. From those who provided "free text responses" in the surveys we see that earlier trainees did not have pleasant experiences:

---

28. I keep the distinction between a candidate for training and cadet in training deliberately vague. There are so few cadets currently that, if a participant were current enrolled in training, they would be easily identifiable.

> There were some classes in college where homosexuality was consistently labelled an abomination, and compared to bestiality and pedophilia.—Survey Response

But more recent trainees, post 2012 and mostly trained in Ringwood or through remote training, were more positive:

> Academic study has had a large part in forming my current state of belief. I feel like it has led me down one of the paths of deconstruction. I used to identify as heterosexual but (someone who) dealt with homosexual sin. But now I identify as bi/pan and am ok with that.—Survey Response

> (I now have a) sound theological understanding of Imago Dei. Sexuality week at college, particularly the day spent with presentations from counsellors with interviews and interaction with Christians with lived experience very much helped—Survey Response

The interview participants were drawn from the following colleges:

Table 7: Interview Participants' Officer Training Colleges

Parkville	4
Ringwood	2
Bexley North	5

We can see clear differences between the approaches of the colleges and the decades in which people trained. To protect interview participants, in this section no names (not even pseudonyms) are included so that the stories cannot be linked to other sections and no-one can be identified.

Bexley North

Those who trained in Bexley North mostly had negative experiences that included referrals to SOGICE. Two referred to inclusion of SOGICE materials in the classroom. A third was referred to SOGICE at another time and a fourth had already been exposed through her local corps/church. It is worth noting that three of the five participants who trained at Bexley North had their SOGICE "therapy" paid for by TSA.

> *I remember an experience at college where it was just like, well if you're gay we're getting rid of you right now. And in fact, someone left my session after the pastoral care session on being gay which was just horrendous.—Interview with former Bexley North Cadet*

> *I'll start by talking about our pastoral care session which was neither pastoral, nor caring. And it was run by two officers, who are—you know—lovely people. They're counsellors; they're lovely people. And it would be interesting to have a conversation with them now, if I could suppress my rage long enough to have a conversation, to say, "Do you understand the damage that you did to people in that session?" So, we had a whole bunch of . . . we had ten . . . in the Eastern Territory at that time we had ten sessions of pastoral care [on topics] that you might deal with pastorally. And this was going to equip you for your ministry. And the bit on homosexuality was a bit, you know, from Sy Rogers—talking about how God had delivered him from homosexuality and how he'd married a woman and how it was all hunky dory. And I'm like . . . so I know that one of my session mates was traumatized by that; we've talked about it since.—Interview with former Bexley North Cadet*

> *There was just a whole heap of discussion about how homosexuals are perverts, they're pedophiles, and none of that conversation was stopped. It was "homosexuals are disordered people," they are one of the things that . . . the officer leading the session said was that they had not ever developed mature, adult relationships and that's why they were gay.—Interview with former Bexley North Cadet*

> *We were shown—the only teaching on this was videos by a guy called Sy Rogers, who was an "ex-gay" who testified about how you can change, and you know all that sort of stuff. And they were the videos that we were showing, and then that was reinforced through any discussion afterwards. But funny thing is, we now know there were several gay people in my session, and we all sat through that. You know, we never knew about each other. Obviously, it was, you know, the shame, and it [the shame] was great there.—Interview with former Bexley North Cadet*

The use of SOGICE material in the classroom has left each of these participants with some degree of trauma. One still expressed significant anger a few decades after their training experience. None of the participants reflected any biblical teaching on diverse sexuality at the Bexley

North college, only derogatory counselling approaches or limited theological reflection and promotion of SOGICE.

Parkville

The Parkville experience was not explicit in its reference to SOGICE for any cadets. One was referred to SOGICE during his out-placement. For most, it was a wildly variant experience depending on their particular training staff and cadet session.

> *I know it came as a surprise to all of my session mates, even though at one stage there I did a talk at college, about people's attitudes towards homosexuality. I was the only one that ever brought it up and I did this long talk about "You never know who you're talking to and about what you're talking about." I got very emotional in it, which they all thought was a bit strange.—Interview with former Parkville Cadet*

> *The lecturer that came in to do our ethics classes on sexuality started the class by saying that he didn't even know what a homosexual was until one of his military colleagues got sent home under a cloud of secrecy. He clearly hadn't advanced his thinking much beyond that point. Then it became a joking matter. One of my session mates was spouting hateful anti-gay gunk, but as a joke one of my other session mates sat on his lap and gave him a kiss to make it all worse. Cleary, gay people were sinners and something we could joke about. And the lecturer did nothing about either of them.—Interview with former Parkville Cadet*

> *It must be said that in my session we had a very supportive training principal and almost all of the college staff, I would say, were people who were ah . . . affirming, if not, supportive of LGBTIQ people. My training principal did pull me aside on one or two occasions, and I was one of two LGBT people in my session, and offered pastoral conversations and check ins to make sure everything was OK. [But in relation to other cadets:] I had a cadet tell me at one point he was upset because he loves me like a brother and he hates the idea that I'm going to spend the rest of eternity in hell, but that's where I'm going to be . . . There was a very loud, and active, opposing voice [from among the cadets] that kept coming up that made that an unsafe place to be. I wasn't at college much, I would stay at friends a lot, because college just wasn't safe, but that came with risks too. At one point I was brought into*

> the training principal who told me if I wasn't present at the college more and stayed onsite overnight, I would be considered for . . . um . . . what's the word—being kicked out because I wasn't immersing in the full experience. And I did try to explain that the experience wasn't safe for me and that I didn't want to be here, immersed with forty highly conservative Christians who let their voice be heard wherever they can, in the hallways, in the dining room, in class, but it was really emphasized for me that I need to be at the college more or else I risked my place there. I was, you know, made to confront my abusers effectively around the clock, seven days a week.—Interview with former Parkville Cadet

These interviews show that there was not a uniform experience at Parkville for gay and lesbian cadets. However, it was not as explicitly driven toward SOGICE in the way that the Bexley North cadets found.

Post 2010s—Ringwood & Remote

The current training environment for cadets is very different to the old residential colleges, especially since COVID. This has seen training conducted remotely, mostly, from the college's base in Ringwood. Of those that have trained since 2012, there is a theme of safety and support from training staff, but some hostility from session mates.

> We had XXX as a lecturer who was challenging the, I suppose, the debate, or more introducing another side around the gay marriage debate. And I remember XXX came and did like a panel session. [But] I had session mates who were sort of like resistant to that, to some of those ideas, and maybe seeing it as a trendy thing for some officers to be supportive of.—Interview with former Ringwood Cadet

> I unpacked, and learned, and understood better this concept of "God in each of us," that was probably the real moment for me when I thought, "Oh . . . there I am, created in God's image, and so my very nature . . . but by very nature of that reflect part of who God is . . . " We actually had a human sexuality week at college, which was amazing. And it focused on the broad spectrum of sexuality, relationships in general, ah . . . singleness, and then there was a whole day that was dedicated to LGTBIQ and they actually had a therapist come in that deals . . . that used to be a—I don't know what denomination—but used to be a minister, and ah . . . . Basically, he presented a day with a few parts. There was

a—*I think it was done by one of the college staff actually, but a list of biblical passages and we went through these to understand the texts in a more helpful way. And then we had this [person] who gave from his perspective as a therapist some of the theological underpinnings of where things are at, the damage that's done in the church, and just painted a picture of normalcy really. And then in the second session in the afternoon he brought in some people that identified as LGBTIQ—I think we had three—and it was basically a panel session where they shared their stories with the group. And it was really amazing forum, and quite eye-opening for everyone including me.—Interview with former Ringwood Cadet*

This was one of the first officers to articulate the theme of creation, which is explored later in chapter 10. Over the course of the interviews, affirming one's sexuality as part of their created being and part of the very good order of creation was important for a number of the officers. Other recent trainee officers also spoke positively about their experience of college, although continuing to distinguish between staff and colleague cadets at times:

College, it was very affirming. Even though I wasn't out publicly to anyone. I knew that it was a safe space to be.—Interview with former Ringwood Cadet

And then I went to college and current college leadership at the time were totally chilled . . . You know, it's like a non-issue . . . My session, on the other hand, were not amused that I was accepted. One even said, "Well, if . . . "—to my face, so I appreciate that they said it to my face . . . "if they've let you in. What next?" It was brought up a couple of times, by session mates, in—What was the class we did?—Christian theology, or something along those lines. [They] got us to watch the trailer for "1946" which started the conversation within the session, but which then created an unhealthy conversation . . . They [the other cadets] took that conversation offline . . . [And] I do know that there were prayer meetings held, and I was brought up a number of times, only because a friend's husband told me it was like an old men's, little men's group, and I know the college attempted to shut them down. But then what can you do? You can't stop people meeting.—Interview with former Ringwood Cadet

I only had one challenging moment with a lecturer . . . other than that it was actually quite affirming.—Interview with former Ringwood Cadet

For the most part, the experience of LGBTQ+ cadets is improving over time. Certainly, in the past decade, apart from some hostility from session mates, there has been a sense of safety in the college environment and more balanced biblical, theological, pastoral, and ethical teaching. While the officer formation and higher education staff are in distinct teams within the Eva Burrows College structure, there appears to generally be an affirming and supportive environment. Historically, however, the differences between the colleges are stark, as is the difference between pre-2010s training and post-2010s training. This is somewhat due to a higher standard of theological education in the University era of TSA cadet training which brings thorough exegesis and analysis to the classroom. While there are no direct links to matters like the bad public relations TSA received during the early 2010s and the internal and external influences for change previously identified, it is a reasonable assumption that the changes have also been influence by these broader vectors for change in and around TSA.

Conclusion

The teaching received by the research participants over time has been highly formative. There are multiple impacts, both positive and negative, that direct their attitudes and emotions toward themselves, as well as their memories and experiences of school, family, church, and ministry. This chapter has considered three highly impactful times in the lives of research participants: growing up, joining up, and then officer training.

It is demonstrated that following 1980 there was a conservative shift seen in the changes in public statements and teaching materials. This is commensurate with the shift seen in wider evangelical circles (discussed in chapter 1) and resulted in many cadets and officers being referred to SOGICE or exposed to it in some way. The trauma experienced by many in this era will be discussed in the next few chapters.

Then, following the early 2010s, there was a different approach that saw many definitive statements removed from circulation and a sense of safety found in training environments. This could, in many ways, be attributed to the higher quality of education provided in the university era of training cadets. It is assumed that there is also some influence from the broader shift in TSA that is occurring through grass roots movements, societal influences, and after bad public relations events, threats to funding and changes in social service accreditation.

Section 2—**Harm**

Chapter 3: Moral Injury

Introduction

THE STORY ARTICULATED BY LGBTQ+ officers is one of both harm and hope. In the next four chapters I discuss the four primary areas of harm that surfaced during the surveys and the interviews: moral injury, religious trauma, Sexual Orientation and Gender Identity Change Efforts (SOGICE), and discrimination leading to internalized homophobia. In some cases, these are simply things that had been experienced and the officers have healed or continued through life relatively unaffected. In other cases, there is lingering hurt and trauma that is carried by the officers and former officers. From chapter 7 on, I discuss the hope found via theological reflection, authentic living, and support groups that have been birthed through grassroots movements. There, the officers tell stories of authenticity, ministry opportunities, affirmation of their sexuality as God-given, solidarity in community, working for justice, and enlivening the grace of God that they have experienced for themselves.

The first area for discussion is the experience of moral injury, which is the focus of this chapter. The study of moral injury has been a developing field of research over the last twenty years. It focused initially on members of military forces who were challenged and confronted by many moral and ethical challenges in both war and peacekeeping operations. Conceptually, it considers the impact of being party to human suffering that confronts one's core beliefs and values. This can include witnessing the actions of others, particularly authorities and trusted leaders, that one cannot morally accommodate and/or being directed to undertake activities that conflict with one's core values and morals.[1]

---

1. Litz et al., "Moral injury and moral repair in war veterans," 695.

I originally assumed that there would be significant examples of moral injury among LGBTQ+ officers, such that it may be the lens or framework for the entire research project. Recent research has indicated that the LGBTQ+ community may be considered high risk for exposure to morally injurious events. This is particularly the case where there is religious trauma associated with SOGICE.[2] The assumption about its presence among LGBTQ+ Salvation Army officers was correct; however, to be faithful to the full experience of the participants who shared their stories, not just the breadth of harms but also the positive stories of hope, grace, and ministry, I have reduced discussion of this area to one chapter.

Here, I discuss the distinction between moral injury and post-traumatic stress, noting differences in symptomology and trigger events and recognizing that a specific trauma does not need to exist for moral injury to occur. I will also discuss the distinction between moral injury that is related to the self-as-transgressor, and that related to the other-as-transgressor.

The first category includes both acts of commission and acts of omission. The second category considers both acts of other people and betrayal by systems. At each stage, I will identify how this relates to the experiences of LGBTQ+ Salvation Army officers, considering where they may have been exposed to morally injurious events.

Defining Moral Injury

Moral injury is a term that has gained increasing currency among researchers. Mostly, researchers believed there was something in the experience of military personnel that manifested itself as a violation of personal values systems and was potentially a sub-set of Post-Traumatic Stress Disorder (PTSD).[3] It first gained prominence in the 1990s through work by American psychologist, researcher, and veterans' advocate Jonathan Shay.[4] From the early 2000s researchers gave more focus to the area, directly as a result of veterans returning from the Gulf Wars. Since 2013 the term "moral injury" has been documented and reported in the

---

2. Jones et al., "Religious Trauma and Moral Injury from LGBTQA+ Conversion Practices," 2.

3. Frame, *Moral Injury*, 2.

4. Shay, "Learning About Combat Stress from Homer's Iliad."

popular press with features appearing in periodicals including the *New York Times* and *Huffington Post*.[5]

Even when patients presented with symptoms not consistent with PTSD, moral injury was treated solely from a psychological perspective as a result of its prior classification. Distinguishing which experiences are trauma inflicted and stress inducing from those which are moral violations, and then understanding the similarities and differences between the two, has been much more recent work. Litz and others have undertaken significant work to distinguish moral injury from PTSD.[6] Essentially, it is now clearly understood that one does not need to be exposed to direct trauma to experience moral injury. However, it is very much the case that many cases of moral injury will be comorbid with some degree of post-traumatic stress.[7]

Such research enables people to differentiate the two more precisely. PTSD will often elicit a fear and hypervigilance response as it is essentially a fear-victim response to danger, for example when a traumatic event triggers ongoing internal judgements about one's safety. It has physiological impacts whereby hormones are produced that affect the amygdala and hippocampus, which connect fear to memory, regulate emotions, and control the individual's responses to fear. The individual remains "on guard" leading to periodic states of hyper-arousal.

Moral injury is, however, essentially rooted in guilt and shame and therefore requires different approaches at times.[8] It is an experience caused by various physical, psychological, social, and spiritual impacts from moral transgressions or violations affecting a person's beliefs, values, or ethical standards. It is due to an individual "perpetrating, failing to prevent, bearing witness to, or learning about the inhumane acts which result in the pain, suffering or death of others and which fundamentally challenges the moral integrity of the individual." Alternatively, it can generate from the subsequent experience and feeling of "utter betrayal of what is right by trusted individuals who hold legitimate authority."[9]

---

5. Frame, *Moral Injury*, 2-3.

6. Litz et al., "Distinct trauma types in military service members seeking treatment for posttraumatic stress disorder," 286-295.

7. Beard, "Conceptual Distinctions," 116.

8. Brock and Lettini, *Soul Repair*, xiii; "Moral Injury," National Centre for PTSD, 26 November 2020.

9. Carey and Hodgson, "Chaplaincy, Spiritual Care, and Moral Injury," Introduction.

Researchers break potentially morally injurious experiences into two categories so as to simplify these definitions. The first are those experiences that are self-generated by commission of acts that betray one's own morals and values, omission of "right" behaviors, or the failure to prevent such morally egregious incidents where it is perceived to be within one's power. The second are those experiences that are other(s)-generated whether via specific acts of individuals or the betrayal by organizational and institutional systems. This useful distinction helps to better understand the different pathological impacts of each, according to whether they are based on individual responsibility (e.g., perpetration of morally questionable acts or failing to prevent harm to others), or others' responsibility (e.g., witnessing disproportionate violence or acts of betrayal by trusted others).

In general, each category of moral injury will result in differing symptomology. Events that are perceived as self-generated are more likely to lead to negative self-referential emotions and cognitions (e.g., guilt, shame, lack of self-forgiveness), whereas those morally injurious events involving others-as-transgressor are more likely to result in negative externally-directed emotions and cognitions (e.g., anger, trust issues, inability to forgive others). Both types of events are often associated with spiritual/existential issues including the sense of self and purpose, potential loss of faith, leaving religious institutions and expressions, and questioning the validity of moral codes.[10] Dispositional shame that results from moral injury—when shame becomes a person's habitual way of navigating life—violates the self in such a way that it affects the ability to support healthy relationships and/or moral activity.[11]

Self-Generated Moral Injury

Self-generated moral injury is where the individual experiences self-as-transgressor and either acts, or fails to act, as their moral and value codes dictate. This is commonly noted in the case of soldiers who kill despite their own moral code forbidding such actions, intentionally or otherwise,[12] or who participate in other extreme combat activities (for example, extreme interrogations of prisoners). Where a person experiences

---

10. Barnes et al., "Moral Injury and PTSD."
11. Downie, "Christian Shame and Religious Trauma," 6.
12. Brock & Lettini note that even when their lives were directly threatened, 75% of American soldiers could not or did not fire at the enemy in World War 2. Brock and Lettini, *Soul Repair*, 17.

significant guilt and shame deriving from committing acts in violation of a moral norm, or a personal moral standard, it is perhaps the hardest area of moral injury to overcome.

In these instances, moral injury occurs when someone violates or betrays their own core values and beliefs. Importantly, while moral injury is commonly understood within high-stakes, life-or-death situations such as military service, researchers are now starting to consider how even seemingly innocuous acts can later be perceived as moral violations by one's self.[13] It may realistically occur at a much lower level. For LGBTQ+ officers, this could be through personally choosing to continue serving in a system that denies the freedom to be who they are, or being conflicted by remaining in a space while not feeling safe to express their sexuality or speak about same-sex relationships due to the perceived oppressive environment. LGBTQ+ officers will experience self-as-transgressor where they are defending or promoting discriminatory policies, or teaching theologies and practices that deny their true self or their moral and value constructs.

Ninety-two percent of survey respondents in this research (twenty-two of twenty-four) said that, at least some of the time, they needed to edit their speech, appearance, dress or behaviors. Five said they consciously edited their behavior all of the time. Only two respondents did not feel the need to self-edit. Considering the importance that so many placed on authenticity (discussed in chapter seven), it would be distressing not to be able to be themselves in their workplace and ministry.

Eighty-two percent of survey respondents (twenty of twenty-four) believed they were expected to speak or act in ways that suggested LGBTQ+ people (themselves) were not acceptable in TSA. To deny one's self and to feel required to speak against one's self or one's experiences would also be distressing and could be morally injurious. Three interview participants explicitly noted such instances:

> [There was] a strong expectation from my corps that I would denounce all the gay people in town.—Mary (Interview Participant)
>
> There were conversations I got involved in . . . where prejudices against gay and lesbian people etc. were being had.—Andrew (Interview Participant)
>
> I was even told once, "No, you can't preach that. Your sermon's great, but you're going to a country corps." . . . Because it was

---

13. Dursun and Watkins, "Moral Injury."

> *around same sex marriage, and I wanted to preach it at the church . . . So, I was stopped from preaching messages that I believe are relevant, and should have been spoken about.—Salome (Interview Participant)*

In extreme cases there may be officers who, having been exposed to SOGICE themselves and desiring to help others, subsequently undertake to lead such practices. This would likely be while having an underlying feeling or realization about both the lie being perpetuated and the harm being caused. Only one officer in the survey indicated that this was their experience. As it was a survey response, there is no understanding of the extent to which this could have been personally harmful, but there is significant likelihood it was harmful.

It can be devastating to violate one's self, one's conscience, or one's values. This can be the case even if the occurrence is unintentional or unavoidable. Over time the individual concerned may have a growing feeling that they no longer live in a reliable, meaningful world and perhaps can no longer be regarded as a worthwhile human being. The resulting cognitive dissonance has been observed to result in responses that include overwhelming depression, guilt, and self-medication.[14] The damaged conscience becomes very good at punishing the self and less effective in applying the balm of forgiveness, as forgiveness is most effectively pronounced from a position of moral authority—a position which the 'self' no longer has. In the absence of forgiveness, guilt may become pathological.[15] One interview respondent carried significant guilt for a number of years, and perhaps still does:

> *I did let myself down and betray my own values in the ways I behaved at one point. It caused damage and hurt people that matter a lot to me. You end up feeling like you don't know yourself, because your behaviors don't align with who you are and what you believe. There are explanations, including not knowing how to deal with my sexuality and the sense of hopelessness I may have had at the time, but they are not excuses. I did the wrong thing.—Joseph (Interview Participant)*

Unravelling this self-as-transgressor sub-set of moral injury can be difficult. A first step may require the individual to be assisted through a process of appraising the normative dimensions of their circumstances

---

14. Brock and Lettini, *Soul Repair*, xv.
15. Beard, "Conceptual Distinctions," 121.

and actions to determine the extent to which they are *actually* guilty, or otherwise. Then they can relativize that appraisal against the degree to which the self is punishing them through pathological guilt and maladaptive experience or behavior.

These experiences of self-as-transgressor can be complicated by the perceptions of others. An LGBTQ+ officer may perceive incongruity between their internal discourse of shame and the empathetic support of allies who posit mitigating circumstances that excuse the officer's behavior. The military equivalent is where a soldier condemns themselves for taking a life, but sympathizers will not join in that condemnation and wish to positively focus on neutralizing a threat. Perhaps they even call them a hero. The notion that these individuals may be struggling with emotional pain related to *their own* actions does not occur to others.[16]

The other type of morally injurious event in the category of self-as-transgressor is the failure to prevent harm to others. This is where the individual has witnessed abuse or a moral failing and not participated, but also not acted to prevent or redress the incident either. Researchers note that more attention needs to be paid in this area. Previously it has been given limited attention because the failure to prevent a trauma did not trigger the same PTSD response as experiencing a trauma. Since we now understand moral injury as distinct from PTSD, researchers have found that the moral injury potential of witnessing or learning about acts that one believes one could have, or should have, prevented has resulted in similar numbers of suicide attempts as compared to control groups.[17]

The most common form of potentially morally injurious event identified in the interviews was the failure to prevent or respond to harm caused to others. The cumulative impact of this on the individual LGBTQ+ officer is worthy of note as a significant stressor. Some of the interview participants described this:

> *It was something else that she said about LGBT people and I felt that I needed to stand up for the community, but I thought that was going to raise too many questions, so I let it go.*—James (Interview Participant)

> *I've not had the emotional energy to then deal with what comes back. Because it's not just me putting my hand up and saying,*

---

16. McCarthy, "An Exploration of Moral Injury as Experienced by Combat Veterans," 28.

17. Bryan et al., "Moral Injury, Suicidal Ideation, and Suicide Attempts in a Military Sample," 154-160.

> *"that's not OK." It's worse. So, the majority of the time I just choose to stay silent, not because I want to, but because I have to for my own safety.* —Simon (Interview Participant)

> *Ministers' fraternal meetings where there was, you know, if I look back on it, pretty overt homophobia and you know, you stay silent, because you're supposed to stay silent.* —Mary (Interview Participant)

Consistently, interview participants discussed being party to conversations and activities which were anti-LGBTQ+ but not feeling safe to do anything about it. Nintey-two percent of survey respondents said that they had witnessed discrimination against LGBTQ+ people in a Salvation Army context. Seventy percent of respondents said that, at least some of the time, they stayed silent when they witnessed such discrimination. Forty-five percent said that this was because they were concerned about the consequences of intervening. Twelve percent said that they, too, experienced discrimination *as a direct result of their intervention*. Following this, there is shame and guilt that they did not stand up for a colleague or that they did not counter a harmful attitude.

Other-generated Moral Injury

There is a second sub-set of potential moral injury events derived from "other-as-transgressor," which, in turn, includes an area known as "betrayal-by-systems." This betrayal occurs where there is a psychological contract between an institution or system and an individual, in which the individual believes they are owed something in exchange for commitment and sacrifice in the organization. For example, in the military, soldiers believe that they are owed welfare and health care given that they are deployable, in harm's way, and commit state-sanctioned violence. As a non-military example, in TSA, officers would expect a stipend or allowance, pastoral care, and housing in exchange for being deployable, exposed to ministry traumas, and expected to sacrifice other careers and personal liberties. Importantly, this contract is often unconscious until it is breached, but a breach through betrayal of leadership, institutional action, or institutional inaction damages an individual's capacity to trust, and results in injury.[18]

---

18. O'Neill George, "Moral Injury, Institutional Betrayal, and Psychological Contract Theory Breach in the Australian Army."

After a LGBTQ+ officer's sexuality becomes known, personal or institutional betrayal becomes more possible. Sixty-two and a half percent of survey participants felt that decisions had been made about them by TSA leadership on the basis of their sexuality. Of these, 25 percent felt this "to a great extent." Given that some of the officers surveyed are not "out" (therefore their sexuality is not known at the time of decision making), this makes the perception by the others about how they are treated even more glaring.

To date, little work has been done in the exploration of moral injury outside of the armed services, even in the area of "other-as-transgressor." This is despite many workplaces, it would seem, being ripe for the development of such an internal conflict where people are asked, or required, to behave in "business" in ways that conflict with their personal beliefs and values. There would also be a number of workplaces where someone may be exposed to the abuse, exclusion, or betrayal of trusted others (or one's self).

It is increasingly recognized that morally injurious events are common within other sociocultural and occupational contexts. These include high-stakes occupations such as child protective services, healthcare, and other frontline professions, but they have been rarely studied.[19] One example was evidenced in a staff survey in Tasmania that revealed 46 percent of staff in a state government department reported they felt morally compromised in what they have been asked to do, or stopped from doing, in their work, as the environment of the workplace was heavily politicized.[20]

More work is now being done regarding moral injury among people who have witnessed or experienced certain types of physical or severe emotional/physical trauma. This may include instances of rape and assault, abortion, car accidents, workplace injuries, and so on. These individuals reportedly often obsess about what they should have done differently to avoid the injurious incident or experience inflicted by another, and carry a sense of personal responsibility for what occurred. In these cases, there is a crossover between the categories of self-as-transgressor (who should have acted) and the other-as-transgressor (who inflicted the injury).

---

19. Grey et al., "Adaptive Disclosure," 407-15; Haigt et al., "Basically, I Look at It Like Combat," 477-489.

20. Killick, "Sick Work Environment," 9.

Blumberg, in one of the first studies to look at moral injury in police officers, compiled a helpful list of the ways in which other-as-transgressor morally injurious events could occur.[21] The following examples are adapted from that list and related to the work of Salvation Army officers.

First, police officers may be directed into enforcement activities that violate their morals or values codes, such as having to relocate people experiencing homelessness. In the case of the LGBTQ+ Salvation Army officer, this would include being denied permission to host or perform a same-sex marriage in their church facility or being directed to remove another LGBTQ+ soldier from the church roll.

One interview participant spoke a lot about the conflict they felt from conducting weddings. In their case, this had not only to do with the gender of the participants, but also some of the vows that were required, making it more a personal objection. Another spoke of how she believed the organization expected her only to assist people who fitted a certain moral behavioral code, something that was in opposition to her own:

> My session mates were appalled that we would give a double bed to a de-facto couple. They'd give them two single beds if they came for help. They definitely weren't going to give a gay couple a double bed. And I can remember that there was a gay couple in town that had a fire, so I gave them everything that I would give any other couple. And someone wrote to the DC about it.[22] —Mary (Interview Participant)

"Mary" also spoke about her own experience of being removed from the TSA roll when she left officership, at the hands of someone she had trained with:

> You know, one of my session mates sent me a letter taking me off the roll and talking about my "ongoing moral turpitude."— Mary (Interview Participant; she added with a sly giggle that she was surprised that her colleague even understood the word, "turpitude.")

A second instance could be where trusted colleagues or supervisors act in ways that betray the individuals' morals and values. This can

---

21. Blumberg, "What Should Clinicians Who Care for Police Officers Know About Moral Injury?" 126-132.

22. Divisional Commander—The leader of a Salvation Army Division, which is a geographic area comprised of corps/churches. In Australia, these now correspond (mostly) with state boundaries.

include direct behaviors that cause the individual to lose trust and security in their leaders or superiors, or could include systems, policies, and procedures that are enforced by leaders and diminish the individual's faith in the organization or denomination. An LGBTQ+ Salvation Army officer who confided in a trusted leader about their sexuality or relationship status only to find that this is used against them would be such an example. The enforcement of a resignation policy against Salvation Army officers, either prematurely in the early stages of a relationship or in an unexpected manner, would constitute another.

Almost all interview participants spoke about a feeling of betrayal after they had made a disclosure to their leaders. These included the following:

> [They] just shared information that wasn't theirs to share in order to provoke a response from my new officer [colleagues] here... But there was an effort then to, sort of, undercut me before I came in which is crap behavior.—Elizabeth (Interview Participant)

> It's almost expected that there will be a betraying within The Salvation Army because of this and it feels like there is an expectation that people will be talking about it behind your back ... So other officers will discuss you, your behaviors or practices before they approach you.—John (Interview Participant)

> I trusted a leader with my sexuality and also discussed an experience that I'd had with them. They unfortunately decided that was the time to instigate an "accountability program" to ensure I was behaving appropriately. It became disciplinary rather than supportive.—Joseph (Interview Participant)

> The Divisional General Secretary, who was absolutely, with no doubt, a lesbian in a lesbian relationship, but closeted ... came out and just ripped into me. Absolutely ripped into me. And I'm like, "You're supposed to back me; you're at least supposed to ask my side of the story."—Mary (Interview Participant)

There was even one instance where a disclosure about their sexuality led to a shocking approach by a senior leader for a "hook up":

> It came as a bit of a shock to me once when we were at some kind of officer's retreat or bash in XXX and one of the Colonels came a knocking at my door one night.—Andrew (Interview Participant)

In terms of betrayal-by-systems, the expectation of a life of ministry that is facilitated by the organization can be placed at risk due to a

Salvation Army officer's sexual orientation, gender identity, or relationship status. This risk affects allowances, housing, training, work placements, and professional development. The research discovered that one of the most common fears for LGBTQ+ officers would be forced resignation due to being "discovered" in same-sex relationships. Former officers participating in the survey were asked how much of a factor (on a scale of 1-10) their sexuality was in their departure from officership. Nine out of ten rated their sexuality seven or higher (out of ten) as a factor in their departure.

This not only affects their sense of theological calling and identity as officers and ministers of the gospel. It also breaches the trust around the sacred contract of religious practitioners with real world impacts such as unemployment and homelessness. LGBTQ+ officers could experience this as a breach of the psychological contract for care and support they have with the organization, action and inaction in the areas of discriminatory policy and practice, or direct betrayal by leadership. Such instances of moral injury have been documented as leading to mental illness.[23]

One interview participant spoke at length about the pain of leaving and how it was exacerbated by pending homelessness:

> [When] I leave . . . there is not money to help me leave . . . I had to fight to get accommodation. I had no work and I said, "Can I take one of the units next to xxx?" . . . I get there. I had no fridge, no bedding. You know, and no-one from THQ[24] made contact with me. None of them checked in on me. If it wasn't for xxx dropping in and giving me food for the first month, I wouldn't have eaten. They didn't give me a separation certificate. —Salome (Interview Participant)

For clarity, it should be noted that disciplinary action can also be taken against Salvation Army officers in cohabiting heterosexual relationships; the difference is that the straight officer can choose marriage whereas the LGBTQ+ officer cannot while also remaining an officer.

Another instance of betrayal-by-systems identified was in the failure to provide a psychologically safe workplace for LGBTQ+ officers. Edmondson, a leader in the field of workplace psychological safety, defines

---

23. O'Neill George, "Moral Injury, Institutional Betrayal and Psychological Theory Breach in the Australian Army."

24. THQ means "Territorial Headquarters." In Australia there were formerly two territories, one based in Sydney and one based in Melbourne. Now there is one which is the national headquarters.

this notion as "a belief that one will not be punished or humiliated for speaking up with ideas, questions, concerns or mistakes, and that the team is safe for interpersonal risk taking."[25] All of our interview subjects that are still in TSA ministry spoke about risks involved in speaking up or standing out and ongoing hostility from colleagues, corps members, and, in some cases, leadership.

Achieving workplace psychological safety may mean quite a journey for some religious institutions. In the first place, it requires that the individuals concerned feel safe, present, appreciated, and wanted. Being "wanted" is far more significant than being "included," which is a goal often touted as an initial step for LGBTQ+ people in church environments. And even being included can feel remote when inclusion policies for employees simply do not apply to officers.

There needs to be safety for mistakes, which is often not the case in Evangelical and Holiness traditions that interpret holiness in terms of behavioral codes. There needs to be an environment where LGBTQ+ people have the confidence to put forward their ideas and their needs without fear of rejection or ridicule. And finally, there needs to be the ability to suggest change and significant policy improvements or new ways of working.

Achieving such change for TSA is something that has been merely discussed. There are ongoing challenges to achieving international progress or permission for local expressions to change policy. Halliday has documented this in his use of force-field analysis to discuss both the motivators and preventors of change for TSA.[26] He concludes that the restraining forces present in the organization remain overwhelmingly strong in comparison to the drivers for change. He notes that these restraining forces are not simply a factor of the numbers of individuals against change, recognizing that in this denomination it is not simply a democratic process. Rather, his analysis has shown the way a host of structural and cultural dynamics within TSA combine to reinforce the restraining factors against change. As such, change will require action at all levels of TSA hierarchy to address these structural and cultural restraining forces and find dynamics of positive valence to convert these restraining forces into driving forces for change. His conclusions include the telling statement: "(TSA) is not a safe church

---

25. Edmondson, "Psychological Safety."
26. Halliday, "Changing Attitudes, Orders and Regulations."

for those who are GSD (gender and sexually diverse), a significant risk for the viability of (TSA)."[27]

TSA therefore, and churches more generally, would be ripe for the development of moral injury through many different types of morally injurious event. Consider the lesbian who has witnessed a member of her congregation exposed to a "prayer ministry" (i.e., thinly veiled SOGICE) and subsequently become distressed. Imagine the impact on a young bisexual when a minister that they have respected all of their childhood years rails against divergent sexualities, or when church leadership disallow a same-sex marriage in their facilities dashing hopes of sharing such a key life experience in a space someone holds sacred. Think of the gay cleric who not only cannot marry the love of his life and, in the case of the LGBTQ+ Salvation Army officer, is also denied the privilege of an ongoing shared ministry that they witness being enjoyed by their heterosexual counterparts.

Finally, it is noted that a key symptom of moral injury is a sense of shame, something that is often tied to religious observance and received theology. This is fundamentally related to perceived or real negative evaluations by others, particularly respected others or cultural majorities. It leads those who experience shame to self-withdraw or hide.[28] In LGBTQ+ language, it pushes people back into the "closet" and slams the door shut. The outward behaviors related to shame in interpersonal contexts inhibit communication and undermine honest interactions with others.[29] By re-entering the closet, or staying closeted, the LGBTQ+ religious person therefore believes they are avoiding condemnation and rejection but concurrently denies their true self and experiences other psychological stressors. This counters the health and freedom discussed by the research participants who were able to live authentically as their full sexual and spiritual selves.

Identifying and Treating Moral Injury

It is not the intention of this book to discuss, at depth, the screening and treatment of moral injury. The cases cited and quotations above are

---

27. Halliday, "Changing Attitudes, Orders and Regulations," 47.

28. Litz, "Moral Injury and Moral Repair in War Veterans," 699.

29. Izard, *Human Emotions*, 386; Keltner and Hacker, "The Forms and Functions of the Non-Verbal Function of Shame," 78-98.

reflective of possible examples of morally injurious events. This does not automatically mean that each of these officers and former officers have experienced moral injury as a direct result. Such direct correlation between cause and effect requires specific screening through tools adapted for the purpose.

This would create a methodological conundrum for my research into the experiences of LGBTQ+ Salvation Army officers. If the primary way of confirming moral injury is through the use of a screening tool, then it could be argued that legitimately identifying instances of moral injury among research participants requires use of such a tool. Then an ethical dilemma would follow in how to advise, support, and respond to people who score badly. As such, I have provided examples of where moral injury would potentially be evidenced, but make no claim that there has been a clinical screening for identification of moral injury, which is beyond the scope of the project.

If such a screening were to take place, there are tools available. Given the differences identified between PTSD and moral injury, it is deemed inappropriate to try to identify instances of moral injury through the use of the diagnostic tools that have previously been associated with PTSD. For clarity, it is noted that these tools can still be appropriately applied to the patient, as we have already identified a frequent comorbidity between the two experiences. However, moral injury must be then identified separately in the individual's experience.

To address this, tools have been developed over time to specifically identify cases of moral injury. Initially these tools were comprised of self-report questionnaires, each designed to assess and quantify moral injury but with sole regard to war-related experiences or military service. They typically take the forms of checklists that work through potentially morally injurious events, such as killing or torture, or may ask about symptomatic reactions deemed common to the experience of moral injury such as guilt, shame, and betrayal. Importantly, none of these instruments measure changes in experience or indicate the things that have assisted in that change, meaning that a person experiencing moral injury would need to repeat tests to gain a comparative analysis after counselling or treatment.

Given that moral injury is not limited to those experiencing potentially morally injurious events in military settings another, non-military-specific, tool is needed. Koenig and colleagues have determined to address this and have considered civilian settings from healthcare to disaster and emergency situations, to journalists reporting on traumatic incidents or relating to traumatized interviewees, and educators in high-stress or special needs environments. They have developed a ten-item measure of moral injury for use in more diverse populations, based on the original MISS-M-SF (Moral Injury Symptom Scale—Military—Short Form).[30]

This team are also taking on the task of considering the factors—personal, behavioral and situational—that may increase the risk of certain individuals or groups becoming more susceptible to incidents of moral injury. Their work is somewhat speculative as validation would require customized and controlled trials. To date they have, via mostly literature review, developed a list that includes the following: previous military experience, previous diagnosis of depression and/or anxiety, younger people (without clarity of what "younger" means), less educated people, lower religiosity (confirmed in a few settings), personality, prior other traumas, and cultural factors. Higher levels of burnout and exhaustion are also shown to increase incidence of moral injury, potentially due to diminished resilience.[31]

Secular and spiritual/religious interventions have been developed and described for treating moral injury. Some have been examined for efficacy through the use of randomized controlled trials, some are currently under review, and some have been described in qualitative and case studies. Koenig and Al Zaben helpfully summarize the various interventions that have been developed in the following table:[32]

---

30. Koenig et al., *Religion and Recovery from PTSD*, 313-15.

31. Koenig and Al Zaben, "Moral Injury," 2989-3011; Mantri et al., "Moral Injury and Burnout in Health Care Professionals During the COVID-19 Pandemic," 720-726.

32. Koenig and Al Zaben, "Moral Injury," Table 2.

Table 8: Summary of Moral Injury Intervention Resources

Secular	Spiritual/religious	Pastoral care
Adaptive disclosure therapy (ADT) (Litz et al., 2017)	Building spiritual strength (BSS) (Harris et al., 2011, 2018)	Healing through forgiveness (Grimsley & Grimsley, 2017)
Acceptance and commitment therapy (ACT) (e.g., Hayes et al., 2011; Kopacz et al., 2016; Nieuwsma et al., 2015; Evans et al., 2020)	Spiritually integrated cognitive processing therapy (SICPT) (Koenig et al., 2017; Pearce et al., 2018)	Structured pastoral care (SPC) (Ames et al., 2018b)
Cognitive behavior therapy (CBT) (e.g., Maguen & Burkman, 2013; Maguen et al., 2017; Purcell et al., 2018)	Religiously integrated cognitive behavior therapy (RCBT) (Koenig et al., 2015)[33]	Pastoral narrative disclosure (PND) (Carey & Hodgson, 2018)
Cognitive processing therapy (CPT) (Hoge & Chard, 2018)		Moral injury reconciliation therapy (MIR) (Lee, 2018)
Prolonged exposure (PE) (e.g., Held et al., 2018; Paul et al., 2014)		Moral injury group (MIG) (Cenkner et al., 2021)
Alternate therapies (e.g., eye movement desensitization and reprocessing (EMDR) Shapiro & Laliotis, 2015; Hurley, 2018)		

Using only secular psychological interventions disregards the reality that moral injury is as much a spiritual issue as it is a psychological one. Moral injury interventions also require exploration of values, morals, ethics, guilt, and shame to appropriately recover. In fact, surprisingly little is confirmed about whether these psychological treatments make a significant difference to the experience of moral injury, but that is admittedly because so little work has been done in formulating assessments that measure change in the experience of moral injury.

This is where the spiritual, religious, and pastoral interventions come into their own. They address the symptoms that are spiritual in nature and still utilize some of the helpful secular elements. Also,

33. RCBT specifically focusses on depression

within the context of researching LGBTQ+ Salvation Army officers, focusing on some validated pastoral responses will provide a more accessible range of supports for those who need them. They will provide support at the individual level, however there are organizational transformations also required to prevent injurious experiences occurring in the first place. Further, consideration must be given to the nuances of clinical work among the LGBTQ+ community. There must be an understanding of the psychosocial, political, historical, and cultural factors that affect LGBTQ+ people.[34]

One antidote to shame and guilt is forgiveness. While forgiveness is often covered in religious and psychological literature as helping people adapt and recover from various harms, the concept of self-forgiveness is less studied. For those who have experienced a morally injurious event at the hands of others, forgiveness can help process that experience. Where the individual has acted against their own moral code, self-forgiveness is critical. This means confronting and addressing self-condemnation and shame.

One intervention that may assist, as it includes each of these necessary elements, is Pastoral Narrative Disclosure (PND). This has been subject to strong research validation, has been developed in the Australian context, training is available in using the approach, and it is accessible for use by chaplains and pastoral counsellors. Carey and Hodgson have adapted this tool following a review of the use of the secular ADT, seeing the usefulness of the approach but recognizing the absence of the spiritual element, relative to an issue that has significant spiritual and moral components. The basic difference to ADT is that instead of the rites taking place before a void, they place the counsellor or chaplain back into the empty chair and thus enhance the role of ritual in the healing process through the presence of moral authority in absolution.[35]

They argue that the sacrament of reconciliation has long been a key part of many religious traditions. Both the spiritual experience of confession to another and absolution that can follow can be key to self- and other-forgiveness, cleansing, and healing. In this act, the clergyperson has a key and unique role in bringing healing through this sacrament. Within TSA this rite is not used in the same sense and there is a stronger history that derives from the evangelistic camp meetings and utilizes a

---

34. Anderson et al., "Moral Injury for LGBTQ+ Individuals and Their Communities," 284.

35. Carey and Hodgson, "Chaplains, Spiritual Care and Moral Injury."

"Mercy Seat."³⁶ While the use of the Mercy Seat as a place of contrition has waned in recent years, Couchman argues that it can be reappropriated both in terms of emphasizing the central theological tenet of grace and also as an act of contrition and surrender to God's grace.³⁷ This advances the notion that PND could be useful to Salvation Army officers as it is built on both appropriate validated therapies and such rituals where they may feel comfortable practically and theologically. As the officers in this research articulated their experience of grace and the way that they can enliven God's grace to others, it seems particularly appropriate to utilize a ritual that centers on this attribute. It is noted that PND is best used by a mental health-trained clergyperson or chaplain, a CPE-trained health care professional, or military-trained chaplain due to the elements of CBT that are built in, and the duty of care to the individual concerned that mental health first aid capacity is at hand during the process.

Conclusion

Instances of moral injury and morally injurious events will likely be part of the experience of LGBTQ+ Salvation Army Officers. This statement is based on the definitions of moral injury that have been considered at the beginning of this chapter. Some of these events will fall into each of the distinct categories of moral injury: self-as-transgressor, other-as-transgressor, and also the sub-category that includes betrayal-by-systems. Complexity could be added to these violations due to the religious dimensions involved, such as religion-based prejudices, the possibility of SOGICE, and betrayal by spiritual leaders.³⁸

Self-initiated moral injuries include two types—those that are acts of commission and those where the individual failed to prevent an abuse or offense. The first group would include participation in SOGICE or the teaching of theology contrary to personal belief structures. The latter would include failing to speak up when homophobic abuses occur to others, or failing to intervene in processes where they have some control.

---

36. From the Old Testament where it was a place of encounter with the divine, Mercy Seats are found in some churches, including The Salvation Army, as places where people will pray, often during a worship service.

37. Couchman, "Not My Will but Yours Be Done," 217-229.

38. Anderson et al., "Moral Injury for LGBTQ+ Individuals and Their Communities," 280.

While this may be due to fear of potential consequences for the self, it can still lead to shame and guilt for not protecting the other.

Other-initiated injuries would include the direct abuse by a trusted leader, the betrayal of confidences relating to sexuality and relationships, or enforced resignation or dismissal over sexuality matters or a discovered same-sex relationship. Betrayal by systems would include the failure to provide a psychologically safe workplace or honor the spiritual and psychological contract between an officer and the movement. As discussed, providing such a psychologically safe workplace will be a particularly difficult journey for churches such as TSA. Creating a space where LGBTQ+ officers are not only just included but also "wanted," where they are able to make mistakes without judgement, where ideas can be safely discussed and where policies can be challenged and change wrought could be a long way off.

The examples given are only potential instances of moral injury. Moral injury is clinically identified through the use of self-assessment survey tools under the supervision of trained clinical or pastoral professionals and there is no clear picture of the dimensions of moral injury within TSA as yet. It would also stretch the scope of research beyond the individual experiences of LGBTQ+ officers, and present ethical dilemmas around care, should assessment tools be utilized to identify confirmed instances of moral injury.

The available tools to intervene and support officers who have experienced moral injury vary, depending on whether support is sought in a secular, religious, or pastoral setting. A review of some of the available interventions has identified Pastoral Narrative Disclosure as one of the most appropriate for use with LGBTQ+ officers. This is due to its accessibility, the training that is available within Australia, and the spiritual and religious components that are included. Increasingly, there are trained professionals in Australia, such as the majority of military chaplains, to whom referrals could be made for such support.

There is more research to be done in the area of moral injury, which is still a relatively new area of inquiry despite its existence and effects on people over time. Most importantly, the more research that can be done outside the military the more that we will see the diverse ways and settings in which moral injury can be experienced. This is critical, as the impacts do not cease when the fighting stops, or in the civilian setting, when the injurious event, abuse, exclusion, discrimination, or betrayal has passed.

Chapter 4: **Religious Trauma**

> *[The] Corps is about 100 meters away, and [the] Uniting Church too, where the minister there is now married to one of my best friends from college . . . and so I'm caught between these two religious experiences. And it was a really strange thing, because I felt really disconnected . . . I didn't feel safe enough to walk into a church.*—Mary (Interview Participant)

"Mary," a former officer, speaks of the experience of religious trauma. She is not alone, and while the experience of being required to leave her calling as an officer was traumatic enough, it has been significantly compounded by also being a lesbian and the organizational reactions to that revelation. She later wryly added in the interview that her tip for anyone with religious trauma is not to start dating someone who has also experienced religious trauma!

In this chapter, I discuss Religious Trauma, the second type of harm identified in the research. Religious trauma is defined as "pervasive psychological damage resulting from religious messages, beliefs, and experiences."[1] It is, most often, the result of spiritual abuse.[2] Spiritual abuse is a form of psychological and emotional abuse occurring when an individual uses ritual, religious practices, or spiritual or religious beliefs, to manipulate, control, hurt, or scare another person. Here I discuss the mechanisms for religious trauma, the ways they manifest in the experiences of LGBTQ+ officers, and some of the resulting damage. I choose to use the term "religious" as it has fewer ambiguities in definition than "spiritual."

---

1. Stone, "Thou Shalt Not," 324.
2. Hollier, *Religious Trauma, Queer Identities*, 168.

Religious trauma results from many things. It could have been an event, a series of events, relationships, or circumstances within or connected to religious beliefs, practices, or church structures, that are experienced by an individual in ways that are overwhelming, disruptive, or which have long lasting effects on their physical, social, mental, emotional, and spiritual wellbeing.[3] While many traumas result from a single incident, religious trauma is more likely to accrue over time from longer-term exposure to messaging that undermines mental health.[4]

Most clinicians, social workers, and psychologists are aware of the trauma that religion can cause. This is especially the case for LGBTQ+ people who are the subject of controversy and isolation in religious circles. Despite this, up to the early 2000s, much of the literature focused on the positive associations and affectations of religious practice and community. It assumed that religion and spirituality were tools of recovery from trauma, rather than causes of trauma.[5]

More recently there has been a growing body of literature considering the ways spiritual abuse is inflicted, resulting in religious trauma. These have included research published by Barnes and Meyer (2012) who were guided by minority stress theory in discussing religious affiliation and internalized homophobia.[6] Cole and Harris (2017) researched the lived experience of LGBTQ+ Christians and the need for social workers and others to be culturally competent in dealing with the traumas that resulted.[7] Gandy-Guedes and her team (2017) considered the impacts of such trauma on the lifespan development of LGBTQ+ people. They noted that perceptions of traumatic events are important, in that an event only needs to be perceived to be threatening or harmful to trigger the same biological symptoms in the human body.[8] Gibbs and Goldbach (2021) considered how spiritual abuse can lead to identity dissonance, especially among sexual minority adolescents.[9]

---

3. McConnaughey, *Trauma in the Pews*, 84-5.
4. Stone, "Thou Shalt Not," 325.
5. Stone, "Thou Shalt Not," 323.
6. Barnes and Meyer, "Religious Affiliation, Internalised Homophobia, and Mental Health in Lesbians, Gay Men, and Bisexuals," 505-515.
7. Cole and Harris, "The Lived Experiences of People Who Identify as LGBT Christians," 31-52.
8. Gandy-Guedes et al., "Trauma Impacts on LGBTQ People: Implications for Lifespan Development," 118-136.
9. Gibbs and Goldbach, "Religious Identity Dissonance," 2189-2213.

While Australian society has mostly moved to a more progressive and inclusive attitude toward many minority groups, this is not always true for queer people in evangelical churches.[10] Even when overt negative behaviors in these environments have decreased, there is still subtle and persistent aggression and hostility toward LGBTQ+ people. Some of this I discussed in chapter 2. These behaviors include comments, statements of the church or individuals, exclusion from activities, social media activity, and derogatory humor, to name but a few. One interview participant described the silence he felt from people in TSA who were previously friends and close colleagues, after he had "come out."

In this chapter, I consider two lenses through which religious trauma can be discussed in relation to LGBTQ+ Christians. These are drawn from the above literature and reflected in the experiences articulated by the majority of research participants, particularly in the interviews. One is Minority Stress Theory, which understands that minority groups in communities experience stressors permeating their everyday existence. Hollier and his team found that LGBTQ+ Christians, as a group, were consistently subject to mischaracterization, viewed as a moral threat, and experienced erasure and social distancing.[11] The second lens is Microaggression Theory, which recognizes that the accumulation of small actions of discrimination can exceed an individual's capacity, leading to the development of allostatic overload, and form substantial experiences of trauma.[12] In this case, it is often the small and perhaps otherwise unnoticed actions of others that build over time to traumatize the individual. Also, as Downie notes, it is the insidious way that this religious trauma is routinely and consisted posited as "love," which exacerbates the harms caused.[13]

---

10. Hollier et al., "Mechanisms of Religious Trauma Amongst Queer People in Australia's Evangelical Churches," 276.

11. Hollier et al., "Mechanisms of Religious Trauma Amongst Queer People . . . ," 275.

12. Allostatic load is the term used to describe the cumulative effects of chronic stress and life events. It particularly refers to the interactions between different physiological systems at varying degrees of activity, due to the cumulative exposure to such stress. See Guidi et al., "Allostatic Load and Its Impact on Health," 11-27.

13. Downie, "Christian Shame and Religious Trauma," 5.

Minority Stress Theory

Meyer conducted a meta-analysis of research into LGBTQ+ people's mental health and proposed that minority stress would explain the higher levels of mental illness in non-heterosexual populations.[14] The effects go beyond psychological harm, however, and it should be briefly noted that sexual minorities are known to experience stress associated with isolation, stigma, prejudice, and discrimination which, in turn, tends to predispose them to both negative physical and mental health outcomes.[15]

Minority Stress Theory was originally used as an explanatory theory for understanding experiences of ethnic and racial minorities. It describes how the minority status of a group can lead to experiences of chronic stress and subsequent health complications. In application to LGBTQ+ communities, minority stress theory usually highlights internalized homophobia (discussed in chapter 6), expectations of rejection from families and communities, including churches, and the experiences of adversity related to one's sexuality or gender identity.[16]

Since Meyer's work was published, there has been an increase in evidence demonstrating how social stigma and prejudice towards non-heterosexuals are linked to mental illness and somatic health problems.[17] It is problematic and insidious. Often it has no discernible beginning and the events surrounding it can be varied according to perception and frequency, making it hard to define.

It is, however, sometimes very clear. This is in cases where homophobia can be easily discerned, mischaracterizations are obvious, and the non-heterosexual is viewed as a threat or intentionally excluded or erased. Among the survey participants in this research, 91 percent (twenty-two out of twenty-four) indicated that they had witnessed direct homophobic discrimination. 79 percent believed that they had personally been discriminated against on the basis of their sexuality. For example, in this greeting from a local Salvation Army church elder to a newly commissioned officer, we see blatant homophobic discrimination:

---

14. Meyer, "Prejudice, Social Stress, and Mental Health in Lesbian, Gay and Bisexual Populations," 674-697.

15. Mays et al., "Chronic physiologic effects of stress among lesbian, gay, and bisexual adults," 551.

16. Hollier et al., "Mechanisms of Religious Trauma Amongst Queer People . . . ," 276.

17. Hollier, *Religious Trauma: Queer Identities*, 168.

> *I was greeted after the appointments meeting by my Corps Sergeant Major who said, "we could have had anyone and we got you and we're not happy!"*[18]—*Mary (Interview Participant)*

Homophobia takes many forms and it does not need to be direct. For many of our research participants, there were direct instances that stemmed often from the attitude of "love the sinner, hate the sin" mentality, but did not demonstrate love at all. Ten out of eleven interview participants indicated instances of spiritual abuse based in homophobic attitudes. For some this was at the hands of congregation members they were pastoring, for others it was from colleagues, and for some it was from leaders.

One of the ways that this was discussed by the interview participants was through the way that prayer was used toward and against them:

> *I was referred to a night of prayer ministry with some retired officers. Now, I didn't know what that was, but when I got there it was very clear that um . . . in fact, it was overt, the person leading the prayer meeting stood up and said, "I believe that, or I understand that there is a spirit of homosexuality resting upon someone in this room and we cast this out" . . . and there was a whole bunch of prayers and words to do that—incantation almost—and I'm sure no-one turned around but it felt like all eyes in the room were on me. Ah and I went away from that very bruised.—John (Interview Participant)*

> *There was a prayer meeting I was taken to. I remember it being quite traumatic. An older officer prayed loud and very strongly against all manner of things. It was really "there's a demon under every rock and we need to get rid of it." I can remember blubbering in the prayer meeting because it was just so scary. The guy that had been leading actually walked up to me in the middle and asked why I was so upset. I couldn't answer him.—Joseph (Interview Participant)*

> *It has certainly been interesting in chatting to people, that because of the way that prayer is used, and justified, the impact I'm picking up is interesting—everything from disengagement to spiritual abuse to all sorts of things in between.—Andrew (Interview Participant)*

---

18. The Corps Sergeant Major is the senior lay leader in a Salvation Army Corps/Church.

The homophobic way in which prayer has been used has also had the effect of reducing the capacity to engage with and believe in the power of prayer for some participants. McConnaughey notes that such trauma often prevents full engagement with spiritual disciplines and that, in turn, the spiritual disciplines themselves will not be sufficient for the healing of these traumas.[19]

Homophobic comments are obviously not confined to prayer meetings. Research participants described being called many things, including pedophiles and criminals. There were tales of LGBTQ+ officers being denied client contact in ministry settings including TSA social programs, because they were seen as "risks." (It should be noted that particular example occurred in Sydney over twenty years ago). And there were cases of direct exclusion on the grounds of sexuality; one former officer describing how she was removed from a former officers Facebook group upon discovery of her sexuality. Rejections small and large accumulate and research has indicated that many LGBTQ+ Christians are led to equate rejection by the Church with rejection by God.[20]

Such comments and behaviors are often reflective of toxic theology and are perpetuated by authoritarian structures. Downie notes that the doctrines of original sin and eternal damnation are often used to induce shame and elicit certain responses among the religious faithful.[21] The requirement for a substitutionary atonement, a key doctrine taught in many churches, makes LGBTQ+ people especially, who are condemned by *who they are* (according to many), prone to trauma and shame. Ways to speak of God's love and mercy that do not perpetuate shame need to be found, unlike the recent Anglican Diocese of Sydney pronouncement that same-sex desire is "an inclination toward evil."[22]

Mischaracterization occurs through misrepresentation of individuals and groups in negative ways. For many of our participants this is through terminology such as the "gay lifestyle," a descriptor that mischaracterizes them and carries connotations of promiscuity. Hollier's research participants spoke to this term as a way in which conservative Christians "other" non-heterosexuals by minimizing and disparaging their

---

19. McConnaughey, *Trauma in the Pews*, xxiv.
20. Fielder and Ezzy, "Religious Freedom for Whom?" 9.
21. Downie, "Christian Shame and Religious Trauma," 2.
22. Koziol, "Sydney Anglicans Say Same-Sex Desire 'an Inclination Toward Evil,'" *Sydney Morning Herald*, 17 August 2023.

experiences, relegating it to a matter of choice. It is a phrase that lacks nuance and is associated with overt sexuality.[23] One participant noted:

> *On the ground colleagues and congregations . . . they just say stuff, not knowing that they are talking about people, and that they are talking about you . . . Obviously it hurts, but most of it just makes me angry.*—Elizabeth (Interview Participant)

For bisexuals and pansexuals there is the mischaracterizations that they are either just undecided or, at an extreme, having threesomes and group sex persistently. One of the survey participants discussed their journey from identifying as heterosexual but struggling with homosexual attraction, to becoming reconciled with their pansexuality. Given the binary understandings of the church, and the struggle to even deal with homosexuality and heterosexuality as a continuum rather than a binary, it is not surprising that this individual has not "come out" publicly as pansexual.

For many it is seen in the sense that they feel "othered" and therefore dismissed:

> *I can't actually speak up here because I'll just be given a label. "He's just the token gay officer . . . so we won't listen to him either."*—Simon (Interview Participant)

Othering someone, or a group, has significant consequences. McCormick discusses this from both a practical and a theological perspective. Practically, he notes that once we are comfortable excluding someone as an "other," then we have no trouble killing the "other." This may not be literal, but will certainly be in the realized cold indifference to the plight of that person. Theologically, he points out that no-one who is also made in God's image can be "other." When we "other" someone we manifest the opposite of God's declared justice, righteousness, and redemptive activity. Simply put, we no longer see or consider that person as God does. "Blindness and callous indifference to those we deem as 'other' have made us idolatrously certain of our holiness and purity and woefully deficient in love for one another."[24] The officers in this research clearly spoke about affirming the place as part of God's creation, in God's

---

23. Hollier et al, "Mechanisms of Religious Trauma Amongst Queer People . . . ," 278.

24. McCormick, "See No-one as Other," 384.

image while also LGBTQ+, and about the solidarity and support they found in community that embraces and does not "other."

There is also the mischaracterization that someone could not be LGBTQ+ and Christian at the same time. Fielder and Ezzy open one of their articles with the assertion that "LGBTQ+ and Christian identities are often seen as incompatible."[25] "Mary" (the interview participant quoted at the start of the chapter) discussed this as an issue clearly articulated to her during her growing up years. "Joseph" (interview participant) discussed how his boyfriend's mother refused to accept that Christianity and homosexuality could be compatible, yet also struggled to reconcile the evidence she perceived of the Holy Spirit working in her son's life. The authenticity he felt and expressed could not be comprehended by some in his family despite the evidence of an affective spiritual difference in his living.

The perception of LGBTQ+ officers as a threat varied. But there were times, as also discussed in Hollier's work among the broader evangelical population, when LGBTQ+ officers were told that they were threats to society, threats to the organization, and definitely a threat to orthodoxy.[26] In extremes this was discussed as the "gay agenda," with experiences of such mischaracterization during both the Safe Schools debate and same-sex marriage postal survey being quite pronounced (see chapter 1). In some respects, this perception of threat is a more extreme form of mischaracterization, but the severity of its tone and ramifications warrants a distinct mention.[27]

One officer recalled being sent on an ecumenical leadership course where his sexuality came to light. As a result, other Christian leaders on the course approached the course management to ask if separate ablution times or facilities could be arranged for the officer so that he was not a threat to their safety. Others were cut off by friends who thought they were a threat to their families and children:

> I had one friend who said, "I don't ever want you to visit my house again and I don't want you to have anything to do with my children."—Mary (Interview Participant)

---

25. Fielder and Ezzy, "Religious Freedom for Whom?" 1.

26. Hollier et al, "Mechanisms of Religious Trauma Amongst Queer People . . . ," 278–9.

27. Hollier, *Religious Trauma: Queer Identities*, 177.

> *Part of the response of people around me was to stop people visiting me because I was speaking about this, you know, in a public way.* —Matthew (Interview Participant)

Rivera has also written on the various harms caused to LGBTQ+ people in the church. The first harm she discusses (she uses the term "burdens") is the way in which the church treats non-heterosexuals as a threat. She theorizes that this results from the "Protestant sexual revolution" which saw sexuality as a necessary good, but in contradiction (and even in accepting that there were LGBTQ+ people) required them to remain celibate. One participant in her research describes this theology and demand of celibacy as a slow suicide, driving a futile effort against natural inclinations in a terminal torture.[28] Rivera argues that this harm, in its full realization, is a product of the culture wars of the twentieth century where evangelical leaders posited any form of sexual liberation as a threat to society.[29]

Erasure is another way in which minority groups are diminished. If a person (or group) does not exist, then they are easier to ignore, stigmatize, marginalize, and eventually dismiss altogether. After advertising this research to potential participants, one officer corresponded that I should find that there were no subjects for this research as there would be no such thing as an LGBTQ+ officer.

Erasure overlooks a group of people. This can be where TSA's human resources department look at the retention and wellbeing of LGBTQ+ staff, as they did in 2023, but deliberately exclude officers. In congregations, the absence of visible LGBTQ+ people shapes congregational thinking and in turn shapes denominational thinking—if they are not there we do not need to think about them.[30]

Messaging that there is no such thing as a LGBTQ+ Christian it leaves LGBTQ+ people of faith with a crisis of identity. Fielder and Ezzy note that the harms caused by the denial of religiosity among LGBTQ+ people can lead to emotional, psychological, and social damage.[31] Some resolve this for themselves in spite of the church. Others make choices to remain under secrecy or to leave to other places more embracing and affirming. I discuss this positively in chapter 7, noting that many

---

28. Rivera, *Heavy Burdens*, 21.
29. Rivera, *Heavy Burdens*, 22-23.
30. Hollier et al, "Mechanisms of Religious Trauma Amongst Queer People . . . ," 279.
31. Fielder and Ezzy, "Religious Freedom for Whom?" 10.

participants have been able to resolve their faith and their sexuality, and live authentic and integral lives. Here, however, I also note that the process to arrive at that point can be traumatic and, for some, the results are not always positive:

> I guess I just reached a crisis point of going, "I can't live authentically as I am within this system." And while I was wrestling with those thoughts, I didn't think it was fair for me to continue in a ministry role or a leadership role in the Salvation Army and I wanted to, I guess, have a bit more agency over my life decisions, including who I dated.—Martha (Interview Participant)

Microaggressions

Microaggression Theory is a close relative of Minority Stress Theory. The similarity is in the way that chronic exposure to even small doses of stress will accumulate to high levels of stress and anxiety. Robinson and Rubin's research into the experience of ninety LGB and eighty heterosexual participants revealed this proximity. Their findings suggested there was a link between homonegative microaggressions and traumatic stress symptoms.[32] These microaggressions may be unintentional or unconscious, but they are statements and behaviors that convey derogatory or hostile messages to members of the targeted groups.[33]

Microaggressions are far more common than overt discriminatory behaviors. Quite often they are perpetrated by leadership, friends, family, or trusted people in the individual's sphere, adding to the trauma caused.[34] When Kimbal discusses why the church is seen as homophobic, he notes that it is often the small comments, jokes, exceptions, or lack of visible welcome (including flags and icons) that create an environment of cumulative stress and lack of safety.[35] One participant noted some of the ways they sense this:

> It's like living with constant anxiety about who will say something, who might post something, or whether or not you will have a job

---

32. Robinson and Rubin, "Homonegative Microaggressions and Posttraumatic Stress Symptoms," 57-69.
33. Hollier, *Religious Trauma, Queer Identities*, 169.
34. Hollier, *Religious Trauma, Queer Identities*, 170.
35. Kimball, *They Like Jesus but not the Church*, 142-3.

> *next week because of the attitudes of whichever leader may be in place.—Joseph (interview participant)*

Church leaders set the example and the atmosphere for the congregations and denominations. When these microaggressions start from the top of the organization, it permeates the whole and other members will feel free to express the same behaviors and use the same language towards minority groups.[36] The interviews for this research were conducted at a time when there was a change in the Territorial (national) leadership in Australia. Many of the participants expressed concerns about this because of their understanding of how leadership can impact the whole organization:

> *I'm not sure how I'll be under the new Territorial Leadership—Simon (interview participant)*

> *There is a change of divisional leadership here, and a change of territorial leadership. I won't be having those conversations again. I don't think the game is the same as it was.—Elizabeth (Interview Participant)*

> *[There is a] lack of concrete policy or overt promise to support LGBTIQ+ Salvationists or corps members and free rein those who hold anti-LGBTIQ+ views. The change of territorial leader brings renewed risk and uncertainty.—Survey Participant*

Quite often, the role of church leaders in religious trauma generates hurt through incongruence. While providing her commentary on the Old Testament book of Jonah, van der Walt speaks of her own experience in this regard where she had been physically man-handled by one leader in an attempt to remove her from a synod meeting, following which another leader of the event "welcomed all." The incongruity of the situation was then exacerbated when both she and her attacker needed to show mutual grace in the sharing of the communal sacramental meal.[37] It is an example comparable with those articulated by the research participants, where enlivened grace was needed in the face of clear hostility.

A change in leadership at local level makes a big difference as well. An officer who wrote a letter, rather than being interviewed, pointed out that a change of officers could mean that LGBTQ+ congregation members who had previously felt welcome, are then rejected from the corps.

---

36. Kimball, *They Like Jesus but not the Church*, 143.
37. van der Walt, "These are the Days of Raw Despondence," 12.

He states, on this basis, that he doesn't believe that The Salvation Army should claim to be welcoming, inclusive, or non-discriminatory.

The source of a microaggression makes a significant difference. Very few people speak of such microaggressions coming from strangers, but rather leaders, close family and friends, colleagues, or members of a congregation.[38] Not many studies aside from Hollier noted the potential for relational proximity to be material in the impact of microaggressions.[39] However the participants in my research, as with Hollier's, indicate a qualitative difference in the impact of a joke or snide comment coming from someone we have relationship with, as opposed to (say) a random street preacher.[40] In movements such as TSA, the lines between officers, leaders in general, families, friends, and co-workers is often blurred which simply makes the rejection harder to deal with.[41]

The source of these microaggressions is found in the culture and assumed norms of the organization. Heteronormative attitudes, based on a "natural heteronormative order" seen by some in their reading of Scripture (e.g., Genesis 1:18-25), are another problem that is experienced. This is seen in many ways, from the way men's and women's events are shaped (and that the church has gendered activities in the first place), through to congregational worship and church life including things for (only heterosexual) "couples." These attitudes and activities have a powerful impact on individuals who are conflicted. They reinforce the distinctions between groups in the church, separating those who are to be "othered" from the (supposedly) "normal."[42]

Consequences of Religious Trauma

There are a number of major consequences resulting from the perpetration of spiritual abuse that leads to religious trauma. These range from those that are general to a denomination or congregation as a whole, through to those that directly impact individual people. In some cases, the psychological damage leads to significant ongoing mental health concerns. For some, it leads to a loss of faith. One interview participant indicated they had lost their faith within a few years of leaving officership.

---

38. Hollier, *Religious Trauma, Queer Identities*, 170.

39. Robinson and Rubin, "Homonegative Microaggressions," do not note this, for example.

40. Hollier, *Religious Trauma, Queer Identities*, 170.

41. Hollier et al., "Mechanisms of Religious Trauma," 279.

42. Fielder and Ezzy, *Lesbian, Gay, Bisexual and Transgender Christians*, 97.

At a macro level, TSA is simply not safe for LGBTQ+ people because of the various forms of spiritual abuse, or other harms, that occur. When asked if they believed TSA was committed to ensuring a safe working environment, LGBTQ+ officers responding to the survey in this research scored the organization 5.13 out of ten, compared to the broader workforce scoring the organization at 8.34 out of ten. As a result, when asked if they would recommend TSA as a place of work, survey participants nominated a level of 'five' (on a scale of one to ten) compared to the broader employee and officer workforce that gave a rating of 7.67 in the TSA national staff engagement survey of 2023.[43]

That indicates lack of safety in the workplace for TSA's LGBTQ+ clergy. However, most of the spiritual abuse and harm caused, as discussed in the interviews, seems to be originating in the church or congregation setting. This is observed by the survey participants in two ways. First, they are more likely to be "out" to leaders (62.5 percent) rather than their local congregation (29 percent). Second, the ways they described the sorts of reactions that are expected in TSA congregations, in comparison to other denominations, is telling. These reactions are summarized in their responses to the question, "What are the attitudes toward LGBTQ+ among the majority of people who attend the worship service or event that you most often attend?"

Table 9: Congregational Attitudes to LGBTQ+ People

	Percent
Welcoming	29.2
Loving	16.7
Tolerant	54.2
Cautious	20.8
Ignorant	41.7
Judgmental	25
Regard LGBTQ+ people as sinful/ wrong	29.2
Regard LGBTQ+ practices/ behaviors as sinful/wrong	54.2
Don't know	8.3

---

43. The Salvation Army, National Engagement Survey 2023.

The main thing to note here is that only 29 percent believe their congregation would be welcoming of LGBTQ+ people. Only 16.7 percent believe their congregation would be loving. These would be challenging statistics for the majority of TSA congregations who would claim to be both welcoming and loving, but are clearly not seen that way by LGBTQ+ people within the movement. It is tragic that more than half seem to think they could be merely "tolerated." It is also telling that just under one in three also believe that members of their congregation would believe that their *identity* is sinful, regardless of any particular behaviors.

By way of comparison, research by Ezzy, Fielder and McLeay shows 60 percent of LGBTQ+ Christians in Australia believe that their congregation is welcoming and 55 percent say that it is loving.[44] This shows that TSA congregations are perceived to be much less welcoming, at least by LGBTQ+ officers, and much less loving (around one third of the average) towards LGBTQ+, when compared to other Christian denominations. In the spirit of transparency, this comparison may be a little skewed: The majority of Ezzy, Fielder and McLeay's research participants would be lay people who could choose their congregation and therefore choose a more progressive congregation. It also appears that some more inclusive denominations such as the Uniting Church and Quakers promoted the research, again skewing the results to a more welcoming environment. Regardless, TSA officers, mostly, do not have the opportunity to choose their worshipping community because they are appointed by the organization to a particular location or congregational setting, something which, perhaps, adds to the risk they face.

These negative experiences of church have "profound, long-lasting impacts" on the psychological, social, and spiritual health of people.[45] The stress that accumulates on LGBTQ+ people as part of an oppressed minority within a denomination accumulates over time to have significant ramifications. Trauma produces psychological changes in people, including a recalibration of the brain's warning systems, increases in hormonal stress activity and hypervigilance, and alterations to our systems so that they can no longer process what is relevant and irrelevant information.[46] This can become even more dangerous for the LGBTQ+ officer who would struggle consistently to process the stimuli around them and subsequently struggle to remain psychologically regulated. Acting without

---

44. Ezzy et al., "LGBTQ+ Christians in Australia," Table 9.
45. Hollier et al, "Mechanisms of Religious Trauma," 282.
46. McConnaughey, *Trauma in the Pews*, 92.

reflection (where one's capacity has been diminished) could lead to even more reactions from leaders and colleagues, and even less safety.

Spiritual trauma sometimes has an added element, especially in churches such as TSA that often preach purity cultures. Among these churches there is a message that the individual needs to control themselves, be more disciplined, or try harder through spiritual practices. When the LGBTQ+ person is first told that they are "broken" or "sinful," and they are then told to be "better" or more "holy," a cycle of shame begins as the individual cannot rectify the "brokenness" that others perceive (but which does not, of course, exist). This is rooted in the false idea held by some Christians that all things are spiritual in nature, therefore all solutions to problems (perceived or otherwise) are either theological, doctrinal, or spiritual in nature.[47]

The resulting shame is a powerful emotion whereby the LGBTQ+ members of churches feel defective or fear rejection from their community. Moon and Tobin identify "Sacramental Shame" as something that is particularly toxic. This is where the Christian community unjustly stigmatizes a group with shame, typically deeming them unworthy of membership, fellowship, and relationship. LGBTQ+ Christians are constantly confronting entire theological constructs dedicated to the idea that they either do not exist as persons, or if they do, it is as defects. Sacramental shame is that form of shame which is complicated by posing through love and concern for the individual, while concurrently locating the shame in the individual's lack of, or failure of, will. It makes being recognized as a person of worth, by God and the community, contingent on changing, by will, things that an LGBTQ+ person cannot change. This instils shame as an enduring, conscious mental state.[48] The ensuing sense of spiritual failure is a result of trauma and also a trauma in itself.[49]

A Way Forward

It will take significant cultural change at all levels of TSA to counter the beliefs and behaviors producing the abuse and traumas that LGBTQ+ officers face.

---

47. McConnaughey, *Trauma in the Pews*, 7.
48. Moon and Tobin, "Sunsets and Solidarity," 451-468.
49. McConnaughey, *Trauma in the Pews*, 10.

Other denominations have started to pursue addressing generalized religious trauma, but not often with their LGBTQ+ members and congregants. One such denomination is the Southern Baptist Convention of the United States when considering the impacts of sexual assaults in their churches. Their guidance to churches is that, when the "village" fails, there is a number of steps to be taken towards healing, including: a) acknowledgement of the abuse and associated trauma, b) apologizing to the victims, c) making a tangible gesture of contrition, d) providing compassionate care, e) providing and pursuing dedicated advocacy on behalf of victims, and f) establishing a survivor compensation fund.[50]

While the last point may not be applicable to LGBTQ+ officers, the other steps give a clear way forward for leaders and boards at denominational level. As they take these steps, they also need to consider how they will be received. When considering marginalized groups through history, such as LGBTQ+ people, Christians have often been at the forefront of perpetrating such traumas as discussed in this chapter, and many others. While some of this may have come from a place of error, misdirection, or misguidedness, the lived experience of the LGBTQ+ people was still trauma and marginalization. Christian leaders trying to reach out to this group therefore need to remember that they have forfeited any moral ground or right to speak. Shotsberger and Freytag say it like this: "Christian leaders have had their turn and their actions have spoken clearly—power and influence have been used to hurt and marginalize others."[51] To be well received, any acknowledgement or apology needs to be authentic and prominent. The current acknowledgement and apology to LGBTQ+ people that was issued by TSA Australia in early 2023 is hidden on a webpage under the heading "Rainbow Tick Accreditation," given the impression that it was only issued as part of the pursuit of accreditation and not as a genuine sign of contrition by leadership.

For the record, the apology states:

> We acknowledge the past mistakes made by The Salvation Army and the hurt that many LGBTIQA+ community members still hold. We are sorry for the harmed caused. As a movement we commit to ongoing improvement, learning from past mistakes, and growing in understanding, acceptance, and respect. In particular, we are focused on having an open dialogue with all community members around our inclusive practices.

---

50. McConnaughey, *Trauma in the Pews*, 169.
51. Schat and Freytag, "What Can Christians Learn from Care Theory," n.p.

In addition to the above steps from McConnaughey, there is need to address toxic theology and to start to listen and love. This love must, however, be complete and not conditional. It must also be *completed*, that is to say it must be successfully communicated and enlivened.[52] Love is not love if something prevents it being received as love.

Finally, TSA and other churches, need to recognize the holy strengths, grace and resilience of the LGBTQ+ community in the face of the trauma they have experienced. Like the Old Testament prophets Job, Jeremiah, and Jonah, they are examples just because they survive and share their stories—showing that others in traumatized and victimized communities may also survive.[53] The LGBTQ+ Christian community are modern prophets to all who do not fit in, or who suffer.

---

52. Schat and Freytag, "What Can Christians Learn from Care Theory," n.p.

53. Claassens, "Resilience in the Book of Jonah: Surviving the Unsurvivable," online seminar, 1 February 2024.

Chapter 5: Sexual Orientation and Gender Identity Change Efforts

The truth cannot be converted. —Garrard Conley[1]

SEXUAL ORIENTATION AND GENDER Identity Change Efforts (SOGICE) is an umbrella term to generically describe a range of practices. More commonly known as Conversion Therapy, Conversion Practices, or Reparative Therapy, they are neither conversional or reparative in nature, but are those practices used with the intent of changing a person's sexual orientation, gender identity or expression.

In this chapter I intentionally use the term SOGICE as these practices may include a lot of effort, but are not therapies. The chapter provides a background to SOGICE in Australia and beyond, and discusses these efforts as experienced by LGBTQ+ officers in The Salvation Army (TSA) with their potential impact, as indicated by the participants in the survey and interviews. The current environment in Australia is revisited, as well as the current official position of TSA, which is evidently at odds with some continued beliefs and behaviors in the organization.

SOGICE in Australia and Beyond

From the outset, I claim there is no clinical or therapeutic basis for these activities. While the initial programs in this area took their lead from Freud and were delivered by psychoanalytically-oriented practitioners, the evidence base for their efficacy was soon shown to be wanting.[2] Despite this, after the decriminalization and de-medicalization of homosexuality,

---

1. Conley, *Boy Erased*, subtitle.
2. Drescher et al., *Sexual Conversion Therapy*, 7.

SOGICE were still, and are still, championed and delivered through conservative religious groups, across a range of faith groups.

While Christian groups proposing SOGICE are best known in Australia, it is notable that this is not confined to Christianity. StraightWay Foundation is an Islamic group that offers such practices, which came to the fore during controversy surrounding links to former London mayor Ken Livingstone. Their literature goes beyond the usual condemnation of homosexuality as sinful, stating that you cannot, in fact, be a "Gay Muslim" because the constituent parts of that phrase are contradictory, a claim made in some conservative Christian circles also (i.e., that you cannot be a "gay Christian").[3] StraightWay add that same-sex attraction is a test from Allah and condemn "gender-blurring lifestyles" such as effeminacy in men.[4] In parts of the world, Jewish groups such as "Hosen" runs hotlines and programs to support young Jewish men with "reversed inclinations." They operate in Israel, despite condemnation from the Israeli Medical Association, offering help in "the changing of sexual preference and sexual reorientation" using "therapies for (the aforementioned) reversed inclinations."[5]

SOGICE are offered on the basis of an underlying assumption that a person's sexual orientation or gender identity is fundamentally changeable. Moreover, there is the firm assertion that an individual not only can change their sexual orientation, but that they *should* actively seek to become heterosexual.[6] The methodology is variant, but is typically based around a range of aversion therapies designed to distract from homoerotic impulses, psychoanalysis of childhoods, reconstruction of perceived gender relationships, discussion of same-sex intimacy struggles (e.g., supposedly derived from histories with distant fathers or overly protective mothers), and a range of spiritual practices.[7]

Research predominantly indicates that SOGICE do not change a person's sexual orientation. There are some minimal research exceptions with varying degrees of credibility. Hollier notes that the *New Report of the*

---

3. StraightWay Foundation UK, *Statement on Homosexualist Campaign Against Muslim Scholar*, 4.

4. StraightWay Foundation UK, *Statement on Homosexualist Campaign Against Muslim Scholar*, 4.

5. Hofstien and Sharvit, "Gay conversion therapy to fix 'reverse inclinations' is alive and well in Israel," *Times of Israel*, 24 June 2020.

6. Hollier, *Religious Trauma, Queer Identities*, 28.

7. Burack, "From Heterosexuality to Holiness," 222.

Kinsey Institute concluded that people do not "necessarily maintain the same sexual orientation throughout their lives" and that "programs helping homosexuals to change report varying degrees of success."[8] This may simply indicate some fluidity in the experience of some people's sexual orientation and is based on self-reporting by research participants, indicating perhaps a *desire* that the change was effective. Also, at one point, the Chair of Psychology at Wheaton College, Stanton Jones, claimed his research indicated that, "Anyone who says there is no hope [for change in sexual orientation] is either ignorant or a liar."[9] This last claim, however needs to be understood in the context of a college such as Wheaton that has a College "Community Covenant" affirming "chastity among the unmarried and the sanctity of marriage between a man and woman," and denounces "sexual immorality, such as the use of pornography, pre-marital sex, adultery, homosexual behavior, and all other sexual relations outside the bounds of marriage between a man and woman."

Notwithstanding, almost all research shows that SOGICE cause serious harm to those involved and do not effect change in sexual orientation or gender identity. This has led professional health bodies in Australia to oppose SOGICE, including the Australian Psychological Society.[10] Their updated 2021 position statement clearly states that there is no clinical evidence to support the efficacy of such efforts, there is evidence of negative impacts including higher rates of depression, and that these practices compound discriminations already experienced by the LGBTQ+ community. It goes on to say that the attempt to use such a practice by an Australian psychologist would most likely be in breach of their Code of Ethics.

One Australian study explicitly outlines the harm of such religious practices and beliefs towards people from the LGBTQ+ community. These harms included immense trauma, grief, and pain at the perceived need to choose between their faith and their sexuality. They also included psychological harm and spiritual abuse through rejection by their community (covered in chapter 4).[11]

Researchers are improving their approach to documenting harms caused by SOGICE. A 2021 report from La Trobe University was able

8. Hollier, *Religious Trauma, Queer Identities*, 30.
9. Hollier, *Religious Trauma, Queer Identities*, 30.
10. Higgins, "Push to Outlaw Gay Conversion Therapy in the US Should be Mirrored in Australia, Gay Rights Group Says," *The World Today*, ABC, 27 July 2015.
11. Jones et al., *Preventing Harm, Promoting Justice*.

to establish that survivors commonly experience Post Traumatic Stress Disorder symptoms related to religious trauma and may require support with: integration of their self-concept; improving self-care; correcting misinformation about LGBTQA+ people and communities; repairing and rebuilding their social support and community networks; navigating their relationship with faith; and recovery from the impact that involvement in conversion practices had on their civic and economic participation.[12]

Among earlier studies, Shidlo and Schroeder (2002) were the first to document harms. They included low self-esteem, depression, suicidal ideation, suicide attempts, relationship problems, sexual dysfunction, alienation, loneliness, and social isolation.[13] These authors noted the limitations of their own research in that they didn't document the percentages of respondents reporting specific harms, while 13 percent of respondents did report that they still believed the conversion practice experience to be effective. Since then, clinical psychologists, such as Haldeman, have described reports of depression, intimacy issues, sexual dysfunction, and abandoning spiritual beliefs by their patients who had been exposed to SOGICE.[14]

Despite the harms, at the peak of SOGICE popularity (1970s-1990s) there were even significant conferences for "ex-gays"—and those hoping to be—around the world. These were offered by various organizations and often had high profile speakers representing the "hope" for change. Among the most prominent people to speak to the impact of this era is Anthony Venn-Brown, a renowned former Assemblies of God preacher known for his involvement in the establishment of the "Youth Alive" events. His autobiography presents a graphic yet balanced perspective on his experiences of exorcism, fasts, and psychiatric treatment over the course of more than twenty years—to no avail. The SOGICE failed to achieve any change and inflicted major trauma throughout its delivery.[15]

Despite being discredited SOGICE are still currently offered in Australia. One report noted that up to 10 percent of LGBQ+ Australians are still vulnerable to religion-based pressures and attempts to change or suppress their sexuality and/or gender identity.[16] Another, more recent,

---

12. Jones et al., *Healing Spiritual Harms*.
13. Shidlo and Schroeder, "Changing Sexual Orientation," 249 and 254–6.
14. Haldeman, "Therapeutic Antidotes," 117.
15. Venn-Brown, *A Life of Unlearning*.
16. Jones et al., *Healing Spiritual Harms*, 3.

report noted that 63 percent of LGBTQA+ Australians reported hearing messages promoting SOGICE "often" or "frequently."[17]

These may be current figures, but they hide a more extensive historic reality. A report from the United Kingdom found that 22 percent of LGB people from religious backgrounds have been subject to someone trying to change, "cure," or suppress their sexual orientation or gender identity at some point in their lives. Tragically, that number climbed to 43 percent of transgender people and 36 percent of non-binary people.[18] In Australia, the figure sits at a high rate of 45 percent of LGBTQA+ people having experienced at least one type of informal conversion practice "often" or "frequently."[19]

SOGICE and The Salvation Army in Australia

Among the participants in my research, the frequency of exposure to SOGICE was higher than these reported averages. Given the option to skip ahead, all twenty-four survey participants explicitly chose to complete the section about SOGICE in the survey. 46 percent (eleven of twenty-four) reported experience of or exposure to some form of SOGICE, which is directly comparable to the 45 percent of LGBTQA+ Australians reporting such experiences.[20] Four of these respondents placed this experience within the last ten years. It is clear in the interviews, and in the survey of TSA membership material, that the position of TSA in this regard has changed significantly since 2012 to be officially opposed to the use of SOGICE. That makes the four that have some experience in the last ten years even more significant: SOGICE are still being practiced even though it would not be officially sanctioned and would, in theory, be organizationally rejected. Clearly, even when the denomination stands against SOGICE from an official perspective, there are still leaders and congregants who encourage their use and administer their practice.

Almost all of the survey respondents that indicated exposure to SOGICE had experienced this in the last twenty years. Rather than just indicating recency of the practice, this may, as much, indicate the recency of service of the officers surveyed. However, it does show the continued

---

17. Jones et al, "Improving Spiritual Health Care for LGBTQA+ Australians," 5.
18. Carlisle and Withers Green, *There Was Nothing to Fix,* 6.
19. Jones et al., "Improving Spiritual Health Care for LGBTQA+ Australians," 5.
20. Jones et al., "Improving Spiritual Health Care for LGBTQA+ Australians," 5.

practice in TSA, long after the historic peak of SOGICE in the 1980s and 1990s. There were a range of practices and change efforts noted by the survey participants, described in Table Ten:

Table 10: Types of SOGICE Practice in TSA

Type of SOGICE practice	Percentage of respondents
Prayer ministries	37.5 (N=9)
Seminars or conferences about changing sexuality	12.5 (N=3)
Rallies/ "ex-gay" events	4.2 (N=1)
Counselling sessions	29.2 (N=7)
Retreats for intensive treatment	8.3 (N=2)
Exorcism	8.3 (N=2)
Books on how to change or suppress my sexuality/ gender identity	25 (N=6)
Videos on how to change or suppress my sexuality/ gender identity	25 (N=6)

Note that as these experiences are discussed here, I do not identify (even with pseudonyms) the participants. I am also not providing ages and dates, and I am altering or omitting some locations. This is because some participants could easily be identified in this way. I have still included some indication of location as there were different practices evident in different states, with the former Australian Eastern Territory being far more overt in the delivery of SOGICE, but some very underground and dangerous activity occurring in the former Australia Southern Territory.

Prayer is one of the spiritual practices commonly utilized as a form of SOGICE and was mostly covered as a form of spiritual abuse in chapter 4.

Seminars and conferences were attended by survey participants and interview participants. These varied in intensity and it is of note that the former Australia Eastern Territory funded the attendance at such events by two interview participants. The first participant funded by the Eastern Territory felt uncomfortable but able to discern what was happening:

We kept going to the "how to deliver people from homosexuality" and that was not a comfortable experience for me. And I . . . along

> with two other people, I think we all felt targeted. You know—constant offers for special prayer, you can come and see someone confidentially, we've got [people] here who've successfully left the gay lifestyle. (Interview Participant)

The other was sent overseas for intensive treatment and seminar exposure, again at the expense of the Eastern Territory. In their case, it led to a mental breakdown and time in a psychiatric medical facility upon their return to Australia:

> I was, you know, sent overseas to be cured . . . When I was out [there], the Army looked after me, put me in the house there . . . and I went to groups almost every day. There, in a ministry called "Redeemed lives," which was run by a supposedly ex-gay Episcopalian priest. He was the minister of the church. In fact, basically, later on, after I came back to Australia, I heard that he'd been thrown out of the church because he'd "regressed," and got involved in a gay relationship again . . . I went to a psychiatrist over there. I was part of a group meeting. I wanted to believe it was all possible. So, everyone was telling me it was all possible. This was finally my chance to be cured and to be made well, so I believed that and I went into it. (Interview Participant)

In Victoria, participants experienced seminar and conference exposure in different ways. One participant noted that a speaker whose keynote topic was promoted as "healthy male sexuality," and who had previously publicly humiliated homosexuals in his audience, was still being used by TSA as a speaker at men's events in Victoria in 2022. Another participant noted that someone need not be sent away to another group to experience this type of SOGICE. They noted their experience of taking some transgender youths to a TSA camp in Victoria where young people were first separated along gender lines and then, when the transgender identity of the young people became known, that prayer ministry was specifically offered. They stated:

> They, you know, they do it under the guise of "I'm going to pray for you." You pray for them—for what you want them to change. That is conversion therapy. Sorry, but that is what you're doing to them. You're telling them that they need to change.

Almost one third of survey participants (29 percent, N=7) experienced counselling sessions aimed at SOGICE which varied in type and intent. The survey question did not distinguish between pastoral counselling, psychological treatments, pastoral, or professional supervision sessions, or counselling specifically associated with SOGICE organizations. One interview participant noted that the Australia Eastern territory paid for him to travel to another major city each month for counselling around matters related to sexuality, although it turned out to be somewhat farcical:

> And I went to counselling for several months. I was actually living in XXX and used to travel [to XXX] once a month, or every six weeks or so, to see an Army counsellor. He was an officer... and I said something to him about being attracted to men, because his initial solution... cleverly... was to try and notice women more. (Interview Participant)

Some carried deep suspicion about the counselling sessions that they were sent to:

> I was sent by the Army, who suspected that I might be gay, and I'm really quite angry about this one, and I know it's nowhere near as bad as some of my colleagues were subjected to... but, sent to a psychologist and told that there would be no repercussions if I admitted to them I was gay, and I knew damn well that if I decided to tell them that I was then I was out. (Interview Participant)

For another, counselling was proposed by the officers he was sent to for placement during his officer training:

> On my very first Sunday, the officers took me out to lunch and said that they were very pleased to have me, that they had asked specifically for me to do my placement at their corps. They had been praying that I would come, because one of the officers in that team had a business on the side as a counsellor helping people get back to the "Straight and Narrow." (Interview Participant)

Exorcism attempts were only reported by a few survey respondents, and it is important to note that they were proposed or carried out in both former Australian territories. Importantly, one of these was within the last ten years, while the others were quite some time previous (1990s). The low numbers do not indicate much, except that this extreme form of spiritual practice aimed at SOGICE was used in TSA and, in recent years, was still considered (in one place at least) to be a reasonable option. In the broader context of TSA, exorcism is not a standard or regularly practiced spiritual exercise, demonstrating that this is a significant outlier.

One officer noted that she had not experienced exorcism attempts, but that she had a friend who had experienced them. A second spoke about how it seemed the logical conclusion to those who had counselled them, because of the way that homosexuality was treated as a demonic occurrence. A third participant comically told the story about how a former officer colleague had come to their workplace, on behalf of TSA, for support with government funding, but had tried to exorcise them during the conversations that were held. She noted with a grin, "Casting demons out of somebody is not a good way to get funding out of them."

The original exposure to SOGICE varied among research participants. For some it was with family, for some it was at their corps (church) and for others it began when they entered training to become TSA officers.

Family is often the first place where SOGICE is discussed. In these cases, it is a concerned family member who is the instigator of SOGICE out of concern for the salvation of their "loved one." This is the case in over half (56 percent) of reported cases in the United Kingdom.[21] One participant noted that it was his father who first gave him a book on how to renounce the "spirit of homosexuality." He discovered that others had the same experience and knew the materials well:

> I mentioned before that my father gave me a book on how to pray against the spirit of homosexuality. It turns out this was quite a widely distributed resource as I've met others who were given the same material. A lesbian friend and I had a laugh once reciting the prayers to each other from memory . . . "I renounce the lie that the spirit of homosexuality reflects God's plan for me . . . " While we laugh, we had to concede just how deep these things reach into our psyches. (Interview Participant)

That interview participant also discussed the influence of Christian friends. He talked about how following his father's intervention, a close friend went and obtained a series of videos for him to watch. They were intended to ensure he acted like the heterosexual, masculine man he was "meant to be," and covered how to behave like a man: not crossing his legs when sitting or standing, how to have a firm handshake, and how to concentrate sexual interest towards the opposite sex, as examples.

For others, it was the corps setting where they were first exposed. One interview participant discussed how SOGICE videos produced by

---

21. Carlisle and Withers Green, "There Was Nothing to Fix," 7.

Sy Rogers's ministries were still being shown at their corps around 2000. His work and materials would come up quite often in the interviews, as if they were the materials of choice for many in TSA.[22] Another interview participant gave her pulpit over to her Corps Sergeant Major one week (in the late 2010s) only to find that he used the opportunity to promote SOGICE to the corps. She intervened:

> I said, "Actually, I won't have you say that here. I will not. The Salvation Army does not believe in conversion practices. We have spoken out against that. We have policy, now, that speaks to how we think that that is harmful. So no, thank you, sir!" (Interview Participant)

Exposure through church environments is that which is most commonly discussed in the Australian context. Materials for individuals and church group settings are still for sale on websites such as Koorong Australia (as at November 2024). These include Keane's book *What Some of You Were*, which includes testimonials from Australians claiming to be ex-gay with Bible Study materials re-asserting negative readings of the six "clobber" passages of Scripture.[23] This book was awarded Australian Christian Book of the Year in 2002. Some denominational environments are also more likely to offer SOGICE. David Marr's essay, "The High Price of Heaven," speaks from the context of Sydney Anglicanism and notes how shame-driven LGBTQ+ Australian kids hungry for a spiritual life will follow whatever formula for salvation being offered through their churches.[24]

One participant in my research spoke about how coming out led to an immediate referral to SOGICE from the corps officer:

> When I first came out, I was told that I should be going to Exodus, and that I was going to be referred to Exodus. And I've since heard from the officer who made those referrals that they regret

---

22. Sy Rogers (1956-2020) was an American-born president of Exodus International, an organization promoting SOGICE, who also spent many years as a pastor in New Zealand. He claimed to be "ex-gay" and had at one stage lived as a woman, before later "de-transitioning." Exodus International closed in 2013, with Alan Chambers, the president at the time, denouncing its mission. Rogers later said in private conversations he no longer supported SOGICE but never made the statement publicly. See: Ring, "'Former Gay, Trans Pastor Sy Rogers Dies, Memorialized by Right Wing," *The Advocate* (Online), 22 April 2020.

23. Keane, *What Some of You Were*.

24. Marr, "The High Price of Heaven" (1999), republished as "Shame and Forgiveness," in *Growing Up Queer in Australia*, 8.

that, and that they just believed that was the right thing to do at the time.

Exposure during training to become a TSA officer was also discussed by a number of research participants. While one officer from the former Southern Territory was exposed to invitations to SOGICE during placement (mentioned above), it is alarming that many former Eastern Territory officers spoke about how SOGICE materials were promoted and used during their time in the Sydney college.

In a previous chapter, a former officer was quoted regarding a couple that came to run pastoral care lessons at the Eastern Territory college. These included sessions on working with people of diverse sexualities. She had reported how their material included Sy Rogers's testimony of "deliverance" from homosexuality. Another cadet from that era confirmed the story:

> *The only teaching on this was videos by a guy called Sy Rogers, who was an "ex-gay" who testified about how you can change, and you know all that sort of stuff. And there were the videos that we were shown, and then that was reinforced through any discussion afterwards. But funny thing is, we now know there were several gay people in my session, and we all sat through that. You know, we never knew about each other (back then). Obviously, it was, you know, the shame.*

Interestingly, some younger officers who hear about these stories expressed guilt. One participant discussed their consciousness that "that could have been me." They looked back in their own story and saw a number of instances that could be identified as "indirect conversion therapy practices" (their term), but wondered at the grace that they had been born a little later and may have been insulated as a result.

Current Environment in Australia

In recent years there were still ten registered religious organizations in Australia or New Zealand advertising the provision of ex-gay or ex-trans therapies.[25] And while SOGICE may no longer be extensively delivered in Australia by organizations incorporated specifically for such a purpose, there is strong evidence that within conservative congregation settings they occur under the direction of the local pastors and priests. Further,

25. Jones et al., *Preventing Harm, Promoting Justice*, 16.

the SOGICE movement now attempts to present itself in more ethically acceptable postures, cloaking anti-LGBTQ+ ideology in the language of spiritual healing, mental health, and religious liberty, making it harder to distinguish from pastoral care until very much entangled in its web.[26]

The danger presented by these activities, still used in many faith-based environments, is increasingly being recognized. Various governments around the world are seeking to legislate against their use. Within Australia, Queensland, the Australian Capital Territory and Victoria have led this move. New South Wales and South Australia have now also passed legislation against the use of SOGICE, both in 2025. In a previous chapter, I noted the Australian Christian Lobby campaign that was supported publicly by three Salvation Army officers in opposition to the Victorian legislation. While the Western Australian Attorney-General promised a ban in 2022, no legislation has been forthcoming to date. Tasmania's government also previously promised legislation, but the draft legislation was extraordinarily flawed, offering defenses to SOGICE rather than bans, and has not yet been tabled in parliament.

In making recommendations for legislation to the Tasmanian government in 2020 the Tasmanian Law Reform Institute did, however, give one of the best comprehensive working definitions:

> (SOGICE) are acts or statements that are aimed at changing, suppressing, or eradicating the sexual orientation or gender identity of another person and are based on a claim, assertion or notion, either expressed or implied, that non-conforming sexual orientation or identity is a physical or psychological dysfunction that can be suppressed or changed.[27]

The Salvation Army in Australia did not explicitly provide a statement condemning SOGICE until March 2024. The statement opposes vilification or discrimination of anyone on the grounds of sexuality. It argues that same-sex attraction is not rectifiable at will, so therefore there is no basis for referral to, or engagement in, any form of "gay conversion therapy." It recognizes the social, emotional, psychological, and spiritual harms caused by such practices.[28] When drafts of guidelines for members were first prepared, there was recognition of the

---

26. Jones et al., *Preventing Harm, Promoting Justice*, 4.

27. Tasmania Law Reform Institute, *Sexual Orientation and Gender Identity Conversion Practices*, x.

28. The Salvation Army, *Guidelines for Salvationists: Conversion Therapies*, 4.

ideological divide in the organization. The first draft paper concludes, "It is our hope that we would show love and compassion to all, and that even in our disagreements we can continue to work alongside each other, united in our mission and love for Christ."[29] Commissioner Robert Donaldson, then Territorial Commander of TSA Australia, summarized this difficulty just prior to the draft guidelines being developed. Of TSA in Australia, he said, "Our challenge, however, is not in serving without discrimination. There are polarizing views in the church and this is where we are struggling."[30]

Other TSA territories were more advanced that Australia in this regard. TSA New Zealand Territory published guidelines that note that TSA had an international position statement on homosexuality as early as the 1990s which states that homosexuality is not "rectifiable at will." Therefore, they say, SOGICE are illogical. The New Zealand guidelines also state that knowingly approving of "conversion therapy," which is known to bring harm, is "not consistent with the love of God."[31] TSA Canada Territory followed New Zealand within two months and published their own statement, specifically addressing the laws being proposed before the Canadian parliament. After discussing the harms, among their commitments were, "To not act, directly or indirectly, to encourage, refer to or engage with any form of conversion or reparative therapies or practices."[32] TSA United Kingdom and Ireland Territory boldly titled their statement, "Conversion Therapy: We stand against this practice."

Various TSA Territories have clearly denounced SOGICE, now including Australia. The gap between these moves and statements, and the reality across the TSA in Australia, is still there, however.

Ways Forward

The Australian Psychological Society has outlined some of the ways in which people can respond healthily to disclosures of exploring sexual orientation and gender. This is especially important for people of faith who sometimes struggle to reconcile their sexuality or gender identity

---

29. The Salvation Army Policy, Research, & Social Justice Unit, *Draft Gay Conversion Discussion Paper for Salvationists*, 3.

30. Donaldson, *State of the Territory*, Webcast, 19 February 2021.

31. The Salvation Army New Zealand, Fiji, Tonga and Samoa Territory, "Guidelines for Salvationists: Gay Conversion Therapies," September 2020.

32. Tidd, "Salvation Army Responds to Bill C-6," 4 December 2020.

with their received teaching and tenets of their faith. They recommend psychological approaches that challenge negative stereotypes, develop affirming social supports, promote self-acceptance, and increase mental health literacy.[33] Even without psychological professionals, churches can adopt these measures to some degree.

These recommendations reflect the contrast between helpful and unhelpful approaches published by Ryan in her research. She notes that gay and transgender youth rejected by their families are: eight times more likely to attempt suicide; six times more likely to suffer high rates of depression; three times more likely to use illegal drugs and alcohol; and three times more likely to become infected by HIV and other STIs.[34] Alternatively, talking with your child about their identity, expressing affection, providing emotional support, advocating for and protecting your child from mistreatment, attending affirming churches and events, connecting your child to positive role models, welcoming your child's partner into your home, and speaking to them positively about their future can promote well-being.[35]

An approach which acknowledges and apologizes for the past, while promoting a positive way forward, would be appropriate for TSA in Australia. This positive way forward would include acknowledgement that members of TSA in Australia identify as LGBTQ+. It would actively discourage offering, referring people, or supporting SOGICE within Australia, and support government legislation to outlaw such practices. It would need to include training for officers and soldiers particularly in how to demonstrate sensitivity to the social, emotional, and spiritual needs of LGBTQ+ people, and it would include forums for listening to the lived experience of SOGICE survivors to promote understanding and prevent their delivery within the organization ever again.

---

33. Australian Psychological Society, "Use of Psychological Practices that Attempt to Change or Suppress a Person's Sexual Orientation or Gender," 3.

34. Ryan, *Supportive Families, Healthy Children*, 5.

35. Ryan, *Supportive Families, Healthy Children*, 9.

Chapter 6: **Discrimination, Internalized Homophobia, and Suicide**

THIS CHAPTER IS THE last that deals with the darker experiences of LGBTQ+ Salvation Army officers. It incorporates those areas that did not fit neatly into the other chapters, or which may result from the accumulative effects of the experiences discussed therein, including discrimination in the workplace, internalized homophobia, and suicidal ideation.

These concepts are not disconnected. Discrimination leads to internalized homophobia and higher rates of mental illness in LGB communities.[1] Suicidal ideation can be a product of internalized shame, fear and loss of hope. While some studies (e.g., Igatua et al., 2009) do not find that internalized homophobia directly predicts suicidality apart from depression, others note that experienced homophobia (regardless of source) was positively associated with a history of suicidal ideation and suicide attempts *because* it led to significantly higher risk of depressive symptoms.[2]

In turn, discrimination and homophobia are products of living and operating in non-affirming environments. They are a key feature of the failure to support LGBTQ+ people, and failing to confirm that they can experience wholeness and holiness while living as their authentic selves. They are tied to a lack of understanding that the pronouncements and actions of church leadership, and members, can be profoundly harmful.

1. Hanekom, "Internalised Homophobia."
2. Igartua et al., "Internalised Homophobia," 15; Tan et al., "Experienced Homophobia and Suicide Among Young Gay, Bisexual, Transgender and Queer Men in Singapore," 349-358; Lee et al., "Internalised Homophobia, Depressive Symptoms, and Suicidal Ideation Among Lesbian, Gay, and Bisexual Adults in South Korea," 393-399.

Workplace Discrimination versus Psychological Safety

It must first be recognized that, for Salvation Army officers, there is no regular workplace. The nature of calling and covenant that are bound so intricately to the nature and operation of officership make their circumstances far more complicated. They psychologically and spiritually bind the officer to service in a way that makes them more likely to remain in places and situations that are far from healthy.

Also, the nature of remuneration for service for officers creates psychological and financial dependency unlike other workplaces. Officers are paid very low amounts relative to the rest of the workforce (mostly around $25,000 - $30,000 depending on years of service)[3], and therefore rely on the supply of housing, health insurance, and vehicles owned by TSA. Many simply cannot afford to leave and start over, and saving up to do so can take many years. Asking the question, "Why don't they just leave?", fails to understand each of these issues, or even the nature of community that is felt among many officers. Further, many religious institutions can be "greedy" (using a term from Jennings), in that they demand undivided commitment, maximizing loyalty.[4] This loyalty is often given freely, without coercion, due to the religious earnestness of the individuals, but leads to the church becoming the center of someone's life.

The survey clearly pointed toward workplace discrimination for LGBTQ+ officers in Australia. Twenty-two out of twenty-four (92 percent) survey participants said that they had witnessed discrimination. Ten said that they had witnessed it often or regularly. Nineteen out of twenty-four (79% percent) said that they had personally experienced discrimination. This is compared to just 39 percent (arguably still too high a figure) in the broader community.[5] Sadly, when I cross tabulated the survey data against which survey participants were "out" in the organization, it became clear that the sole protective factor for LGBTQ+ officers was to not be "out". Four out of five officers that had *not* experienced personal discrimination were not "out".

> I've been afraid to share who I really am with other people . . .
> For fear of being rejected and all the hard questions. And you

---

3. This can be compared with the Australian minimum wage for employees from July 1 2024 of $915.90 per week or approximately $47,626 per annum.

4. Jennings, "My Whole Life Was the Two Suburbs that Surrounded the Church."

5. D'Almada-Remedios, *Inclusion@Work Index 2023-2024*, 12.

> think, "Ahh, I really don't want to do this." For the fear of being rejected.—James (Interview Participant)

This leads to many officers editing their behaviors, speech, and dress. While it may not be obvious, given many still wear uniforms and branded clothes in their workplaces, for the officers concerned there is a constant feeling that they must check their presentation so as not to give reason for comment or backlash. More than 90 percent of the officers surveyed said that they edit their behavior or speech at least some of the time. This requires an incredible amount of effort and can be tiring.

> I think it's a lot around being very careful around my disclosure. Yeah. Because it's mainly because you just don't know what position somebody comes from, or if it's then going to be turned into a defense. . . I don't have the energy for it, so it kind of creates a bit of a low level, like, anxiety and hesitation.—Martha (Survey Participant)

> I came to the point where I was honest with myself about my sexual orientation, [but] I was never even going to have a fulfilling life as an officer because I'd be watching my back every five minutes.—Mary (Interview Participant)

There is some understanding, at least in headquarters and social services centers, that workplace safety needs to be improved. A webinar presentation and subsequent conversation between Salvation Army members from around the world in July 2021 sought to find ways in which the safety and wellbeing of people with diverse sexual orientations and gender identities could be assured within the organization.[6] While the focus of that event was initially intended to look at Salvation Army congregations, by necessity the break-out rooms moved to considering the conditions and "workplaces" for LGBTQ+ officers. Specifically, the group discussion led to calls for better understanding of workplace psychological safety for officers.

Workplace psychological safety is a shared belief that the team environment is safe for interpersonal risk taking, for example, "coming out".[7] It is a state of feeling included, safe to learn and flourish, safe to contribute, and also safe to challenge the status quo.[8] Further, it needs

---

6. Included, "Included: Connected," 24 July 2021.
7. Edmondson, "Psychological Safety and Learning Behaviour in Work Teams," 352.
8. Clark, *The 4 Stages of Psychological Safety*, v.

to be possible for all four of these things to occur without fear of being embarrassed, marginalized, or punished in some way.

Clark sees these stages as the natural progression of human needs in workplace settings.[9] When human teams of all kinds progress through the four stages, they create deeply inclusive environments, accelerate learning, increase contribution, and stimulate innovation. Initially a model designed to improve workplace learning, psychological workplace safety has conceptually evolved over the last twenty years to help organizations also consider broader matters of inclusion.[10]

Psychological safety in a workplace encourages vital behaviors that enhance the team environment and team effectiveness. These include: asking a question, admitting a mistake, disagreeing, saying "I don't know," sharing an alternate point of view, sharing something personal, challenging the status quo, giving feedback, sharing your emotions, sharing an idea, asking for help, doing something you're not good at, or simply saying no.

The Salvation Army is not alone in failing to create safety for its LGBTQ+ officers. Across the board, psychological safety is not shared by LGBTQ+ employees in many companies. In a 2014 survey of Fortune 500 employees, it was observed that over 35 percent were not comfortable being "out" at work and 53 percent were not comfortable being "out" to clients or other stakeholders. Worse, in terms of psychological safety, 81 percent of non-LGBT respondents felt that gay and lesbian co-workers should hide who they are in the workplace.[11] While this survey is now dated, and is US based, it can still be safely assumed that in some Australian workplaces, especially those with an evangelical Christian heritage, the figures would translate. Also, while employee protections are stronger in Australia for LGBTQ+ employees, this is not the case for clergy as faith groups have statutory exemptions in legislation allowing the regulation of their members.

More recent work in Australia by Fielder and Ezzy recognizes that the landscape is complex. There are some Australian religious workplaces that are affirming, but many are not and some are explicitly and legally discriminatory. They found there were many variables such as the variant views on LGBTQ+ sexualities by denominations and individuals in

9. Clark, *The 4 Stages of Psychological Safety*.

10. Edmondson, "Psychological Safety and Learning Behaviour in Work Teams," 350.

11. Fidas et al., *The Cost of the Closet and the Rewards of Inclusion*, 3,9.

religiously-affiliated workplaces. Also, the immediate experience of the individual can be directly affected by the support, or otherwise, of their immediate line manager.[12] In my survey, it was noted that LGBTQ+ officers were more likely to be out to their line manager (54 percent) than their congregation (29 percent).

This is not surprising; it is most likely the local congregations that will actively reject, or clearly not affirm, LGBTQ+ officers. One survey respondent spoke directly to this:

> My concern is local congregations, particularly older Salvationists, won't accept LGBTQ, and especially people in loving monogamous marriages—Survey Participant

This has many underlying factors which may include a lack of education in theological and socio-historical criticism among congregation members. It is likely also tied to the fears of loss in many congregations that are diminishing in size and influence, which some connect to societal acquiescence. Fielder and Ezzy note that Christians' rejection of diverse sexualities and gender expressions is tied with the churches' loss of influence, power, and privilege in broader society and the perceived societal undermining of conservative Christianity's hegemonic heteronormativity.[13]

The primary reason to address workplace discrimination and psychological safety for LGBTQ+ officers is obviously their mental health. Another key reason is to address the basic need to connect with others and belong. A Boston Consulting Group report noted that 75 percent of LGBTQ+ employees had a negative interaction with a colleague in their workplace during the previous year (2019) and 41 percent had more than ten such interactions. They add, "Despite meaningful progress, the unavoidable fact is that most LGBTQ employees do not feel truly included in the workplace."[14] This could be assumed to be higher for Salvation Army officers who interact with people of varying theologies within a culture that protects traditional viewpoints.

Nearly every workplace requires some degree of personal sharing. It is natural that we get to know our work colleagues. Everyday conversations around home life, dating, politics, and social lives are prevalent in almost every workplace and where people cannot safely be themselves,

---

12. Fielder and Ezzy, "Religious Freedom for Whom?" 7.
13. Fielder and Ezzy, "Religious Freedom for Whom?" 1.
14. Duprelle et al., *A New LGBTQ Workforce Has Arrived*, np.

they are automatically excluded. For some officers it may even be empowering to set personal boundaries when deciding what information is confidential or private and not for sharing in the workplace. Nevertheless, it is stressful being forced to conceal something all the time, when the rest of the team are sharing.[15]

Ensuring psychological safety allows people to contribute and make a difference. It ensures environments where people feel safe to speak up with the intent of making things better. No one wakes up in the morning excited to go to a workplace where they are perceived as less worthy, intrusive, or perceived in any other negative way. This is especially the case in a setting where one senses "calling" to serve, is perceived to be failing or is deemed a "sinner" in a purity culture.

Where people feel treated as intrusive by colleagues and managers, they stop asking questions or offering ideas. Where they are treated as less worthy or dirty, they will not admit weakness or failure. Where they are belittled or treated negatively in any other way, they are less likely to challenge the status quo, including their own mistreatment. This is "impression management". It works to protect LGBTQ+ people and many become very good at it at a very young age.[16]

The homophobia generated in conservative circles would exacerbate the experience of isolation and the subsequent protection mechanisms employed by LGBTQ+ officers. A lack of psychological safety is very costly, not just for these officers but for the whole organization. Where it is not present, there can be disastrous outcomes.

First, the organization will bleed out some of its best talent. In The Salvation Army this is not just through the departure of LGBT officers and their allies, although this continues to occur. It is also through the departure of more conservative officers in progressive countries where they do not feel there is psychological safety for conversations around (non) inclusion and diversity issues. The Salvation Army in some parts of the world is trying to address this through the implementation of Faith-Based Facilitation conversations (mentioned in chapter one).[17] These are facilitated conversations on issues of divergence within communities, for small groups of eight to twelve individuals, with no goal other than creating safe conversations.

15. Headstart, "LGBTQ+ in the Workplace: Supporting Authenticity," Headstart, accessed 28 July 2021.

16. Edmondson, "Building a Psychologically Safe Workplace," 5 May 2014.

17. The Salvation Army, *Building Deeper Relationships Using Faith Based Facilitation*.

Second, the organization will experience a failure to innovate. Environments that do not reward vulnerability lead not only to closeted and hurt individuals; they also fail to provide space for new ideas and/or to conceptualize the necessary innovations for recreating organizational life cycles.

Third, a lack of psychological safety leads to hostile work environments. While the trauma behind this is obvious for the individual, it also has significant long-term costs for the organization. Harassment, bullying, and public shaming should not be allowed to become normalized in any workplace. They present not only productivity, quality, and innovation risk, but also legal risk. At the time the research was conducted, the clerical employment status of Salvation Army officers had meant that there has not been a legal challenge to the organization for medical, psychological, or discrimination reasons from LGBTQ+ officers. Since that time, a case has been accepted for conciliation between a former officer and TSA through the Tasmanian Anti-Discrimination Commission.

Further, a lack of psychological safety for officers leads to a lack of positive ministry. It hurts the officers, and it hurts those whom they are trying to serve.

Newman, Donohue and Eva note that, "Every time [people] withhold (to keep themselves safe), [they] rob [themselves] and [their] colleagues of small moments of learning."[18] Every time someone withholds, they perpetuate the pain and isolation for both themselves and others. Therefore, it is incumbent on any organization to ensure that they include all members of their workplace in all areas of organizational life and decision making, collaborate well across diverse demographics, and create a culture of safety for all.

Research has offered organizations a way to address the need for psychological safety in the workplace, and some antecedent conditions can be fostered.[19] These include inclusive leadership behaviors, such as the top-down release and modelling of the Inclusion Statement by The Salvation Army Australia Territory in 2021.[20] Other organizational inclusion practices are a second antecedent, such as the Australia Territory seeking Rainbow Tick accreditation to ensure external validation of its inclusive practices in headquarters and social service provision. Relationship networks, both informal and formal, provide support, and

---

18. Edmondson, "Building a Psychological Safe Workplace."
19. Newman et al., "Psychological Safety," 521-535.
20. The Salvation Army, "Inclusion."

while in The Salvation Army this is mostly done through social media at the moment, there is a sense in which it provides both support and semi-unionized advocacy.

However, these initiatives are still being met with skepticism:

> *They are inconsequential. Rainbow tick accreditation only comes in to play with regards to social [program] and was necessary for funding. Whether we have it or not is barely even known to most Salvationists at a corps level. The Let's Talk (faith-based facilitation) gear feels like tokenism and nothing more.*—Survey Participant

> *Until IHQ [International Headquarters] relinquishes its stranglehold on how territories operate, and what they can/cannot do in this and other spaces, true equality is unattainable, irrespective of local desire or action.*—Survey Participant

> *Some of these, like the faith-based facilitation sessions, have taken too long to roll out. And there's not enough explanation to people in our corps about what they are about.*—Survey Participant

Finally, consistent lack of safety due to intolerance, discrimination and stigma can be internalized. LGBTQ+ officers can be led to believe that some, or all, of the negativity is true, which leads to a form of self-hatred. I turn now to discuss this internalized homophobia.

Internalized Homophobia

Internalized homophobia is a term describing the effects of LGBTQ+ people absorbing negative messages about themselves and internalizing those messages.[21] The messages are often associated with the accumulative harmful effects of social stigma and forms of discrimination experienced in heterosexist and anti-homosexual societies and/or community groups such as churches. In such areas of society, theological conservatism means that gains in civil liberties and social understanding in broader Western societies do not automatically translate into religious or other homonegative environments.

Internalized homophobia has three clear outworkings. These are: negativity toward other LGBTQ+ people, negativity towards oneself, including the subjectively homosexual traits one identifies in oneself, and

---

21. Gruenhage, "Internalized Homophobia."

anxiety about one's homosexual identity being disclosed to others. It results in self-corrective behaviors to limit the impact of such negative messaging as a self-protecting mechanism, 'closeted' identities and discrete, sometimes unsafe, activities. It can therefore diminish the indicators of positive adjustment to sexual identity in the individuals affected. At its worst, this leads to a suppression of behaviors as the phobia is internalized, as well as subsequent feelings, often lifelong, of self-loathing, embarrassment and shame, and rarer cases even leading to violence towards those reflecting their own denied nature.[22]

Among the survey and interview participants there was not a significant level of reported negativity toward others. One interview participant, Andrew, did talk about how this occurred during his time prior to becoming an officer, while working as a public servant:

> *There were a couple of gay guys that were employed around there and they were really, really under the—in the firing line as far as prejudices and really bad attitudes go, and that's when I sort of started to think, "Oh, that's me that they're talking about," and so I become fairly anti-homosexual and homophobic myself.*

What was far more common was the accumulative experience of homophobia leading to negativity towards oneself. These accumulative effects can be very detrimental. It is over 40 years since Maylon identified the pathological effects of internalized homophobia including depression, suppression of identity, and hyper-functioning of the superego in an attempt to make the ego behave "morally" rather than realistically. He claimed that these outcomes were a result of a suppression of homosexual feelings, a forced appearance of a heterosexual identity, and the interruption of identity formation.[23] As one of the survey respondents wrote:

> *The overall feeling I struggled with was the need to hide my sexuality and dealing with the discrepancy between my belief of my worth as a human being and TSA's definition of homosexual acts as being sinful.*

Psychologist Alan Downs, reflecting on his own experience, wrote, "We hid because we learned hiding is a means to survival. The naked

---

22. Kort, "How Therapists Often Fail Their LGBTQ Clients."
23. Malyon, "Psychotherapeutic Implications of Internalized Homophobia in Gay Men," 59–69.

truth about who we are wasn't acceptable so we learned to hide behind a beautiful image."[24]

This process of perceiving and internalizing negative messaging starts when LGBTQ+ people are very young. Kort describes the process in this way: "With no external affirmation of their feelings from adults, children must develop their own narrative about their non-heterosexual orientation—a daunting task. The overwhelming message they get is clear: I'm bad, I'm wrong, the world is dangerous, I'm unsafe, and must keep my true feelings secret."[25] The perceived lack of affirmative support can be crippling not only due to the lack of recognition and acknowledgement of feelings through positive information and teaching, but also through a lack of endorsement of same-sex relationships, an absence of LGBTQ+ examples in leadership, or a clear lack of welcome into community spaces and rituals. While TSA does have a strong sense of corporate injustice (and justice) in its responses to Aboriginal and Torres Strait Islanders, poverty, and family violence, as examples, many of its members and leaders continue to see LGBTQ+ people through a "sin" lens rather than a justice lens.

Some of the interview comments reflect this:

> *You get given a theology—while it might be quite mainstream—you sit there and think about how that's being presented by someone and then you think, "Actually, I shouldn't exist if that's true."—Simon (Interview Participant)*

> *It emphasised that there was something wrong with me. It sent me in a decades-long cycle of prayer and crying and grief and hiding.—Joseph (Interview Participant)*

Research by Barnes and Meyer indeed supports the hypothesis that non-affirming religion was directly associated with higher internalized homophobia. They also confirmed that internalized homophobia was a predictor of depressive symptoms and other mental illness.[26]

Given the circumstances that lead to internalized homophobia, it would seem logical and reasonable for LGBTQ+ individuals to leave religious communities. Barnes and Meyer boldly state, "We conclude that non-affirming religious settings present a hostile social environment

---

24. Downs, *The Velvet Rage*, 21.

25. Kort, "How Therapists Often Fail Their LGBTQ Clients"

26. Barnes and Meyer, "Religious Affiliation, Internalised Homophobia and Mental Health," 505,511.

to LGB individuals, so why would they stay?"[27] It would perhaps make more sense for LGBTQ+ Christians to denounce their faith and perhaps even become atheist or embrace agnosticism. While many LGBTQ+ people will leave the non-affirming environment, others will retain affiliations with non-affirming settings because of the spiritual significance and history they associated with that setting and the ongoing personal meaning derived from service within that faith expression. This significance and meaning are something they are accustomed to, often since childhood.[28] More simply, in separate studies, Haldman and Pitt have both shown it is just hard to leave a religious setting where there is some form of affiliation and connection; leaving can be spiritually, culturally, and socially distressing.[29]

Ultimately, belonging is such a critical social construct that it can override other emotions and cognitions. Being a member of a cohesive group that has a shared mission or shared task commitment insulates members of that group from negative cognitions and emotions by focusing attention on achieving group mission. Belonging and task cohesion encourage both action and coping.[30]

There appears to be limited correlation in research between the levels of religious commitment and positive adjustment to sexual identity. Similarly, scriptural literalism (i.e., biblical interpretation with limited attention to historical context or textual analysis) does not seem to be related to internalized homophobia or sexual identity development. However, Harris and her team have reported that a higher level of post-conventional religious reasoning, which they define as capacity for religious decision making apart from defined religious authorities, did predict higher levels of positive adjustment and lower levels of internalized homophobia.[31] Matty emphasizes this in her research and adds, alternatively, that having less homonegativity toward oneself and being willing and/or able to "come out" is

---

27. Barnes and Meyer, "Religious Affiliation, Internalised Homophobia and Mental Health," 514.

28. Barnes and Meyer, "Religious Affiliation, Internalised Homophobia and Mental Health," 514.

29. Haldeman, "When Sexual and Religious Orientations Collide," 691-715; Pitt, "Killing the Messenger," 56-72.

30. Costello, *Primer to Support IGADF Directed Discussions*.

31. Harris et al., "Religious Attitudes, Internalized Homophobia, and Identity in Gay and Lesbian Adults," 205-225.

statistically associated with higher levels of appropriated and experienced grace along with reduced levels of shame and guilt.[32]

It should be noted that the term *internalized homophobia* does not meet universal acceptance. Some LGBTQ+ people do not relate to the expression and end up rejecting the idea. The word "internalized" presents the first barrier. Williamson points out that the concept suggests weakness rather than resilience shown by LGBTQ+ people and therefore distracts from the "external structures of inequality and oppression."[33]

These structures are those that emphasis heteronormativity and produce biases in society that pre-suppose and reinforce heterosexuality as the norm. Therefore, some authors suggest that *heterosexism* is a more accurate descriptor because of the way it draws attention to societal issues at the root of the phenomenon. I disagree with this approach, as heterosexism refers more to external structures and biases, while internalized homophobia relates more to the internalized, developed psychopathologies, emotions, and conflicts within the LGBTQ+ person.

The alternative to internalized homophobia, the real reparation, is the appropriation of grace and love in oneself and toward oneself. Through such grace and love we reduce fear (1 John 4:8—"Perfect love casts out *all* fear") and continue to pursue healthy relationship with God, even where a healthy relationship can no longer exist with a faith community. Through such grace and love we come to see ourselves as part of the "very good" creation (Gen 1:31), forgiven of God and embraced as God's children. In this grace, sexual identity is something to be embraced with gratitude and therefore internalized homophobia is reduced. Authentic living is further discussed in chapter seven, and enlivened grace is a major theme of chapter 10.

For some of our interview participants, arriving at such a place of grace was very hard:

> *From Sunday through the rest of the week it was always, "Yeah, I've got to fight this. I've got to fight this. This is not God's will for my life."*—Martha (Interview Participant)

> *I did believe for years that I was making choices to be gay somehow. That I'd allowed sin in my life.*—Matthew (Interview Participant)

---

32. Matty, "Faith and Homosexuality," 2.

33. Williamson, "Internalized Homophobia and Health Issues Affecting Lesbians and Gay Men," 97-107.

Another Downs reflection sums up much of this section well: "peel away the well-crafted layers, for only then can you see the secret clearly for what it is: [their] own self-hatred."[34]

Suicidal Ideation

This section discusses difficult and potentially traumatizing material concerning suicidal ideation. At its worst, homophobia and internalized homophobia remind LGBTQ+ people of heteronormative expectations and emphasize their failings in that regard. Cis-heteronormativity may not be sustained with malicious forethought but it is still emphasized in everyday innocuous behaviors, from uniform and dress standards to an assumption of different-gendered partners. It is the emphasis of these things that establish being cisgender and heterosexual as the desired norm, and create a climate where queerphobia is possible. This makes living an authentic LGBTQ+ life in a safe manner potentially unimaginable.[35]

There are a range of factors that contribute to suicidal distress. Suicidal ideation and attempts can be conceptualized as a means of escape for LGBTQ+ people: from stigma, discrimination, harassment, and as a means of embodying the rejection and isolation that is felt.[36] While there are currently no national data sets on the rates of suicide among LGBTQ+ communities in Australia, research demonstrates that LGBTQ+ communities experience higher levels of mental ill health, suicidal ideation, and self-harm compared to the general population.[37] 30.3 percent of LGBTQ+ people aged over eighteen in Australia report having attempted suicide at some point in their lives, a rate that rises to 48 percent of transgender and gender diverse people aged fourteen to twenty-five.[38]

For many people, active involvement in faith communities can produce an antidote and many positive life outcomes. These can include higher levels of positive socialization, better overall well-being, and

---

34. Downs, *The Velvet Rage*, 17.
35. Marzetti et al., "Am I Really Alive?" 7.
36. Marzetti et al., "Am I Really Alive?" 3.
37. Australian Institute of Health and Welfare, "LGBTIQ+ Australians: Suicidal Thoughts and Behaviours and Self-Harm."
38. LGBTIQ+ Health Australia, *Snapshot of Mental Health and Suicide Prevention Statistics for LGBTIQ+ People*, 3.

better mental health outcomes.[39] But this is seen in several studies to *not* always be the case for LGBTQ+ people.[40] For those who don't conform to the cis-gender heteronormativity of their particular religious setting, involvement and service in that church can lead to higher instances of self-hatred, depression, and suicidal ideation.[41] The distress can be summed up in one of Hollier's research participants, "Katie." She had got to the point where the pain involved as an LGBTQ+ person in the church led to the cry, "Make me straight or make me die." Ultimately, the only healthy thing for her was to leave the church and separate her religious experience (the church) from her spirituality.[42]

It is therefore no surprise that there were discussions of suicidal ideation among the research participants. Four out of eleven interviews discussed suicidal ideation and two discussed complete mental breakdowns. All of the contributing factors that led to suicidal thoughts among these people cannot be known, but the context of their disclosure suggested that all, bar maybe one, were directly contributed to by the rejection, internalized homophobia, discrimination, and shame experienced during their service, or conflicts between their perceived self and their identity as officers.

So as not to project onto the disclosures of suicidal ideation that were made, I simply cite them here as they were shared:

> *And if we want to keep talented people that God has called, we need to make living out their vocation better than not living out their vocation. And I think that for me the choice was always, "Live out my vocation and die," or "Leave and have some hope of living." By the time I left I was not very far off self-harm. I remember driving home from "pubs"[43] and thinking, "There's gravel road, and a bunch of trees and no-one will ever know that I've done it deliberately." I don't think I've ever told anyone else that. But, you*

39. Ellison and Lee, "Spiritual Struggles and Psychological Distress," 501-517.

40. Hollier, *Religious Trauma, Queer Identities*, 40; Hiller et al., "I Couldn't Do Both at the Same Time," 80-93; Wood and Conley, "Loss of Religious or Spiritual Identities Among the LGBT Population," 95-111; Schuck and Liddle, "Religious Conflicts Experienced by Lesbian, Gay and Bisexual Individuals," 63-82.

41. Schuck and Liddell, "Religious Conflicts Experienced by Lesbian, Gay and Bisexual Individuals," 63.

42. Hollier, *Religious Trauma: Queer Identities*, 114.

43. "Pubs," for TSA officers is a shorthand for "hotel ministries" where people are offered magazines, the opportunity to talk about life matters and sometimes asked to make a donation to TSA. "Driving home from pubs" in this quote refers to returning from hotel ministry.

now, and I'm not prone to wanting to do myself in, but that was a real "I just want to end it all."—Mary (Interview Participant)

It is noted that one at least felt some support from a section of TSA when this occurred:

> At that point my CO [Corps Officer] was actually a good support too. I remember ringing them in a real mess. My whole world had crashed around me and I didn't know what I was going to live for anymore. I was at a phone booth [in XXX place], and just a mess. And they said, come over, let's have a chat and, again, very pastoral, very supportive.—John (Interview Participant)

"Joseph" also thankfully found support at the right time:

> At least twice in my life I've been suicidal. Once was not long before I came out the second time and thought there were no more options. The second, was not long after I had come out and separated from my wife. At that point I thought I had ruined everything and that it was never going to heal for anyone. I almost drove my car off the road at XXX and I honestly believe God saved me by shocking me back to my senses when a stone flew up and cracked my windshield. The second time I stood crying with a knife in my bathroom and thankfully had the where-with-all to call a friend [my Corps Officer] who came around, took the knife, and sat with me for the rest of the day.—Joseph (Interview Participant)

And for one other, it was a sense of divine intervention that saved them:

> [I had] medication I was on, and I contemplated taking it all in one go and hoping that that would, you know, end the torment that I felt. But in that moment, I heard God say to me - I've only heard his voice once, and so not audibly, so I wasn't in psychosis—but say, "It's okay."—Simeon (Interview Participant)

While some of the interview participants (such as two of those above) reported helpful and appropriate interventions by their TSA colleagues, it is not always the case:

> When some of the wheels started to fall off there, that then impacted the one friendship that I had because, obviously, I become a little more unhinged. Um . . . and . . . it again, that whole singleness thing and I actually became quite unwell from a mental health perspective. And at a point where I was not mentally well and did not have the capacity to fight the thing. Particularly when,

> as a XXX year old, you are being told [by TSA leaders] that you are being put on a plane back to your parents' house, who you have not lived with for twenty years. Because that's where "you're going to best get better." And I was like, "Actually, no! Mum and Dad aren't a safe place!"—Lazarus (Interview Participant)

Conclusion

Among both the survey and interview participants instances of direct and indirect discrimination were described. Many found that this, along with the negative messaging and "norms" perpetuated by the culture and teaching of the denomination, became internalized and led to internalized homophobia. This self-hatred was one of the issues, along with shame and rejection, that led to a notable proportion reporting suicidal thoughts and behaviors.

The history and teaching of The Salvation Army has contributed to such significant harms to LGBTQ+ people within its membership, particularly its officers. Over the preceding chapters we have also seen that this is experienced as moral injury, religious trauma and, for many, had led to sexual orientation and gender identity change efforts. It has been observed in workplace discrimination and led to instances of internalized homophobia.

From this point, I will turn my attention to more positive indicators expressed in the surveys and interviews. Namely, the final chapters will discuss the healing power of authenticity, new ministry opportunities discovered by the research participants after "coming out", ways forward for The Salvation Army with its LGBTQ+ Officers, and their positive theology of creation, grace, community, and ministry.

Part 3—**Hope**

Chapter 7: **Authenticity**

> *Homophobic and transphobic people want to silence us. They want to question our very existence, fill our heads with their negativity, and stop us from being who we are. So, our greatest victory, in the face of hatred and intolerance is to live our best lives . . . Be completely you. Be happy. Be fabulous.* - Jack Guinness[1]

I NOW TURN TO the positive witness of the LGBTQ+ officers in this research. In coming chapters I discuss the positive ministry and theological reflection that has eventuated because they are both faithful disciples of Jesus and LGBTQ+.

In this chapter I discuss the experiences of LGBTQ+ officers who have come out and are finding ways to live authentically. The process of coming out, for those who do so, can be positive, leading to self-acceptance, liberation, and community affirmation. For many, however, it is noted that this is not the case; coming out can be harmful, leading to stigma, psychological distress, and discrimination.[2] This chapter considers the responses to participants' coming out, their theological considerations in doing so, and the benefits of living authentically. It also notes the disconnect occasionally felt by individuals in both the Christian and the LGBTQ+ communities, making living authentically harder for those who identify as both.

---

1. Guinness, "Introduction," 9.
2. Sahoo et al., "'Coming Out'/Self-Disclosure in LGBTQ+ Adolescents and Youth," 1012-1024.

Coming out

> *I'm definitely gay, definitely proud, definitely happy, definitely an advocate, an activist, um, more so in the last five years than perhaps before.*—John (Interview Participant)

Twenty-three out of twenty-four survey participants were "out" to somebody, in that they had disclosed their sexuality. Eighteen out of twenty-four were "out" to somebody in The Salvation Army. Each person's story is highly individual and it would be unfaithful to present a particular trope for either the performative experience of coming out, or the choice to remain closeted. I do not attempt to formularize the process or theorize a particular common motif as it is far too broad a concept to cover in this space. Rather, along with others, I simply note that it is a critical stage in sexuality identity development and is often a source of both trauma and healing.[3] This is particularly relevant to note for those who provide a pastoral response to LGBTQ+ people in Christian settings, as is the variant degrees of processing involved for individuals before, and after, coming out.[4]

There are a few commonalities, such as the way that the process is fundamental for identity integration and authentic living among LGBTQ+ communities.[5] However many personal factors, historical and social contexts, and the age of the individual concerned, all affect the relationship between coming out, health outcomes, and social outcomes.[6] Generational factors come into play, with younger people more likely to identify themselves as queer, pansexual, or fluid rather than with more concrete sexuality labels such as heterosexual, gay, lesbian, or bisexual.[7]

The nature of coming out in religious settings is fraught. It is notably difficult because the theological teaching of the church is often explicitly discouraging (see chapter 2). Discussions that individuals

---

3. Hollier, *Religious Trauma, Queer Identities*, 138; Fielder and Ezzy, *Lesbian, Gay, Bisexual and Transgender Christians*; Brumbaugh-Johnson and Hull, "Coming Out as Transgender," 1-30.

4. Hollier, *Religious Trauma, Queer Identities*, 134.

5. Rosati et al., "The Coming-Out Process in Family, Social and Religious Contexts Among Young, Middle, and Older Italian LGBQ+ Adults."

6. Bishop et al., "Sexual Identity Milestones in Three Generations of Sexual Minority People," 2177-2193; Dunlap, "Changes in Coming Out Milestones Across Five Age Cohorts," 20-38.

7. Rosati et al., "The Coming Out Process in Family, Social and Religious Contexts . . ."

encounter before they come out as LGBTQ+ are often about a "them" (being "othered" is discussed in chapter 4), or a set of behaviors perceived to be sinful, such that the conversations do not consider a person's intrinsic identity, let alone involve them specifically.[8] This is derived from a historic pathologizing of LGBTQ+ desire in ways that does not occur with hetero-erotic desire, something problematic for the LGBTQ+ Christian because of their desire to be authentic in the eyes of God and accepted in their community of faith. Further, where more open discussions *are* held in the church around human sexuality, there is an ongoing sense that is a threat to the unity of the fellowship, despite growing and significant support in many denominations.[9] As an example, a survey conducted among UK Anglicans, in the lead up to bishops allowing same-sex marriages to be blessed in churches, showed that more supported same-sex marriage than did not, yet it still faced a severe conservative opposition campaign.[10]

For many LBGTQ+ Christians there is therefore a familiar dilemma. In many denominations and in many Christian families the two identities (being gay, and being Christian) are mutually exclusive: one is told that one cannot be openly gay and also be Christian. This leads many to a difficult choice between one's religious commitment and one's sexual or gender identity. Wilcox positively observes that there are a few that refuse to make that choice and instead "reconfigure the map."[11]

Articulating such a reconfiguration is disruptive. Such actions counter the cis-heteronormative attitude and power structure of religious institutions, but do so using truth—truth developed in periods of discernment and declared as an ongoing pursuit of justice using practical theology.[12] The oft-heard catch cry, "We are queer, and we are *here*," takes on theological and ecclesiastic significance—within the church it is an explicit prioritization and statement of truth and authenticity over authority and assumed traditions.

For some this has led to formation of a specifically LGBTQ+ church, such as the Metropolitan Community Church (MCC), a group

---

8. Wilcox, *Coming Out in Christianity*, ix.

9. Runcorn, *Love Means Love*, 2.

10. Hensman, "The Church of England, Same-Sex Love, State and Society," Ekklesia, 7 February 2023.

11. Wilcox, *Coming Out in Christianity*, 11.

12. Talvacchia, *Embracing Disruptive Coherence*, 5-6.

that was first studied by Enroth & Jamison as early as 1974.[13] Sadly, their book was written from a cultural perspective that still portrayed the gay man (it was mostly focused on gay men) as psychologically abnormal and the churches as dressed-up versions of bathhouses—a new place to cruise for sex that was marginally more respectable. They did, however, start the conversation about how cognitive dissonance could be resolved for the gay Christian, something picked up by Bauer and Gorman who both showed that these congregations were critical sources of support for same sex couples.[14]

It is this congregational and denominational support, or otherwise, that often defines the experience of coming out for LGBTQ+ Christians. Rosati et al. note simply that LGBTQ+ Christians will find variant reactions along three general lines: acceptance, invitation to change (see SOGICE in chapter 5), or outright rejection.[15] Thankfully, many of the survey and interview participants had positive experiences.

> *The way I have been embraced by friends and some colleagues within the Army has been incredibly affirming. It helped immensely in my journey of "coming out" in particular.—Survey Participant*

> *Probably the first person I spoke to was X; [I was] a little anxious, and yet not—because I trusted him. I knew that it wouldn't be an issue, and I needed that.—James (Interview Participant)*

> *To be now out and free and authentic is just a wonderful experience. There's a freedom in being authentic and being "out", and people knowing that you are a gay person, loved by God, and accepting that that all the freedom that comes from that . . . So, you've got to trust God in the process, and he's been faithful, as I've always known he is.—Matthew (Interview Participant)*

Where people were not certain how to react to disclosures of sexual identity by an officer, it was helpful where they chose to take time to consider their responses:

> *I've been exposed to the actual unconditional love of God in in who my parents are, and so I've never wondered if God hated me.*

---

13. Enroth and Jamieson, *The Gay Church*.

14. Bauer, "The Homosexual Subculture at Worship," 115-127; Gorman, "A New Light on Zion."

15. Rosati et al, ""The Coming Out Process in Family, Social and Religious Contexts . . ."

> I've never wondered if I wasn't worthy, or if I was broken. Like those things, never entered my head . . . And then I spoke to this minister, and, like, said it out loud to someone in a Christian [setting] for the first time, and he was incredibly gracious. He didn't want to say things that were hurtful. And so, he said, "Would you allow me to do some reading?" And, you know, "I've not been confronted by this. Would you allow me to do some reading and some thinking about it? And then can we have another conversation later."—Elizabeth (Interview Participant)

It is worth nothing that the helpful pastoral responses are also needed for the family members of LGBTQ+ Christians. One interview participant found out, after she came out to family, that her mother had sought counsel from pastoral leaders which enabled her acceptance of her child. McGeorge and Coburn discuss how important it is for pastoral leaders to be advocates and allies for acceptance of LGBTQ+ children within family settings, and to assist in processing any fear or grief that the family may be experiencing, for the sake of all concerned.[16] This grief can include areas of life they believe their children will not experience, such as school formals or having children, or what they themselves fear losing, including social status and enjoying grandchildren. McGeorge and Coburn also discussed the need for pastoral leaders to help both individuals and families navigate external discrimination and connect families to helpful resources.[17] That is well and good . . . unless the discrimination and lack of resource is evident within the faith community itself.

It is certainly the case that some of the research participants were not so fortunate as to have a positive personal or pastoral response to their coming out. One person observed that it is much harder to come out to people in congregations in TSA than it is in social or community services settings, or in headquarters settings, and that the majority of the resistance or negativity they encountered was from those corps settings. A second said that they were very careful with their disclosures and would never "out" themselves in an Area Leadership Team meeting because the reactions would be too unpredictable.[18] Following being

---

16. McGeorge and Coburn, "Approaches Mainline Protestant Pastors Use to Work with LGB People and Their Families," 343-369.

17. McGeorge and Coburn, "Approaches Mainline Protestant Pastors Use . . . ," 368.

18. Area Leadership Teams are representative leaders of Salvation Army mission expressions in a proximate geographic area brought together by an Area Officer for collaboration, planning, and implementing strategies for holistic mission in their area. See: The Salvation Army Australia Territory, *Local Mission Delivery Handbook*, 4.

outed, another was told that they should not still be an officer, because a "gay officer" would be an oxymoron. A fourth simply reflected on the shock they encountered:

> *My Divisional Commander was somewhat shell shocked, believing that I was the only one within the Salvos.—Andrew (Interview Participant)*

The performative act of coming out is a recent phenomenon in many respects, part of the post-1960s social protest that seeks "rights," "liberation," and validity. Previously, it perhaps would not have occurred to officers to admit or publicly affirm their sexuality. Even in broader society, homosexuality was previously often seen as a perversion or indulgence. Then in the late nineteenth and early twentieth century it was treated under a medicalized model. From the 1970s onwards a shift occurred in society where a range of sexually related matters previously considered "wrong" were normalized, such as pre-marital sexual activity, abortion, and contraception. More conservative elements of the community, including much of the church, who were no longer able to rely on the medical or legal establishments to keep society "under control," turned to the last bastion of power that perhaps could: religion. For the first time it was deemed necessary for Christian organizations to clarify their positions on issues raised by the visibility and vocal nature of the gay liberation movements; such positions expounded by churches were almost all negative, with many stating that homosexuality was temporary in nature and could be healed. It was assumed that heterosexuality and heterosexual marriage were good, but everything else was wrong and dangerous. This didn't just mean LGBTQ+—being divorced or polyamorous was evil also. Two exceptions were the aforementioned MCC, which arose in response to Troy Perry's defrocking in another church (because he was gay), and the United Church of Christ who were the first non-LGBT-specific church to ordain an openly gay minister—as early as 1972.[19] Much of this historic material is covered more extensively in chapter one.

One younger officer perhaps reflected a more contemporary reality where today's youths do not always see the need to specifically "come out." This is consistent with some queer theorists who question the necessity of coming out and expressing singular identity just to counter the

---

19. Wilcox, *Coming Out in Christianity*, 41-2.

heteronormative world.[20] The argument is that people just love whomever they love.

> *I wouldn't say I am "out." I would say that I'm very comfortable with who I am and anyone who needs to know, or [if] it's a conversation that's happening where it's a crucial piece of information, then I have no issue sharing that. I'm very comfortable with that. For me, I made a conscious decision that I don't think there will ever be a coming out moment for me. Because, for me, I've identified my sexuality as just a part of who I am. It makes no difference to who I am, it's just a part of who I am. I'm still XXX regardless of that piece of information.—Simon (Interview Participant)*

Earlier, a younger officer was quoted regarding how they needed a combination of new language and deep study to reconcile their faith and their self-identification as "bi/pan." It can take some time to come up with such language or do the necessary hard work of theological reflection. Being both Christian and LGBTQ+ requires intentionality to reduce the cognitive dissonance, unsustainable internal conflict, and immense psychological pressure generated between their identity and their received doctrine.[21]

While undertaking this personal work, the research participants were also often required to make choices about the extent of information they disclosed to others. Sometimes, these decisions needed to be made on the spur of the moment as they quickly assessed the situation they were in and the danger that it presented. As such it can be quite demanding:

> *Every time that you engage with a new person, a new line manager, a new congregation (especially given I would preach in perhaps ten different corps each year), a new situation or working group, you need to decide just how much of yourself you let out—how safe is this new person or environment. It drives you nuts when you know that the straight people don't even have to think about that.—Joseph (Interview Participant)*

For many coming out is of theological significance. One interview participant described it as a soteriological event worthy of any Salvation Army testimony period.[22] Wilcox agrees, noting the similarity with

---

20. Talvacchia, *Embracing Disruptive Coherence*, 5.
21. Wilcox, *Coming Out in Christianity*, 155.
22. Salvation Army church services, "meetings," often have included "testimony

Christian conversion stories in its before, crisis, and after elements and Edman shares the observation in her book *Queer Virtue*.[23] This is because coming out often has thematic threads and stylized forms that (re)frame the story of an individual's experience. These could be along the lines of perceived difference as a child compared to adulthood or construction of the importance or meaning behind a certain critical moment.[24] Althaus-Reid encapsulates this beautifully in the story of a man who came out as gay, and in doing so chose to change his name to "Renato," meaning "Re-born." He explained that the old life had shame and pain, but after a "crisis moment" and declaration of faith (in his affirmed identity), he had a new life of love and truth.[25]

In the biblical narrative there are a number of coming out stories, and queer readings of Scripture enable the LGBTQ+ Christian to draw strength from such passages. Research into the experiences of gender diverse Christians on religious university campuses in the US found that highly religious and spiritual students believe that they can "turn to God (and Scripture) for positive support, even for identity-related support that may be at odds with their embedding Christian community."[26] Kearns points out, for example, that Jesus had to come out, even if not in relation to his sexuality (although this is not known).[27] While there could be conjecture and debate about when Jesus realized his divinity and his role as messiah, and we will never know that discernment process, we can suspect that in living as "truly and properly man"[28] Jesus would have had the experience of forging his identity and working out who he, indeed, was. Like many LGBTQ+ people, he tested the waters with trusted friends. In this case it was with his disciples where he asked them who people thought he was, what were the rumors on the streets (Luke 9:18-20). He then was, just eight days later, transfigured on the

periods." These are times in the service where people give testimony to the change in their life because they now follow Jesus, or an event in their week where they have seen God at work.

23. Wilcox, *Coming Out in Christianity*, 77. Edman, *Queer Virtue*.

24. Wilcox, *Coming Out in Christianity*, 30-1.

25. Althaus-Reid, *Indecent Theology*, 123.

26. Yarhouse et al., "Listening to Transgender and Gender Diverse Students on Christian College Campuses," 4494.

27. Kearns, *In the Margins*, 136.

28. Doctrine 4: *We believe that in the person of Jesus Christ the Divine and human natures are united, so that He is truly and properly God and truly and properly man*. The Salvation Army, "The Doctrines of The Salvation Army."

Mount with a full declaration of his divine identity for the world to know (Luke 9:28-30). He was seen clearly and his disciples are invited to also, in following him, be seen clearly.[29]

Throughout this discussion, we have reflected on the conscious choice to come out. There have been instances where people have been involuntary "outed." While this was only raised by a few in the interviews, it is worth noting that such non-consensual disclosures are particularly traumatic for people.[30] It is also worth noting that at least two participants were required to confirm their commitment to celibacy upon coming out. One felt compelled to write to his leadership and put this commitment in writing.

There is then also a second coming out, or admission, for those that find partners while serving as officers. This can also receive many responses. One participant found the "don't ask, don't tell" approach of his leaders, while well intended, to be distressing and inauthentic. To meet his authenticity with inauthenticity was not just ironic, but hurtful. This does open up new discussions for each individual, or couple really, around identity and "practice" in the eyes of the church. Matthews talks about the disconnect and pain that is felt when some in the congregation affirm the LGBTQ+ person and their partner, while at the same time they are being told by church leaders to "conform to (narrow interpretations of) Scripture" or even summarily "thrown out" by leadership.[31] Runcorn notes that those Christians who are both gay and partnered are sometimes accused by opponents of taking the "easier choice" and living according to their desires rather than God's will for them.[32]

Coming out, therefore, carries elements of both risk and authenticity. It can generate both conflict and self-empowerment. Each of these things occur as a person speaks out, immediately contravening the hetero-normative expectations of religious society, creating new legitimacies, and expressing a uniquely LGBTQ+ Christian experience.[33]

There have always been, and will always be, LGBTQ+ people within The Salvation Army. It is no surprise when we consider how queer a movement TSA is. TSA was famous for its disruption of religious and community norms, especially in the late nineteenth century. Dressing

29. Kearns, *In the Margins*, 138.
30. Hollier, *Religious Trauma, Queer Identities*, 143.
31. Matthews, "Ever, Honestly, Truly Me," 40-41.
32. Runcorn, *Love Means Love*, 113.
33. Fielder and Ezzy, *Lesbian, Gay, Bisexual and Transgender Christians*, 23.

up and going on a march with music, tambourines, and ribbons sounds as much like a Pride March or Mardi Gras as it does a TSA "march of witness."[34] A previous lack of visibility of LGBTQ+ officers does not mean absence, especially in such a queer religious setting, albeit one where many remain closeted or wear another public persona.[35] The majority of participants in this research found themselves in a place where they could declare their queerness and posit that being authentic and honest is closer to the central tenets of Christianity and TSA than unquestioned heteronormativity and patriarchy.

Authenticity

> *So, it was nice to kind of think that I could be just "me."—James (Interview Participant)*
>
> *Authenticity and integrity are really big for me. And so, whenever I couldn't be my authentic self, you know, all the time, I felt like I let myself down.—Mary (Interview Participant)*

Fielder and Ezzy argue that LGBTQ+ are often inspired and led by an "ethic of authenticity" that drives towards lives led as their true, sexual, gendered, *and* religious selves.[36] This is magnified through a paradigm many can articulate, whereby they perceive their sexuality as God-given. By claiming one's identity and desires, many find themselves released from the imposed sense of sin articulated in religious settings and able to walk a new journey of wholeness and holiness rather than secrecy and shame.[37]

Taylor speaks about this ethic of authenticity. In part he worries about individualism in society, that is to say that people are no longer sacrificed to the demands of the "supposedly sacred" or transcendent.[38] And yet this is what the LGBTQ+ Christian is explicitly undertaking to do in seeking to be authentic: be themselves *and* be dedicated to the divine. The drawback

---

34. A "march of witness," still held in many countries, was a parade of Salvation Army personnel, often with bands and timbrels, to declare their presence and witness to their faith within their community. They are often held in conjunction with "congress," a regional or national gathering of Salvationists.

35. Yarhouse et al., *Listening to Sexual Minorities*, 281ff. Here they note how normal it is for LGBTQ+ Christians to hide their identity and assume disguising behaviours.

36. Fielder and Ezzy, *Lesbian, Gay, Bisexual and Transgender Christians*, 2.

37. Osinski, *Queering Wesley*, 16.

38. Taylor, *The Ethics of Authenticity*, 2.

identified by Taylor is where relative individualism means that the establishment of a personal values system leads some to lose sight of concerns that transcend them. The extreme of this is seen as new forms of conformity arise, somewhat as an absurdity, as people who are insecure in their own identities turn to other "guides."[39] For those who are not comfortable in their own identity, or dedicated to a higher purpose, there is a risk that this could lead to an attempted conformity with stereotypical images of LGBTQ+ "lifestyle," some of which include problematic body image and hyper-sexuality. One needs to be balanced in this observation however; we cannot pathologize individualism in problematic ways that prevent us from remembering that people can be moral and ethical without commitment to a deity or religious framework. Hardy and Easton give one of the most famous examples in their development of an ethic for polyamorous or otherwise sexually diverse individuals through communication, emotional honesty, and safe sex practices, in *The Ethical Slut*.[40] Nor can we automatically assume that dedication to the transcendent leads to adoption of a moral or ethical code, let alone a pastoral one.

When individuals come out later in life this could lead to a second adolescence and sometimes replication of destructive behaviors. Sahoo, Vanketesan, and Chakravarty note that this process of self-exploration and self-articulation is meant to be a result of work during the first (biological) adolescence, leading to self-disclosure (coming out).[41] But this is not possible for all, especially in the church, potentially hindering their psychological development. One survey participant noted how she had seen many of her gay male friends fall into this trap (and joked about the embarrassment of men in their forties behaving like teenagers as they have a second adolescence). Downs, in discussing the necessary attributes for living an authentic life as a gay man, says this "adolescence" is not finished until certain skills are developed, such as accepting the reality of one's situation, one's body, and one's relationships.[42]

For most that do successfully navigate their coming out, and find ways to live as both authentically Christian and LGBTQ+, there is release, freedom, and peace. This release is felt, often regardless of the reactions around the individual:

39. Taylor, *The Ethics of Authenticity*, 15.
40. Hardy and Easton, *The Ethical Slut*.
41. Sahoo et al., "'Coming out'/self-disclosure in LGBTQ+ adolescents and youth," 1012.
42. Downs, *The Velvet Rage*, 169ff.

> *But know I feel that I am myself. Even if some of The Salvation Army can't accept me, I can accept myself, and I know I am loved and accepted by God. I am authentic and whole knowing that I'm not trying to be someone I'm not—although I do have to conceal a bit at times. Increasingly there is freedom. It has taken a long time.*—Joseph (Interview Participant)

Rejection in the church is often argued along theological lines, despite such rejection, in reality, being a product of the medicalization of sexuality and the politics of fear.[43] This makes it very hard for LGBTQ+ Christians to be authentic in their churches, simply because to do so subverts the patriarchal and heteronormative boundaries upon which these contexts are often predicated. However, the perfect love required to live a holy life cannot be achieved without authenticity because honest assessment and expression of one's self is necessary for salvation and transformation.[44] If a person cannot be honest about who they are, and who they love, then authentic and honest relationships are not possible, with one's self, others, or with God.[45] As Ru Paul Charles asks, "If you cannot love yourself, how in the hell are you going to love someone else?"[46]

> *It's who you are, so to not be out you're not being honest. For me, anyway, you're not being honest. You're not being your true, authentic self with people.*—Salome (Interview Participant)

It is this necessity of truthfulness and authenticity that leads Cheng to talk about the "sin of the closet." He describes it as such, because of the devastating, dysfunctional, and unhealthy outcomes that result from secrecy and shame, and counters it with the health and grace experienced through openness, honesty, and acceptance.[47]

> *You know that there was no option, to be honest, because I knew that to get well, I had to be authentic. It was a breaking of chains; psychological salvation, really.*—Simeon (Interview Participant)

---

43. Fielder and Ezzy, *Lesbian, Gay, Bisexual and Transgender Christians*, 6.
44. Osinski, *Queering Wesley*, 21.
45. Moorman, "The Grace of Coming Out," 27.
46. This is the phrase that Ru Paul Charles uses at the end of every episode of "Ru Paul's Drag Race," a television phenomenon over 17 seasons in the US (at the time of writing) and with franchises now in at least 15 countries including Australia and New Zealand (as "Drag Race Down Under").
47. Cheng, *From Sin to Amazing Grace*, 85.

The breaking of chains occurs through reconciliation of sexuality and faith, whereby the LGBTQ+ Christian reclaims their own image of God, their place in the diverse and very good creation.[48] It is where many come to understand that Christianity itself, and its expression of radical love for all, can be seen as queer, and therefore being gay and Christian are very compatible. It is understanding that the fundamentalist rejections they experience are coming from people who claim Christian faith but, hypocritically, reject the central tenet of the Christian faith: love as displayed in the life of Jesus Christ.[49]

One survey participant found it extremely necessary to remember such concepts as they found their authenticity threatened by negative periods during their service as an officer:

> *At the end of last year, though, the last few . . . or August onwards . . . at XXX I became very aware that they had stolen something from me. Or, I had my supervisor describe it as someone had put a cup over my flame. Because I live so authentically, because of the nature of my upbringing, and all of that, I can't compartmentalize like some people can. I just can't.*—Elizabeth (Interview Participant)

Many of our research participants found that TSA was somewhat welcoming when they were living authentically. When they compared it to other environments in which they circulated however, TSA was nowhere near as gracious an environment as the broader communities in which they were situated. Moorman notes that if the church cannot allow people the freedom to be themselves as they experience in other places, then the church cannot claim to offer them grace in a theological sense.[50] Grace expounded must be grace practiced. Quite often the contrast between the corps and the community was palpable:

> *[Someone was] connected to the Corps through the community work but not from a faith perspective. And I gendered my partner to them. We talked about that, and I had a number of incredible conversations with the elderly people in the Lions and Rotary Club who came to our community meal about the church's perspective on stuff like that.*—Elizabeth (Interview Participant)

---

48. Osinski, *Queering Wesley*, 17.

49. Springer, "Why Authentic Christianity is Actually Queer," Medium, 22 June 2019.

50. Moorman, "The Grace of Coming Out," 27.

> *There's something really lovely about it, to just be able to have those moments where I can be a Christian, a minister of religion, a gay woman, in a relationship with a Christian . . . like, all the parts of me, all kind of come together, and I can be just be my whole authentic self. It's incredibly life giving. Sadly, the majority of those moments happen with community members. Or, you know, "new to church and organized religion" members.* —Phoebe (Interview Participant)

To live such an authentic life is to live a life that is constantly questioned. This may be experienced as an external stimulus, but is just as often an internal, reflexive necessity. Taylor explains that, "The powerful moral ideal . . . accords crucial moral importance to a kind of contact with myself, with my own inner nature, which is in danger of being lost, partly through the pressures of outward conformity."[51] The officers who participated in this research mostly resist this outward pressure toward conformity in attempts to be true to themselves. It is in doing so that they make possible a deeply integrated and meaningful Christian and LGBTQ+ life.[52] Forging an integration of Christian doctrine, spirituality, and sexuality enables the LGBTQ+ Christian to find what O'Brien calls a raison d'être, and no longer live by an apology or compromise.[53]

There are a minority for whom living authentically as a LGBTQ+ Christian will include living a life of celibacy. In Fielder and Ezzy's research, six out of twenty-eight participants had chosen celibacy *for a period* as a means of managing the tension between their conflicting aspects of identity.[54] Wesley Hill, a biblical scholar who identifies as gay, feels that we need to be careful not to relativize all potential "identities" in the light of being reborn. He believes that all previous identities (e.g., identity tied to diverse sexualities, ethnicity, and social class) are societal constructs that cease when we are born again in Christ.[55] This, coupled with his traditional reading of the commonly cited anti-LGBTQ+ Bible texts, leads him to say that he is called to "spiritual friendship" with others and a life of celibacy.

However, he is in a minority. Very few people can embrace celibacy, and many in the churches feel shame as a result. In Matthew 19:11-12,

---

51. Taylor, *The Ethics of Authenticity*, 27.
52. Fielder and Ezzy, *Lesbian, Gay, Bisexual and Transgender Christians*, 64.
53. O'Brien, "Wrestling the Angel of Contradiction," 179-202.
54. Fielder and Ezzy, *Lesbian, Gay, Bisexual and Transgender Christians*, 70.
55. Hill, "Christ, Scripture and Spiritual Friendship," 143.

Jesus says that very few people are capable of celibacy. In 1 Corinthians 7, Paul also notes that very few people can accept the demands of celibacy and that they should marry to provide a holy way forward. Essentially, he leaves the choice between celibacy and marriage to the individual Christian to determine for themselves according to how God has enabled them. Marriage or sexual abstinence are "determined in his own mind" (1 Cor 7:37). It is a choice and there is no scriptural warrant for the mandating of celibacy. In 1 Corinthians 7 it is described as a gift (charism—same language as the gifts of the Spirit in 1 Cor 12), providing the grace and resources for celibacy to a few.[56]

The quandary created by the teaching of celibacy in TSA, which fails to understand celibacy as a gift for "some," not "all," was well described by two participants:

> *The bottom line was that gay people had to be chaste. It didn't matter that both Jesus and Paul explicitly say in the Bible that chastity is a gift that not everyone has—or that the solution they offer is marriage which was not available to LGBTIQ people in Australia at the time, let alone in the church. There was no option. The other clear message was that they were only to be accepted in the church if they were single.*—Joseph (Interview Participant)

> *I am sure of two things. Number one, I am called to be an officer in The Salvation Army. This is my life's purpose. Nothing else makes sense. No other job, no other role, no other use of my time makes sense. The other thing that I'm sure of is that I'm a gay man who does not have the gift of celibacy, who does not work well, live well, in isolation. And like many, I am designed to be in partnership with another.*—John (Interview Participant)

Sexuality is a profound moral dilemma for LGBTQ+ Christians. Firstly, they need to deal with the ancient Christian dichotomy of spirit and body. Second, they need to deal with the discrimination where non-procreative heterosexual marriages are acceptable, but not homosexual marriages. They need to discover meaningful ways for the expression of sexuality, but find it to be denied to lesbian and gay Christians who are expected to stay celibate. Further, the predominant conservative Christian understanding of sexuality that views it as hidden, private, and shameful, means that those that come out face stigma for violating this

---

56. Runcorn, *Love Means Love*, 112.

hidden aspect of life—and then significant sanctions, strongly enforced, for any perceived sexual activity.[57]

Freedom from anxiety around the expression of sexuality permits the joy, committed desire, and expression of intimacy—both human and sacred. As expressed in the Song of Songs, freely expressed sexuality need not be casual or indulgent, but can be enduring, harmonious and, for some, a means to come into contact with the ecstatic and spiritual dimensions of life.[58] Rather than sexual expression being an obstacle to the holy life, for many it is the avenue to connection with the divine and truly expressing the person God created them to be.

But to live in such freedom, LGBTQ+ Christians have to be absolutely committed to their faith. Research participant "Liz," in Fielder and Ezzy's work, says that this is because it is "just so hard. It is hard because you are rejected by the Christians in your community; you are rejected by the gay community. Unless you are totally dedicated you won't last."[59] The officers in this study were very conscious that the word "Christian" has itself become a weapon of violence in the minds and experience of the queer community. While homophobic, transphobic, and hateful theologies are an affront to the Christian ethic of love itself, they continue to mar the name and experience of the Christian religion and traditions. The face of the Christian Church has become, for many people, the face of intolerance and hostility.[60] This creates a problem for the LGBTQ+ officer, who can find it difficult to explain themselves in either sphere and an unnecessary complication to their professional practice of ministry.

Queer communities and the Church have often reacted to each other as if the "self" and the "other" are absolute binaries, like opposing political parties. However, this false binary can create painful "spiritual quandaries" for those who live with both identities.[61] Victorian researchers have established the mental health cost of this battle for authenticity, discovering that LGBTQ+ youth from religious backgrounds are more likely to feel worse about their lives and are more likely to think about, or succeed in, self-harm than those from non-religious families.[62]

---

57. Fielder and Ezzy, *Lesbian, Gay, Bisexual and Transgender Christians*, 62.

58. Runcorn, *Love Means Love*, 116.

59. Fielder and Ezzy, *Lesbian, Gay, Bisexual and Transgender Christians*, 64.

60. Edman, *Queer Virtue*, Introduction; Fielder and Ezzy, *Lesbian, Gay, Bisexual and Transgender Christians*, 3.

61. Edman, *Queer Virtue*, Part 1, Chapter 1.

62. Hillier et al., "I Couldn't Do Both at the Same Time," 80-93.

Yet we have seen in this chapter that there is a similarity between the queer experience and the Christian experience that can bring the two together. Both start with some form of perceived identity, an identity that progressively you admit to yourself and then tentatively share with others. For many this is the performative process of coming out, that is a step to authenticity and, in Christian language, a testimony to a new life that leads to wholeness and holiness. In Salvation Army doctrine, it is where we would say "whosoever will may be saved" and "[they] that believeth hath the witness in [themselves]."[63] Both sexuality and faith require engagement with others to fully explore the identity and it is the receptivity of others that can determine the degree to which freedom, release, and peace are found for the individual concerned.

It is recognized that, while this chapter argues for the benefits of coming out and living authentically, it is not possible or safe (yet) for many—including some who participated in this research. They grapple with both the security of the closet and the guilt found in the privilege of the closet, in that they can *choose* not to reveal something about themselves in a way that others cannot (e.g., one cannot hide one's skin color). Ironically, another similarity with the Christian life is that one can "closet" one's faith.

"The lived experience of LGBT Christians is at times traumatic and painful, yet it is also transformed into experiences that are deeply rewarding."[64] While they are treated with hostility both within the church and within the LGBTQ+ community, they tend to be a people who act with sustained grace and authenticity as they seek to express their true sexual, gendered (or non-gendered), and spiritual/religious selves. This leads also to unique opportunities for ministry, which are discussed in the next chapter.

---

63. The Salvation Army, Doctrines 6 & 8.
64. Fielder and Ezzy, *Lesbian, Gay, Bisexual and Transgender Christians*, 159.

Chapter 8: **Opportunity**

> *We, like Paul, must look directly to Jesus Christ and God the Creator for our commissions . . . We are called by God to share in Paul's boldness in asserting God's call of us.* Patrick S. Cheng[1]

IN THIS CHAPTER, I discuss the sense of calling and opportunity felt by the officers participating in the research, which led to their unique contributions in service. They have overcome prejudices, including their own, in order to be able to serve freely. Their presence and visibility challenges norms that would otherwise ignore them or diminish them, while providing hope and support to others. I will look at how this has led to opportunities to serve the community, through the unique gifts and characteristics that LGBTQ+ officers felt they bring to service, the effect this has had on the organization, including some opportunities to influence its leaders, and the support networks that have evolved.

In his commentary on Galatians, Patrick S. Cheng asserts and affirms the ministry of queer Christians in the face of legalism and erasure. He does so from the position of a queer Asian man, and also with a strong theological critique of the status quo. He notes that Paul was not commissioned to ministry according to human standards, but rather directly via a revelation of Jesus. He observes that Paul, like the officers in this research, had to overcome his own prejudices, as well as those of the community, to minister to those around him. He challenges the notion of compulsory conformity and heteronormativity in the church, citing the challenge to compulsory circumcision for believers in the New Testament church.[2] He finishes his case by noting that the identity of the believer is in Christ, not gender or ethnicity (Gal 3:28), and that

---

1. Cheng, "Galatians," 624.
2. Cheng, "Galatians," 624-5.

all are free in Jesus from the yoke of slavery to law, free to live and demonstrate the fruit of the Holy Spirit in their lives.[3]

The notion of compulsory circumcision in Scripture, as discussed by Cheng, is picked up also by Osinski. She looks at the practice of compulsory circumcision as feminizing the male Jew, to the point of "menstrual" blood flow from the genitals, and therefore as a queering activity. She looks to Wesley who called his listeners to the "circumcision of the heart" (following Deut 10:14-18 and Jer 4:4), meaning marked and set aside for service. If we are marked and set aside by such a queering act, albeit internally, then all Christians are called to be non-gendered and non-conformist in their spiritual identity and their service of the world.[4] The acts of love, service, and caring that are offered to the world are never confined to, or only delivered by, heterosexual or cis-gendered Christians. LGBTQ+ officers have a part to play, and perhaps a leading role in this.

The participants in this research affirmed their ministry in the face of patriarchal and heteronormative opposition and discrimination within The Salvation Army. All interview subjects were able to identify ways in which their queer identity enabled their ministry and how certain opportunities arose *because* they were officers who identified as LGBTQ+. Some had to overcome their own prejudices and internalized homophobia. All of the participants who were also "out" were discovering that people often sought them out for support as safe and visible signs of hope and support within the denomination.

Responding to Calling

One blogger, while reviewing the Netflix movie *Pray Away*, unhelpfully and offensively criticized LGBTQ+ Salvation Army officers who stay in ministry within TSA. He likened them to battered spouses who don't know any different or are too afraid to leave, a notion problematic both in its attitude to family violence victim-survivors and also to the LGBTQ+ officers he criticized.[5] A New Zealand-based Salvationist, Colin Daley, responded thus:

---

3. Cheng, "Galatians," 626-7.
4. Osinski, *Queering Wesley*, 26-27.
5. McPherson, "Not 'Prayed Away.'"

> My calling is that this is where I stay
> It's not my choice, but God has made a way
> For me to be the person I should be
> And celebrate that God has given me . . . .
>
> A ministry that's mine, a holy task,
> So really is it too much that I ask,
> You stop attacking those who still remain
> For your comments are not helpful once again.[6]

This response hits a key factor for the LGBTQ+ officer—the notion of "calling." This is a vocational term laden with nuanced meaning depending on your faith background, Christian denomination, and personal understanding, but for many it is a critical element to their *raison d'être*, let alone their reason for remaining in Salvation Army service.

The concept of calling as a cause for entering service and driving or motivating factor was important for those who participated in the survey. One third (eight of twenty-four) felt the same sense of calling to Salvation Army officership that they did when they first considered application for officership or entered training. Two felt that their sense of calling had deepened. Half (n=12) felt that their sense of calling was more complex or nuanced, but it nonetheless remained intact. Importantly, this means twenty-two of twenty-four had a similar, deeper, or nuanced sense of calling, while only two had a lesser sense of calling —one of whom is now totally disassociated with TSA.

This is significant when discussing the ways in which LGBTQ+ officers have had to work through their personal and practical theologies. This demonstrates that the majority retain a high spirituality, personal identification with their ministry and a compulsion to serve. It is also significant that there are nine survey participants who have left officership, but on the whole they are not indicating a lesser sense of calling. It may be that the sampling strategy for the research, which concentrated on TSA channels and the personal networks of the researcher, led to engagement with a group that remained committed through or alongside the denomination. Also, generally speaking, we can surmise that TSA officers are more likely to be people with high levels of religious commitment and sense of calling anyway. What we cannot know is whether

---

6. Colin Daley, August 2021. Used with permission.

there are numbers of officers who have identified as LGBTQ+ and then completely dissociated from TSA who were out of reach of the survey, who may present an alternate view.

Broadly speaking, in Christian theological circles there are two types of call. One is a general call on all Christians to live a life of discipleship. The second is a call to a more particular role or vocation, religious task or type of service. Both carry a sense of *apologia* in that if a person perceives a call by God to a vocation, and some discernment affirms this calling, then that can be regarded as constituting a sufficient defense of a person's commitment to that vocation.[7] The call to discipleship in the Wesleyan tradition, to which TSA belongs, is heavy with meaning and could be expanded into sub-themes such as the call to holiness, the call to serve in purposeful work (in a generic sense), and the call to be hospitable. In this all Christians follow the example of Christ in a ministry of healing and reconciliation.[8]

The receipt of a particular calling leaves the individual with very little doubt about what is being required of them. It still, however, requires discernment as to whether that call can be conceived to have originated in the Divine. In the case of a calling to pastoral ministry, it is usually expected that this discernment takes place within a church or parachurch agency that is subsequently going to recognize the ordination of that person to the appointed task.[9] In the case of a LGBTQ+ Salvation Army officer, there has *already* been a process of discernment and endorsement prior to appointed ministry that has affirmed their calling and accepted them to ministry. In most cases, this is through a prolonged candidature process that includes workplace, church, and personal references, consideration by committees ("Candidates Councils") and written testimony to their understanding of their calling. This is important to note in subsequent discussions as to their ongoing suitability for the role of Salvation Army officer.

One person wrote about the strength of their sense of calling:

> *I know that God is not finished with The Salvation Army. God is still calling people like me to serve. Some days, this is the only thing that stops me from resigning and joining an already inclusive denomination.*—Mark

---

7. "Calling, Vocation," in *Dictionary of Biblical Imagery*.
8. Macquiban, "Work on Earth and Rest in Heaven," 47-70.
9. Trodden, *The Shape of Calling*, 5.

Remarks like this stand against the heteronormative hegemony that still dominates the TSA's notions around ministry. The research participants declared that they had been called to service within that movement, in the face of that heteronormative social structure that would seek, at times, even to deny their existence. Participants regularly spoke about the need to "hide" or diminish who they were, in order to survive while living out their calling, and two interview participants spoke about being offered overseas appointments where they may be more accepted—but also "out of sight" from Australia. The very nature of hegemony means that it has such power that even when new truths emerge, or new realities are pronounced, these new revelations must still relate to the hegemony.[10] Many of our participants found this difficult to navigate, but nonetheless followed the apostle Paul, Cheng, and others in asserting their calling, and following through to offer for service.

The research participants are TSA officers, which I have noted means that their calling to ministry has already been discerned and affirmed through their acceptance, ordination, and commissioning. Their ongoing acceptance, however, seems altered by perceptions of how their identity must somehow affect their calling and capacity. Despite knowing their truth within themselves, they, along with many LGBTQ+ clergy, are considered a disobedience problem or at the very least a difficulty to be accommodated.[11] It is at this point that many leave, despite their ongoing sense of calling; in fact, while some participants in the survey and interviews noted that their sense of calling had changed over time, only one noted that it had lessened *and* that they had lost their faith.

Some are driven out of denominations like TSA through exposure to that which Wilkins et al. refer to as "zero-sum beliefs" about LBGTQ+ individuals and Christianity. These are those notions expressed by heterosexual cis-gender Christians who deny that one can be LGBTQ+ and Christian, while expressing a perceived threat that anti-LGBTQ+ bias has decreased over time while anti-Christian bias has supposedly correspondingly increased.[12]

One participant observed the impact that this could have on TSA as a denomination:

---

10. Carlström, "Tensions, Power, and Commitment: LGBTQ and Swedish Free Churches," 22.

11. van der Walt, "These are the Days of the Raw Despondence," 15.

12. Wilkins et al, "Is LGBT Progress Seen as an Attack on Christians?" 73-101.

> *It's hard. We're called, but condemned. We're playing a long game for change, but understanding that the change may not come soon enough for any of us—or for the organization if it really wants to survive in Australia and retain its evangelical arm.*—Mary (Interview Participant)

Among those that do leave, the majority found ways to continue to serve and live out their calling. For some it was in a social service of TSA, for others it was in other organizations. Many continued in explicit Christian ministry. One participant wrote in the survey:

> *I was privileged to bring the sermon two weeks ago . . . My topic was "Who calls unclean, what God calls clean!" I was six and a half when I gave my heart to Jesus, becoming a child of God. At nine, though, I knew I was attracted to same sex persons. However, at fourteen God still called me to ministry in The Salvation Army. I am still ordained and have preached at the [location] LGBTIQA church on regular weekends for the last 10+ years—* Survey participant

Others stay, or leave and return. For one participant, the sense of calling brought them back to TSA after some time out wrestling with their sexuality.

> *So actually, then I thought, "Now I can do this . . . . God's call is bigger than this."*—Paul (Interview participant)

This participant went on to discuss how this attitude drove them and went "really well until it didn't." About twenty years later, they state that they felt their life started to fall apart, showing however that a sense of calling and willfulness can drive someone to persist for long periods of time.

Those that do stay issue the invitation to TSA to join them in the wider work of God in the world. Many queer Christians in ministry note that it is not up to the church to "include" them. It is up to the church to let go of any power structures and forces that would reshape Jesus and his church into something that is other than an expression of the all-embracing love and grace of God—including heteronormativity. To this extent, queer Christians note that the church in general has the question of inclusivity backwards. Rather than looking to be included as called ministers of the gospel in the church, queer Christians in ministry wonder if some Christian movements are interested in really being the church with them.[13]

Finally, for one, it was their sense of calling and the wish to articulate that to the broader community that encouraged their participation in the research.

> *I'm encouraged that such research is taking place and wanting to participate from my perspective as a gay man called to officership.*—Joseph (Interview Participant)

Opportunities to Serve Community

The officers in this research affirmed that which many queer people in ministry discover: being "out" as serving religious ministers creates opportunities that only evolve *because* they are LGBTQ+ and follow their calling. Crowder Noricks articulates this well: "As (people) became aware of my ministry I started getting confidential phone calls and emails. Youth pastors wanted to know how to love and support their LGBTQ+ teens. Pastor's kids confided in me. One mother said, "Thank you for talking to my daughter. You're the first person to give her any hope.""[14]

Consistently, those who were "out" noted that they had opportunities that were there because they were both queer and Salvation Army Officers:

> *So, being an officer gave me a passion for being involved and being supportive in people's lives. As a gay woman, as a lesbian, I have doors opened that wouldn't otherwise be possible.*—Mary (Interview Participant)

> *In XXX there was a volunteer who was attached to the church for a period of time, and then sort of fell away, but continued to volunteer in the community kitchen, my community meal center. And I was quite authentic with her, and she then shared with me the struggles of her grandchild, and how she just can't fathom that people don't see it the way she sees it. And so . . . I feel like there was a moment of healing for her—to hear a minister of religion talk about who they are and to affirm that the gospel she's encountered isn't wrong just because other people say it is, and actually the God she still has a relationship with is the same. But she removed herself from a church environment because they couldn't*

---

13. Severson, "The Queerness of the Holy," 417.
14. Crowder Noricks, "The Rejected Calling," 30-31.

accept a difference of theology. Essentially. Not that she would call it that, but she just couldn't fathom that people weren't inclusive. And so, she removed herself from that environment. But to be able to have multiple conversations, every couple of weeks we had multiple conversations, and that was really—the chances of me being in that moment in that place, with being able to have that . . . there is more chance of her getting a straight officer, right? But it was lovely I got to . . . I think I got to be in that moment because of who I am, and I am grateful to have been able to share that with her. And hopefully she can remember that, when other people try and remove those thoughts from her. That actually, God is so much bigger than people say God is.—Elizabeth (interview participant)

For some, these opportunities to minister explicitly led to people rediscovering Christian faith and finding hope in general:

Now I've seen and had so many really positive conversations with people, both LGBTIQ+ people and not, around what it means to be a gay person in The Salvation Army, a gay person and a Christian, and they've been incredible. I've seen people come back to faith through sharing of testimony and story and modelling inclusion, and being a walking example of acceptance and inclusion, and I've seen small groups flourish, have new members. Yeah, I've seen others inspired—and I don't use that word lightly and I don't want to put myself on a pedestal in that regard, but I've seen allies who sometimes come close to losing hope and see someone who is queer and an officer and see that as some kind of an illustration of a glimmer of hope.—John (interview participant)

For me, some of the most liberating and amazing moments in my ministry have been where I have been able to share my story to support someone else. For me, a turning point . . . was for the first time, well, realizing that telling my story was no longer about me but about others. So, it was this shift from, something that was happening for that individual in the corps setting, and they were trying to make sense of everything that was going on, and I was sitting there thinking, "Well there's no problem here. If this guy actually knew I was gay the whole conversation would be a moot point because suddenly he knew someone and it was all ok." So, in that sort of process, I said, "Well, you're struggling with this and you're not sure about that, so what happens if this example was true?" And he was like, "um . . . well . . . I don't know." And so, it was like, "Well actually, you're already doing that. And he's sitting across the zoom call from you." And it was like this lightbulb

> *moment when in an instant the whole... everything shifted in one instant.—Simon (Interview Participant)*

For some it has led to inclusion in, and requests to conduct, "ceremonies." In TSA, "ceremonies" is a broad term that encapsulates a range of important events in a person's life marked by a religious liturgy or observance: child dedications, marriages, funerals, enrolments into Salvation Army membership, and commissioning to local church leadership, as examples. These are often privileged times in the lives of people and mark significant life milestones. It is noted that there is a sense of personal risk in facilitating or participating in such rites at times, particularly where the ceremony affirms a non-heterosexual relationship or family unit, and the officers involved noted that this will draw the ire of others in the denomination.

> *Other churches embraced me. Other ministers and priests they all embraced me, and when it was okay, and I was embraced within the church all the way through. One time I did a funeral for them. Every time they would all be welcoming and accepting.—Salome (Interview Participant)*

> *I've been invited to participate in same sex weddings. Again, a little controversial, but these are people that want God in their wedding and want a church person they respect to participate. On another occasion, a woman I was working with asked me if I would "christen" their children even though she was in a lesbian relationship. I responded positively, while discussing what a child's dedication looks like in The Salvation Army—why wouldn't I show up for her family and pray a blessing over them as they commit to raise their children well and teach them about the Christian faith?—Joseph (Interview Participant)*

Some felt that God had placed them in certain positions or places for a particular time. They found that their sexuality and their officership concurrently enabled them to serve in that particular setting, when perhaps others would not have been as effective:

> *The first people that came to me for pastoral help when I arrived at my first appointment were a lesbian couple. And I'm like, "Oh my God, you have got to be kidding me"—Mary (Interview Participant)*

> *I twice had community groups pull back from supporting us [in fundraising efforts] because of the perceived discrimination*

against LGBTIQ+ people by the organization. The first time enabled me to sit with the leaders of that group and talk about myself, what the reality is—including the great work our social services do to support vulnerable LGBTIQ+ people, especially young people. The second time I was able to reassure the group that their money wasn't going anywhere near the church and those that would be assisted would include LGBTIQ+ people that had experienced domestic violence.—Joseph (Interview Participant)[15]

It has been critical for many to support families of other LGBTQ+ people that they encounter during their service. The LGBTQ+ officers have become safe people for those who feel that they have nowhere else to go to ask their questions. They also become the safe people with whom families can celebrate their love, or express their concern and seek help, for their LGBTQ+ family member:

Oh, well, being able to share, having platforms to share, and the feedback, and the fact that so many people have reached out to me and said this was helpful. You know parents have reached out to [me]. Even on the Pride March in (XXX), I have three parents who are marching. They said to me, "We thought this day would never come." A couple of them are officers who have got gay children.— Matthew (Interview Participant)

Interestingly, some officers found they were supporting families in such situations—even before their own identity and sexuality were disclosed:

I do recall an officer spoke to me about one of their offspring who, it would appear, was gay. Just late teens, if I recall rightly. So, I didn't really experience joy, but I did experience frustration because I felt an affinity with the person that I was trying to help. But in this case, I couldn't do it by being out. I didn't feel that it was actually safe enough for me to reveal that I was in a similar boat.—Andrew (Interview Participant)

Living out their authentic identity and sexuality during their service has led some to explore specific areas of professional development to assist their ministry. This research is arguably an example of that. For

---

15. This reflects a historical situation where all Red Shield Appeal funds in Australia were centralised for distribution through the social trust to programs supporting people nationally. Now it would be harder for the research participant to give this assurance as (since 2019) the "Red Shield Appeal Initiative" allows local Corps to use community fundraising efforts to support local programs.

others it was because they found themselves driven to join groups that specifically supported LGBTQ+ people through pastoral care:

> *Although I'll never forget Princess Diana holding the hands of the man with AIDS in hospital. That meant so much. It's one of the reasons I chose to do one of my pastoral care placements with the AIDS carers at [a hospital in their home city].*—Paul (Interview Participant)

We have seen in previous chapters that opportunities within churches may be limited and limiting for many LGBTQ+ people. For some of the research participants there was a perception that they could only be used in ministry if they were straight, or at least appeared straight. Some submitted willingly to SOGICE in attempts to conform. But in reality, their sexuality enables their service and often in unique ways. Justin Lee, an American theologian who identifies as gay, talks about how this comes about:

> We're Christians who know firsthand what it feels like to be outcasts and hurt by the church, and that gives us an important perspective the church needs. We've become very aware of our reliance on God's grace at a deep, personal level in a way many Christians haven't. We've had to fight for our faith, questioning everything and making us rebuild our faith from the ground up, truly claiming it for ourselves . . . For these and dozens more reasons, I think God wants to use gay Christians—along with bi Christians, and trans Christians, and others in similar situations—to help the church become what she is supposed to be.[16]

Indeed, one of the most effective arguments for equity for LGBTQ+ Christians in service opportunities is seen in the lives and service of those very people. As they fulfil their calling and follow in the footsteps of Jesus, offerings their lives in service, they witness to the transformation of the Holy Spirit within them and utilize their gifts for the salvation of others (in all the senses that salvation can be perceived). Over 30 years ago, queer theologian John Boswell also noted this. While conceding that it is important for all Christians to engage with the Scriptural concerns of their Christian siblings, he observed that "it is much harder for most people to remain hostile to and unmoved by a living brother [sic] than it is to rail against an abstraction . . . Gay Christians are *logoi* in this sense, arguments incarnated in persons," persons who make their

---

16. Lee, *Torn*, 243-244.

"commitment, their lives, their beings an unanswerable, living statement of faithfulness and love."[17]

God calls and uses LGBTQ+ people in service and has always done so. The first Gentile convert to Christianity, the "Ethiopian Eunuch" (Acts 8:26-39), is recorded as a foreigner, a person of color, *and* a sexual minority. (Bolz-Weber jokes, "if only the guy were also "differently abled" and gluten intolerant").[18] The "inclusion" argument appears to have commenced immediately after the commissioning of the first disciples, and God's persistent response is seen in how God's calling to faith and ministry has gone to "whosoever," regardless of the attitudes of the establishment.

Continued Ministry, Even After Officership

I reckon I have more ministry now than I ever did as an officer. So, it's the officer training that allows me to do that; it's the being gay that opens doors. I think I'm valued, by what I broadly call the inclusive community in the Army in Australia, as someone who's vaguely got their head screwed on right. —Mary (Interview Participant)

All except one of the former officers who participated in this research expressed how their ministry has continued after they had left the formal ranks of Salvation Army officership. Here we see how, for most, the notion of calling never leaves. The form that it takes can be the determinant for how it is lived out, whether within a recognized ministry in a denominational setting, or outside of that construct. Former Catholic Priest, Julian Punch, states that his calling was pragmatic as he saw the priesthood as a way of leading his life in a "meaningful and socially responsible way." Later in life, when his sexuality came into conflict with his priesthood, as did his personality with that of his Archbishop (Sir Guilford Clyde Young, Archbishop of Hobart), he wrote that he could still fulfill his calling, and serve the disadvantaged further, *outside* the confines of the Church. Notwithstanding, he still states that leaving was the hardest thing he ever had to do: "Entering training for the priesthood

---

17. Boswell, "Logos and Biography," 360-361.
18. Bolz-Weber, *Pastrix*, 89-90.

is very easy because you are welcomed and set apart as a special person, but leaving requires enormous courage."[19]

To this end, when contemplating leaving a ministry, there is much to consider. The individual must not only wrestle with life purpose and direction, but also with their concept of the Divine, whom they believed "called" them to this life in the first place. If they perceive a judgmental God, then they will perceive that they will be judged for their decision to leave the ministry to which they were called. Alternatively, if they view God as a compassionate authority, it may be easier to view their calling as seasonal, or adaptable to other settings. Further, if they then find themselves called to a new environment, God will grow what God has already established where they have been at work to that time, and then, as Trodden says, "continue to provide support and community for (people) to flourish. This will help us trust Him and ultimately guide our decision-making process."[20] If they see God as unconditionally loving, if they know that God accepts all, loves all, values all, and cares for all, then they can make such significant life decisions out of a place of peace, security, and even joy.

In a study of clergy who had left their ministries, it was discovered that in general they were people who previously (in ministry) had to live behind a professional façade which would impose considerable demands on their mental and emotional health.[21] That study did not disaggregate clergy based on gender or sexuality. It can only be assumed that this may be a more significant concern for LGBTQ+ clergy.

Arriving at a point of departure comes most often after a long period of hard and painful discernment of one's future. Countering the internal battle for authenticity and freedom that is believed to be found outside of officership, is the understanding that "you cannot change a thing if you leave a thing."[22] In addition to leaving the expression of their calling, they sometimes also feel that they are abandoning their LGBTQ+ colleagues.

That said, the capacity to continue in ministry after leaving TSA officership, and thus fulfil their calling, was a common theme for former

---

19. Punch, *Gay with God,* 52, 217, 148.

20. Trodden, *The Shape of Calling,* 13, 21.

21. Spencer et al., "Validating a Practitioner's Instrument Measuring the Level of Pastors' Risk of Termination/Exit from the Church . . . ," 1.

22. Temple, "Exploring the Lived Religious Experiences of Gay and Lesbian Ordained Clergy in the United Methodist Church," 73.

officers who were interviewed. Most discussed the opportunities that continued to come to them as people of faith who had some pastoral and theological training. This even included service back to people in TSA who found them to be a safe option for funerals or weddings—including same-sex weddings:

> I'm a marriage celebrant and it was being an officer that taught me there was something I could do in that. And ... Um ... people repeatedly come to me who say, "I grew up a Salvo, or I am a Salvo, or in one case, we're Salvo officers from overseas and we'd like to get married and not tell our territory." Ah... "Could we get married in Australia and could you do the wedding?" And I'm like, "Sure, we can do that . . . and shall we all wear paper bags on our heads for the photos?". . . I have no intention of telling the Territorial Commander that they're married. I don't happen to think it's the TC's business. —Mary (Interview Participant)

Living and Ministering According to Their Spiritual Gifts

The officers in the study, like all Christians, sought to express their service according to their perceived personal characteristics and gifting. Theologically speaking, these are spiritual gifts as well as talents and skills, such spiritual gifts being those characteristics bestowed by the Holy Spirit on Christians in order to "unite the Christian fellowship in its life together and its mission," and to enable the "many different ministries the Spirit has given to sustain the life of the Church."[23]

Key to the understanding of spiritual gifts is that they are for the ministry of the church and they should result in good "fruit." Many LGBTQ+ Christians are challenged in their ministry and, as they articulate a personal theology that is increasingly all-embracing and affirming, may even be accused of being "false prophets," the metaphorical "wolves in sheep's clothing" (Matt 7:15-20). Those who embody and speak of life at the margins are often stigmatized, marginalized, and at times removed.[24] But just as Jesus said false prophets would be uncovered because of their "bad fruit," so too will LGBTQ+ Christians be identified by their "good fruit." Vines notes that the first-century Christians applied this simple, experience-based test when deciding whether to include Gentiles in the Church, seeing Peter's declaration, "And God, who knows the heart, bore

23. The Salvation Army, *Salvation Story*, 111.
24. van der Walt, "These are the Days of the Raw Despondence," 16.

witness to them, by giving them the Holy Spirit just as he did to us" (Acts 15:8 ESV).[25] The officers in this study were ministering and finding that their gifts were being used to build up the body of Christ and serve their community, resulting in good fruit:

> *I seem to have a different capacity for caring. Um . . . And I don't know if that's really related to sexuality or not. But a lot of people seem to think so. And that's one of the reasons that I really like this role. And—it's kind of sad, when you put it into words—but I've kind of got a lot of love to give around, to share around, and I've just got to know where to put it. If that makes sense. So, I've got this greater sort of capacity to care for others, if that makes sense.—Simon (Interview Participant)*

> *I was particularly strong in dealing with people in death and dying. And I actually relished—I don't know if that's the correct word—funerals. I didn't have that many to do in that space and time, mind you. But that's where I actually felt I was of greatest use . . . I was on the pastoral care group that was looking after HIV AIDS people within the XXX district. Which was great, I mean I really enjoyed that fellowship. And that was ecumenical and secular as well.—Andrew (Interview Participant)*

> *And I find that God still is using my skills and abilities for spiritual and practical influence in the world. I'm still being invited to speak at churches and I'm still leading sections of our organization, mostly effectively.—Joseph (Interview Participant)*

> *I mean, I don't want to be identified as a gay man. I want to be identified as a follower of Jesus, but being an authentic follower of Jesus means that I'm a gay man too. So, I want to contribute to this, and I want to contribute to the kingdom growing in the area where I am working,—Matthew (Interview Participant)*

One participant found humor in applying stereotypes to demonstrate the effectiveness of LGBTQ+ officers in their ministry:

> *You know, frankly, who would do anything in the church if it wasn't for lesbians. You look around the church, and it's the closeted or uncloseted lesbians that are really running the place and the gay men tend to be in charge of events. It's all good.—Mary (Interview Participant)*

---

25. Vines, *God and the Gay Christian*, 14-15.

As LGBIQ+ officers exercise their gifting in ministry there are still conceptual difficulties that need to be overcome. The very notion of "body," as used in metaphor for the Church (e.g., body of Christ), carries problematic notions of something that can be gendered. Must LGBTQ+ Christians conform to a particular form to be considered part of this body? Can the body of Christ be intersex or transgender—given those people, too, are made in God's image?

Many in the LGBTQ+ community understand bodies better than their cis-gendered and heterosexual neighbors. They understand that you cannot really know who you are until you come to terms with who you are *in the body*.[26] Therefore, many LGBTQ+ Christians can resonate with the notion of an embodied expression of faith. They can and do contribute from their rightful place as Spirit-filled, Jesus-centered, gifted ministers of the gospel. They are critical to the implementation of multi-vocality (engaging multiple voices) in the churches,[27] so that patriarchal and parochial structures are diminished, as are singular or narrow understandings of what the embodiment of Christ on earth should look like. They affirm and are a living expression of faithfulness expressed in ways that can build the whole "body" and bring healing to the perceived divide between the LGBTQ+ community and the churches.

Leading The Salvation Army

LGBTQ+ officers are in a unique position to teach and lead in TSA because of their understanding of God's expansive grace and their affinity with people on the margins. Along with LGBTQ+ siblings in other denominations they enliven this grace as examples of sacrifice, resilience and love. In 2016, over 125 LGBTQ+ clergy of the United Methodist Church expressed this leadership through their "Love Letter" to their church, a declaration to the denomination and a statement of hope for other LGBTQ+ people in the churches.[28]

Within TSA, it is through gestures akin to the "Love Letter" that LGBTQ+ officers teach and lead with grace. This leads to kindly influence on leaders, colleagues, and congregations alike. Specifically, it may

---

26. Hearon, "1 and 2 Corinthians," 612.

27. Hollier, *Religious Trauma, Queer Identities*, 216.

28. Temple, "Exploring the Lived Religious Experiences of Gay and Lesbian Ordained Clergy . . . ," 102.

be through coordinated campaigns or events like the Included webinars, but is also in the quiet, personal interactions that the research participants discussed.

> *Prejudice rarely survives the person. That moment you can put an understanding to a situation—to a person—the prejudice often disappears. And that's been my experience every time I've shared my story.*—Simon (Interview Participant)

Sharing story is difficult in an authoritarian culture. As Althaus-Reid notes, "Authority defines authority, begets authority, and resurrects authority. It is positioned, Darwinian, and self-perpetuating."[29] Many of the research participants noted, however, that they have often had opportunities to speak truth to power and to challenge this authority. Such examples, on the surface, would seemingly diminish previous discussions in this book about how unsafe the work environment of TSA can be at times for LGBTQ+ officers. This is not the case; the opportunities that were presented generated fear and anxiety for many of the officers involved. They discussed a felt obligation to take up the mantle for their LGBTQ+ siblings in these conversations, despite the obvious personal cost through diminished mental health and vocational security.

The good news is that, in some cases, taking up the challenge has met with positive outcomes for both the officer and those with whom they spoke:

> *It has given me new authority in my chaplaincy role where I can challenge staff around their biases and sometimes around their office conduct—challenging those prejudicial and discriminatory comments.*—Paul (Interview Participant)

> *I just think listening to people's stories is important in this space. I mean, I'm fortunately involved in a small group at the moment in the Army that are looking at an apology [for victims of SOGICE in Australia], and it's a great joy for me to be part of this sort of movement. But I think there's a long way to go before we're ready to do that. I think we've got to hear more stories.*—Matthew (Interview Participant)

> *I've been invited into conversations around this in The Salvation Army that I may not have if I was not an officer. I genuinely believe in the possibility of what The Salvation Army can be when it's at its best and I don't believe that we're at our best when we're*

---

29. Althaus-Reid, *Indecent Theology*, 13.

excluding and isolating, or marginalizing. I think when we finally get our head around full inclusion and affirmation and equity, we're going to be a much better, more powerful, Army and perhaps reclaim some of our mantle in terms of missional impact in the community.—Joseph (Interview Participant)

Establishing and Participating in Support Networks

The development of support networks has been a common feature of LGBTQ+ culture throughout time. Contemporary displays of queer culture in television and film, for example, demonstrate this strong sense of camaraderie and support often described as being part of a "chosen family." Chosen families, in which kinship among queer folk is experienced, are an ingenious and resilient model of collective care, often in the face of institutional neglect and religious ostracism.[30] They demonstrate a model of care that the church could learn from—the dispossessed and marginalized coming together as an ecclesial chosen family. This enlivens the calling to a ministry that demonstrates the love and grace of Jesus, which Kelly articulates as individuals surrendering in faith, sharing in the intimacy with the Divine—including through sexual expression, becoming one's full and true self, and then embodying all of this in a community of service marked by love.[31]

Previous chapters have noted the increased risk faced by LGBTQ+ people regarding their mental health, something that is often only aggravated in religious settings. However, it has been found that those LGBTQ+ Christians who had family or acquaintances who were also LGBTQ+ held more positive attitudes toward themselves and their community.[32] A study of LGBTQ+ people in Christian universities in the USA found that the development of their faith, development of sexual identity, and mental health were all enhanced by participation in support groups where they found solidarity and community.[33]

A number of the officers in this study have either directly contributed to the establishment of support groups for others or participated in the forums that have been created. Some, such as *Salvos for a More*

---

30. Davis, "Kin/Folk," 67.
31. Kelly, *Christian Mysticism's Queer Flame*.
32. Heasley and Jacob, "The Experiences of LGBTQ+ Christians in a Support Group and Implications for Practitioners," 41.
33. Heasley and Jacob, "The Experiences of Christians in a Support Group . . .", 45.

Inclusive Church, are inclusive of allies. Others (intentionally unnamed) are exclusively for Salvationists who identify as non-heterosexual. In doing so, they not only create solidarity, but have made it possible for people to find safety and security to explore what it means to be LGBTQ+ in the context of TSA. They tell people they are not alone; they can not only survive—but thrive, and that people care. They echo Rabbi Sharon Kleinbaum in her famous internet speech: "You are not alone. You are sacred and you are beautiful and there are people who care about you. *I am one of them.*"[34]

In this ministry of support networks, participants become role models for younger and newly-out gay and lesbian Christians. Their growing visibility, as people who come out and remain engaged in ministry, is changing the landscape for young people in churches. Unfortunately, there are no trans role models currently visible within TSA officer ranks in Australia, something that is sorely lacking. What appears also to be lacking is the visibility of ethnically or racially diverse LGBTQ+ role models, or explicitly non-binary officers, reflecting the lack of diversity in TSA in Australia as a whole. For ethnic groups where particular cultural and family issues may be present, such as the systemic resistance to notions that homosexuality may be just as prevalent in their community as elsewhere, this visibility matters.[35] If TSA in Australia becomes more diverse in its ethnic composition, having LGBTQ+ officers from diverse ethnic backgrounds will be important.

Most of the officers in the research, particularly those who remain in TSA officer service, mentioned this need for visibility and support:

> *Part of my ministry in the future lies in this area of inclusion, and being a person who helps the church grapple with this issue, which almost every denomination is now dealing with including Salvation Army.*—Matthew (Interview Participant)

> *I'm happy. I'm fulfilled because I have beautiful relationships with gay guys and officers and who speak life into me. You know, I have authentic conversations with people about these issues. No-one previously gave me an alternative story. There was no "Included" back then. No "Salvos for an inclusive church." No alternative story. But now there is, and I know that's making a difference in the world. Thank God, it's making a difference to Salvationists.*—Simeon (Interview Participant)

---

34. Kleinbaum, "A Word to the Bullies," 104. Italics mine.
35. Kathy Baldock, *Walking the Bridgeless Canyon*, 392.

> I've been able to connect with other officers or ministry workers who are allies or part of the community themselves. I have empathy for the officer journey, and I'm new to [this city] as well, because I'm obviously from the old XXX Territory. So, I'm starting to form those friendships with queer people within The Salvation Army, and that's been really nice and edifying. I've attended the Pride March, the Midsumma Pride march this year, as well as the one in Sydney across the bridge. —Martha (Interview Participant)

Just discovering you are not alone can be life-changing:

> And she said, "well I've been with my spouse for 32 years and her name is XXX." And I went, "Right . . . So, this gay officer thing has been going for a really long time." And then there was a whole bunch of us who happened to just find each other and we started [an online support group] by accident one day. And that, that, kind of was the beginning of more positive experiences. —Mary (Interview Participant)

Conclusion

This chapter commenced with observing parallels between the research participants' experiences and Cheng's commentary on Paul's experience as articulated in the letter to the Corinthians. In the same volume, Goss' commentary on Luke discusses the queer dynamic in the writer's portrayal of God's activity through Jesus and his followers.[36]

Goss sees Jesus as a queer prophet—different to all the others—performing dramatic actions with a queer and somewhat camp flair. He sees God's mission in the world being undertaken in usurping ways: servant leadership, voluntary sacrifice, care for the marginalized, hospitality, compassion, and care for the excluded. As such, Jesus' followers would seek to do the same as God uses them, including LGBTQ+ officers, to create kingdom-of-God spaces that appear queer in the contemporary world. Such spaces transgress the normative, usurp the patriarchy, create new chosen families and communities, and include the marginalized.

Like all Christians, LGBTQ+ Salvation Army officers answer the dual calling to discipleship and service. The Jesus they follow took on the sins of the world, as humanity violently sinned "into" him physically and metaphorically, particularly in his betrayal, trial, brutalization, and crucifixion. He also revealed the love of God in that, while he absorbed the

---

36. Goss, "Luke," 530.

worst of humanity, he offered forgiveness. In the cross we see what God endures in Christ as humanity abuses humanity, and we see the ultimate expression of love as God's mercy toward abusive humanity is revealed.

As discussed in this chapter, all except one of the participating officers continue to serve and follow Jesus, to one degree or another. For many it is still within The Salvation Army. In following Jesus, they also absorb some of the worst of humanity from their colleagues: moral injury, religious trauma, SOGICE, discrimination, abuse, workplace danger, homophobia, and erasure as examples. For some this has led almost to deathly consequences as they have become suicidal.

But these same people who are abused and rejected are signs of God's kingdom. They are expressions of God's grace, mercy, and forgiveness as they serve, just as their Lord Jesus was. They are following their calling and finding opportunities for service that only exist because they are *both* LGBTQ+ and Christian. They are influencing a softening of hearts to the hurting and marginalized and they are creating communities of support and faith that are saving lives.

Chapter 9: Writing a Hopeful Queer Future for The Salvation Army

Introduction

TWENTY-FOUR PARTICIPANTS SHARED THEIR stories during this research. Their stories recount their lived experience with a view to create a historical record, discuss the issues that have arisen during their service in The Salvation Army, and articulate the theology that has its genesis in their stories. This theology is grounded in TSA's Wesleyan roots and their expressions of authentic integrated personhood. Despite harms that may have been caused, it is a theology of hope and inclusion, the diverse creation, enlivened grace, community, and ministry.

This is the first of two summary and discussion chapters. It brings together the findings from each of the previous chapters regarding the history of the relationship between TSA and the LGBTQ+ community, and the harms perpetuated on that community particularly within its ranks. Some summaries and recommendations are provided that offer a way forward for TSA and the community. The main discussion of the next chapter will concentrate on expressing the participants' hope in a theologically grounded manner, as a Wesleyan understanding of inclusion and affirmation.

History and Future

History is more than memory and recorded events. It is the collective narration of a group that is contextualized in community. As it is retold, it captures both emotion and intent in conveying something of the culture and story of people groups, associations, localities, and nations.

There are two problems with the way that the history of TSA is recounted. The first is that it is often hagiographical, and one cannot be seen to fault the founding parents of the movement or its elders. The second is that the majority view of history is always dominant and fails to recognize the faults or failures of the movement over time.[1] The organization justifies its own subjectivity when participating in collective memory-making in ways that undermine well-being, selfhood, and agency for minorities.[2] One way that this is demonstrated is in the failure to recognize how initial advances for women in ministry soon gave way to complementarianism and default ministry appointments based on gender and marital status.[3] Within TSA, social power has been, and is, employed in order to preserve its internal social order which is ultimately hierarchical, patriarchal, and heteronormative.[4] This has significant implications in colonized nations, more egalitarian or communal cultures, for women, and for those who are sexually and gender diverse.

This social order and locus of power mean that lived experience and testimony is often rejected because of identity prejudice. Such prejudice is embedded in TSA in ways that mean testimonial injustices can occur. These happen through a credibility deficit or excess, depending on how the individuals or groups providing testimony are perceived. For non-heterosexual officers, sexuality and gender prejudice lead to a credibility deficit in the eyes of the powerbrokers of the denomination. This is not just evidenced in a few instances, but throughout the testimonies of the research participants. When such testimonial injustice is applied in conjunction with structural injustices, such as workplace discrimination, it can properly be termed "systematic."[5]

The officers and former officers participating in this research have pointed out where the collective memory of TSA is incomplete or inaccurate. Like other minority groups, they find their storytelling of selfhood is both directed to and constrained or suppressed by the wider

---

1. Some historians have tried to rectify this, notably Hill in *Saved to Save and Saved to Serve*.
2. See Cover and Prosser, *Queer Memory and Storytelling*, for discussion of how this occurs.
3. Faragher, "Challenging History and Telling Herstory."
4. Faragher, "Challenging History and Telling Herstory," 99.
5. Fricker, *Epistemic Injustice*, 27.

cultural narrative that exists in TSA (and also in broader society).[6] Sometimes they buy into this for the sake of belonging and normative social or vocational participation. In this research, however, it is seen how the collective history hides and, at times, denies the harms that have been caused to the LGBTQ+ community. It also, in turn, denies the voicing of positive stories and theologies that would affirm the lives and ministries of these officers.

In chapter one it was noted that TSA has not enjoyed a positive history or relationship with the LGBTQ+ community. Over the last fifty years this has been most evident through activities that suppress the LGBTQ+ community and support efforts against decriminalization of homosexual activity. While this may be a product of TSA's place in history (as a product of nineteenth century, Victorian, morality and colonialism), more recent negativity has been through engagement with SOGICE and conservative evangelical resources, poor public relations activities, and the use of Scripture in harmful ways that nod to theologies based on fundamentalist approaches.

The collective memory of TSA has long celebrated the Maiden Tribute Campaign (1885). This led to the lifting of the age of consent in the United Kingdom to sixteen. However, this research has noted it as an example of an incomplete history-telling. TSA historians never mention that it also inadvertently led to the establishment of the "gross indecency" laws that criminalized homosexual men as a class of persons. In recent years, the contemporary storytelling of TSA Corps engaging with Pride events fails to also recount the times that TSA groups protested against such events. As noted in chapter one, this included an incident where the band from Sydney Congress Hall Corps joined conservative morals campaigner Fred Nile in a hostile event that publicly condemned the Sydney Gay and Lesbian Mardi Gras.

From the 1970s, TSA joined the conservative churches in mostly rejecting the medical and psychological expertise available. This was while broader Australian society pursued efforts to demedicalize and decriminalize diverse sexualities and gender identities with increasing momentum. In Australia and New Zealand, the denomination made statements against decriminalization and, later, against same-sex marriage. Some of these statements were after TSA's position statement on human sexuality was decommissioned in 2012. The fiasco surrounding the organization's

---

6. Cover and Prosser, *Queer Memory and Storytelling*, 3.

indicative support of, and then rejection of, the Safe Schools program in 2016, immediately following the tragic suicide of gay teenager Tyrone Unsworth, was a case in point.[7]

Critically, the activities of TSA across history represent its operant theology. Regardless of what has been taught in formal settings, or documented in position statements and guidelines for Salvationists, the behaviors of the organization and its people across its history demonstrate an underlying anti-LGBTQ+ sentiment. At those times where these have been accompanied by poor pronouncements, bad public relations interviews or government submissions against such things as same-sex marriage, the operant theology becomes espoused—and quite public.[8] Interestingly, while in Australia the operant and espoused theologies are often more conservative and harmful than much of the current formal theological work being undertaken in academia for TSA, Herben notes that in the Netherlands it is the operant theology—the practice on the frontline in corps and centers—that is far more progressive than the denomination's taught or formal theologies.[9]

There are current grass-roots movements for change, but these are facing into a century and a half of history, mythology, and theology. The majority of the participants in this research grew up in TSA congregations and were not only influenced by the history of the organization but also the direct and indirect theological teachings of TSA. This teaching included the introduction of increasingly negative materials through the 1970s and 1980s, particularly related to human sexuality and often leading to the offering of SOGICE. While the evidence of SOGICE in TSA was not surprising, this research highlighted a surprising scale and recency of such practices.

Negative teaching was facilitated in various formats. This included from pulpits, through discipleship materials, through formal education settings, and in personal interactions. It led many of the research participants to cognitive and spiritual dissonance. The experiences of the participants, particularly those who trained for officership prior to 2012, can be mapped against the written materials of the time to show that some

---

7. Street, "Why I Won't Be Supporting The Salvation Army This Christmas;" Urban, "Salvation Army Retreat on Safe Schools Program." See Chapter 1.

8. Operant and espoused theologies are terms taken from: Cameron et al., *Talking about God in Practice*.

9. Herben, "Working Towards a More Inclusive Salvation Army."

of the worst of times for visible and blatant psychological and spiritual injury for LGBTQ+ Salvationists were between 1980 and 2012.

The teachings received by young people are highly formative, and this was the case for the research participants. During their growing up, the teaching and impressions they gained were from the church as a whole and also from their families of origin. During their process of joining TSA through membership (particularly soldiership), the ever-changing "recruits' classes" (discipleship materials used prior to enrolment as a soldier-member) were used to denounce their sexuality and personhood. Prior to 1980 these materials said little about sexuality. From 1980 to 2012 they increasingly demonized same-sex attraction and behaviors. After 2012, they again went mostly silent.

This uneasy quiet period after 2012, it should be noted, does not automatically mean that things have become remarkably easier or safer. In fact, it may present more danger to some, as the ambiguity allows for unexpected and destructive behaviors and discourse to continue in pockets of the denomination and reduces healthy discourse. If TSA were reflective of the broader Australian population, hidden harms could, in reality, be causing worsening health outcomes as there is evidence that young Australian LGBTQA+ people increasingly report experiencing poor health outcomes and suicidal ideation. Cis-gendered queer men and those in rural or regional settings were also less likely to access mental health services for help.[10]

Those who were trained as officers in the former Australian Eastern Territory may have found themselves exposed to anti-homosexual content and SOGICE at their training college. This included during formal class time, especially in the 1980s and 1990s. Those who were trained in the former Australian Southern Territory were not as likely to experience this as directly, but did find difficulty training alongside conservative colleagues, some of whom were bullies. Some of these cadets (from the Southern Territory) were exposed to SOGICE offerings during their out-training placements. Less harm seems to have evolved from officer training in the last decade, although bullying from fellow students (cadets) was still reported.

The shift in attitude after 2012 was thrust upon the denomination in a moment of crisis following the previously discussed Joy FM interview. It has been evidenced by a change in the experience of officers during

---

10. Amos et al., *Rainbow Realities*, 12-15.

their training and their service. While this makes any change appear reactionary, this research notes that it has been accompanied by better theological training (moving further into higher education and critical thinking) and changes in discipleship materials used in the movement, as well as increased allyship and support.

The biggest concerns expressed by the research participants did not relate to the history or previous teachings of TSA. Most are able to see the historical evolution of the denomination for what it is. For most, the issue is the lack of timely progress and the pontifications from leadership that perpetuate harms. Some have been startling, such as a speech from the immediate past General indicating he was happy for the organization to remain at odds with pastoral care for his LGBTQ+ people, scientific understanding, and many of the cultures in which TSA works.[11] Many now anticipate that they will not see change that enables service on equitable grounds to their heterosexual counterparts (being able to be married and serve alongside their spouse) during their period of service or, indeed, during their lifetime. Often this perception is affirmed in their interactions with TSA senior leaders.

Optimism is therefore countered by realism, or at times despair:

> *There is cautious and measured optimism. [But] until IHQ relinquishes its stranglehold on how [TSA] territories operate, and what they can / cannot do in this and other spaces, true equality is unattainable, irrespective of local desire or action.* (Survey participant)

> *There is far too little to show for the [inclusion] initiatives and we are significantly behind in this regard compared to other churches and general society.* (Survey participant)

> *There are also loud, conservative voices within Australia, that are fed by things such as the religious discrimination debate during the Morrison Government term, who are part of TSA. They are also fueled by the hateful ACL.[12] They are getting louder and more hurtful as we progress conversations around change. It may get worse before it gets better for me and my colleagues.* (Survey participant)

> *Yes, I see . . . crucial steps toward inclusive and better welcoming practices. But it doesn't happen overnight.* (Survey participant).

---

11. The Salvation Army, "ICL 2022, Limitless God."
12. See chapter one for information on the Australian Christian Lobby (ACL).

The experience of the participants is that they continue to be confronted by hurtful attitudes and behaviors in TSA. The antidote is to write a future for the denomination that neither denies nor repeats its past in this regard. Achieving such a change, to many, seems almost impossible, as Halliday discovered in his research on the motivators and preventors for change in TSA.[13] Achieving positive momentum for change is not possible without motivation at all levels of the organization—motivation that currently does not exist. McLaren observes that when a lot of time, money and effort has been invested in the "old," the thought of writing off that investment can seem too high. "Yet every day that passes, the cost of staying silent and therefore complicit rises, too."[14]

Materials used to instruct people prior to enrolment as members of TSA need to be constantly reviewed. This is not just to address the harms that may be caused to LGBTQ+ people but also to consider the needs and perspectives of those from other marginalized communities. This would include migrants and victim-survivors of domestic violence, as examples. Elie Wiesel, Jewish holocaust survivor and theologian, summarizes this well. "Even if the most authoritative teaching, the most sacred text, leads to dehumanization, to harm, then we must reject it . . . Our role in reading sacred-Scripture is to ask two questions: "What does the text say," and "Who may be harmed by this text.""[15]

There is corporate sin evident in the perpetual dehumanization of the LGBTQ+ community within, and by, TSA. There is little consideration of the burdens placed on the LGBTQ+ officers and soldiers. Jesus rebuked the religious leaders of his day, "You heap burdens too great to bear and do not lift a finger to help them" (Luke 11:46). Perhaps he would speak similarly to TSA leaders today. "Anyone who is an obstacle to bring down one of these little ones who have faith in me would be better drowned in the depths of the sea with a great millstone around his neck. Alas for the world that there should be such obstacles!" (Matt 18:6).

Further, TSA needs to understand that a failure to recognize the truth of its past and realign its future will lead to further decline in its membership. The research participants noted that, even if they had not left TSA themselves at the time of their participation, most feel compelled to refer people to other denominations and congregations that are perceived to be "safer."

13. Halliday, "Changing Attitudes, Orders and Regulations."
14. McLaren, "Foreword," xi.
15. Quoted in Burger, *Witness*, 96-97.

> *I literally refer young people to the Melbourne Inclusive Church. Okay, that is an inclusive church. It preaches love for everyone. End of story. You can belong at any stage, in any way, any capacity. That is inclusive church. So, if you want a safe space, go there. (Salome - Interview participant)*

Gushee notes that this decline is something that needs to be faced by all evangelical denominations. He observes that many are leaving these faith groups because of what they believe are specific offences against people they love, family and friends, or against them personally. He lists examples such as clergy sexual abuse, sexist exclusion, and "every kind of indignity against gay, lesbian and trans people," as well as other intellectual and theological issues.[16]

Achieving change will require allies and LGBTQ+ Salvationists to work together. However, their perspectives will need to be theologically and empirically grounded, understanding that countering the culture, theology, and history of TSA is a task of some magnitude. TSA is built on a British colonial, white, male, and conservative world view that is somewhat culturally homogenous and transposed into other cultures rather than adapted. This makes progress explicitly difficult for anyone who is not straight, white, and male, but most notably First Nations people, women, and people who identify as LGBTQ+. Sadly, straight, white men don't always see the significance of their social location and influence in the organization (they comprise nineteen of twenty-two Generals of TSA; and all Generals have been from Europe, North America, Australia, or New Zealand).[17] Cook notes that conservative straight, white men tend to also assert their arguments from a position of "right theology" (rather than rooted in racism, sexism, or homophobia) and denounce other positions as "wrong theology."[18]

Finally, in terms of a discussion on the history and teaching of TSA, there is a caution not to attempt to create a post-memory. Post-memory describes the relationship that the "generation after" bears to the personal, collective, and cultural stories (and traumas) of those that came before.[19] The negative experiences of LGBTQ+ officers in previous

---

16. Gushee, *After Evangelicalism*, 2.

17. I recognise that one general, André Cox, was born in Africa to European missionaries and another, John Larsson, while Swedish, spent much of his childhood in Argentina and Chile, again with missionary parents.

18. Cook, *Worldview Theory, Whiteness, and the Future of Evangelical Faith*, 86.

19. Cover and Prosser, *Queer Memory and Storytelling*, 9.

generations, particularly those who grew up and/or served as officers between 1980 and 2012, will not be automatically indicative of future generations of LGBTQ+ officers. The younger generations may feel more resilient and accepted than the previous generation, and there is hope for institutional change to continue over time.[20] This research is therefore not necessarily a rallying point centered on past injustices. It may, however, present a discourse of knowability that provides confidence and safety for the coming generation.

Harm and Healing

The testimony of the research participants is that there has been much harm done to LGBTQ+ officers during their service in TSA. Noting this cannot be avoided. This has been experienced through its personnel, policy, structure, theology, and the application of direct discrimination. This research was able to identify instances of moral injury (both self-generated and other-generated), religious trauma, SOGICE, internalized homophobia, workplace discrimination, and suicidal ideation.

Much of this has generated from casting the LGBTQ+ officer as sinful due to their identity or orientation. Firstly, this creates an environment where some were expected to constantly repent of something that they could not change. Second, it projects an assumption that they could never pursue holiness because of their presumed perpetual, and willful, sinfulness. This appears to be regardless of whether they had chosen to integrate their spirituality and sexuality within a framework that involved celibacy. Ultimately, it means that the church they engage with is not focused on things that might bring life and health for them, such as Jesus' model of inclusion, love, and healing.

Some minority texts continue to be used as weapons against LGBTQ+ persons in TSA. Scripture will be discussed at depth in the next chapter. But it is noted that, alternatively, the texts that could support LGBTQ+ people if understood in the meta-narrative of God's loving relationship with humanity, can be lost. The most important command—love (Matt 22:35-40), the priority of the poor and marginalized (Mark 12:42-44; Matt 5:3; Luke 6:20; Matt 11:5; Luke 4:18), the welcome to all, the inclusion of gentiles (e.g., Rom 11:11-13), and the consideration of pragmatism over purity laws (Mark 7:1-23), all of which would be of

---

20. Cover and Prosser, *Queer Memory and Storytelling*, 2.

comfort to the LGBTQ+ community, become subservient to less positive writings found in a minority of proof-texts.

The first harm that was discussed was moral injury, in chapter 3. In this research, there is evidence of moral injury occurring via observance and description but not through a clinical assessment. True diagnosis would require clinical engagement and analysis by trained professionals. Despite this, there is evidence of self-generated moral injury which leads to shame, guilt, and lack of self-forgiveness. There is also evidence of other-generated moral injury that leads to anger, trust issues, and an inability to forgive others. Addressing these harms requires a re-appraisal of the normative dimensions of the circumstances in which the officers and former officers participating in this research have found themselves.

Understanding the theological and behavioral dimensions of what may lie behind their own actions, and those of others, is the first step. These officers need to be able to articulate, as they have done in many instances through the survey and interviews, where there have been genuine betrayals of trust and transgressions against their values. Exploration of moral and theological responses that incorporate their own truth and values can provide a way forward. Therapeutic interventions are available, as well as the use of ritual to work through a staged response to recovery.

Religious traumas were evident in the way many participants discussed pervasive psychological impacts. These impacts were from religious messages, beliefs, and experiences within TSA. Often, they constituted spiritual abuse. They could have been in the form of significant religious events, or through microaggressions such as the way that prayer has been used against the participants, or via the mischaracterizations to which they have been subjected.

One of the key theological traumas is perpetuated in the way that penal substitutionary atonement is taught within TSA. As already noted, when an orientation and identity has been described as sin, rather than a problematic behavior being described as sin, then there is the need to constantly atone for something that cannot be changed. There is an unbreakable cycle of shame and repentance inflicted on people. The antidote found by the research participants was in self-love and affirmation, recognizing the love displayed through the crucifixion was for them *as they are*, made in the image of God, including their sexual orientation or gender identity. This shift to focus on the cross of Christ as an expression of love (a reflection of Abelard's "moral influence" theory) does not deny

TSA's doctrine that the death of Jesus has made an atonement for the whole world so that whosoever will may be saved.[21] Rather, it shifts the mechanism of that atonement from penal substitution that pays a debt, to one consistent with a loving and unchanging God whose demonstration of love changes the hearts and minds of sinners back to God.

The research participants have also come to realize that the "demons" that need to be "cast out" are not the demons of gender or sexual orientation. They are the mental health problems so often caused by the practices of religious practitioners and leaders themselves. Osinski observes that Jesus' disciples were often unable to cast out demons in people. If TSA has contributed to the "demon possession" of LGBTQ+ people, then its people will not necessarily be able to drive such demons out. She adds, in paraphrase of Matthew 12:26, "how can Satan cast out Satan?"[22] It is more likely, in time, that a healed and whole LGBTQ+ community may help to cast out the demons of the church. This would be through their visible example of Jesus-centered and Spirt-led ministry that invokes and demonstrates grace, forgiveness, diversity, compassion, respect, integrity, healing, and love.[23] To be free from such demons created by religious trauma (or other traumas) is to be truly free and free to be oneself, part of the whole of humanity (within the diverse creation) that displays the image of God.

Forty-six percent of the participants experienced a corporate denial of this recognition of God's image through invitation (or direction) to change—i.e., SOGICE. While the majority was in past decades, there was evidence of some practices within the last ten years including at least one attempted exorcism. The range of practices discussed was extensive, from prayer practices, to books and videos, to conferences and instances of people being sent to conversion therapy bootcamps or, in one case, an overseas practitioner.

The means to counter these practices, expressed by the research participants, was to seek and appreciate integration of the whole self. This is needed in order to incorporate the physical, sexual, social, mental, intellectual, emotional, and spiritual selves as one coherent and consistent whole. Integration of identity required theological consideration and, in some cases, reconstruction. Helpful to the task was

21. Doctrine 6 of The Salvation Army.
22. Osinski, *Queering Wesley*, 65.
23. It is observed that four of these characteristics are named values of TSA Australia: Compassion, Integrity, Respect, and Diversity. The fifth TSA value is collaboration.

finding support through social networks from other LGBTQ+ officers and allies and participating in conversations that normalized diverse genders and sexualities.[24]

It is important to note where the research participants themselves identified signs of change in the denomination where SOGICE practices are concerned:

> *This is in a sign of change.* We talked about that in the early days I was referred to Exodus[25] and prayer ministry, in recent years—in the past two years—I've been referred by The Salvation Army pastoral care team, for both counselling and pastoral supervision, to someone who is known as an LGBTI ally and who offers specific counselling in affirming queer people and that person sees a number of queer officers, soldiers, people in The Salvation Army. So, I think that paints a really interesting picture of the arc we've been on and the new world that it is. That, you know, where once, when you came out, you were referred to therapy to try to suppress, now, as someone who is out, I've been specifically referred to a counsellor who is known to affirm and support that particular process and experience of faith. (John—Interview Participant)

The final harm discussed by participants was the linkage between workplace and religious discrimination, internalized homophobia and, in some cases, suicidal ideation. Here it was discussed that leadership behaviors often set the tone and, while there is no evidence of an LGBTQ+ officer (or former officer) in Australia completing suicide, there were four officers in this research who discussed episodes of suicidal ideation and two who had complete mental breakdowns requiring hospitalization.

Organizational efforts to counter this are currently focused on employees. The exploration of diversity and inclusion in Australia by TSA has been hampered by the inability to retain staff employed to work on diversity and inclusion programming, both in the operational and governance areas of the Australia Territory. Also, the narrow scopes of working groups that do not consider officers alongside employees (or volunteers for that matter) mean that there is little effort to counter the harms that are caused to those not under employment contracts and therefore covered by anti-discrimination legislation. Accreditation

---

24. Hollier notes the necessity of these steps also; Hollier, *Religious Trauma: Queer Identities*, 76.

25. Exodus International was a non-denominational Christian umbrella organisation connecting groups that offered SOGICE and operating in a number of countries, including Australia, from 1976 to 2013.

processes, such as Rainbow Tick, and affirming assistance from external agencies, such as Pride in Diversity, have been confined to narrow areas of the organization: Social Mission programs (homelessness, youth services, alcohol and other drug recovery services, and family/domestic violence services) or Community Engagement programs (financial assistance, social case work, material aid, children's programs, emergency services, and services to the defense force and veterans). Explicitly, this means that they are not applied at the local Corps (church) level, highlighting an important gap in TSA's approach.

Acknowledging the harms that have been caused is important. Secrecy and denial are the oppressor's first proposed defense but recognizing that sexuality and gender diverse Christians have a claim to justice is the broader church's first act of solidarity. This not only provides moral vindication for the victim-survivors, but also provides a platform for action, as the church cannot admit to an issue without failing to act towards rectification.[26] Furthering this acknowledgement with a genuine apology would provide a promise to LGBTQ+ officers that admission has been accompanied by moral awakening and potential hope that future harm would be minimized. For those LGBTQ+ officers that had been personally betrayed or discriminated against, this would be immensely powerful. Failure to acknowledge harm and maintaining discriminatory practices defies the love-ethic of holiness and the grace-filled approach of Jesus.[27]

Truth needs to be heard from the perspective of the lived experience of sexuality and gender diverse people first, *in order to be acknowledged*. TSA cannot continue to behave as if its leadership are the sole truth-bearers, something symptomatic of its entrenched hierarchical operations. Instead, voice must be given to affected populations, those on the margins. As Hollier notes, this is not only a powerful and humbling act of trust, but one that allows the new and variant ways that people encounter God and enrich community to be recognized and validated.[28]

For those who claim to be allies of the LGBTQ+ officers, the call from the research participants is for allies to be the change that they need to see.

26. Herman, *Truth and Repair*, 77.
27. Oliveto, *Our Hearts Strangely Warmed*, 88.
28. Hollier, *Religious Trauma: Queer Identities*, 221.

> *Our allies won't go with us. This is going to sound really antsy and selfish... they're allies when it doesn't cost them anything. With a few exceptions, and I acknowledge there are a few exceptions. But when we need them to say, "Actually, no! I'm not taking them off the roll." Because if no-one was taking [LGBTIQ+ soldiers/officers] off the roll, what are they going to do? Discipline the whole officer cohort? I've done the demographics. They don't have enough officers for that to work. (Mary - Interview participant) [E/XT]*

> *I'm like "Well, actually, you can. You can speak up. If all of you stood up and spoke up something will have to change. But all you're saying is, 'We'll hide you until those people who are conservative are willing to change.'" (Salome—Interview Participant)*

They also ask that allies do not exacerbate the problems through their activism or reactions:

> *I sat in a meeting where the communications people had again blocked use of a rainbow symbol. The problem was that one of the allies went ballistic towards me (!) with this crazy anger about not knowing this organization anymore and not knowing their place in the organization—as if I could solve their problems or they were the same as mine. And I certainly couldn't fix their problem with the Communications Department! (Joseph—interview participant)*

> *There's another "ally" in XXX who has been warned because of his poor behavior on social media and because he amended the soldiers covenant independently and without approval. He is making out as if he is being punished for his support of the LGBTIQ+ community. We don't need or want his kind of support that is just making life worse for us. (Paul—Interview Participant)*

There is also a call for consistency in appointments that allows for safety at a Corps/ congregational level to be maintained. Where an officer, or officer team, works to create inclusion and safety in a congregation, this can be quickly undone by poor succession planning. As one of the research participants noted, "We know our Corps would welcome them (LGBTQ+ people). However, a change of officers could mean they are rejected from the corps."

The final two areas in which trauma survivors would envisage justice are through restitution and prevention. Restitution, for those who are still active as officers, could be articulated as an affirmation of their service as officers on equal footing with their straight colleagues. This would require recognition of same-sex marriage and the capacity to serve in joint ministry together—something that TSA is internationally not willing to countenance at this stage.

Prevention would require a few things. First, education around the experiences of LGBTQ+ people that hears their voices and acts accordingly. This is not just being "trauma informed," as many social work practitioners will outline. It is about being "trauma effective" and "trauma responsive."[29] This response must also include an incorporation of the religious and spiritual dimensions of trauma and harm, not just the social and personal. Second, it would require consistent public renunciation of certain practices, particularly SOGICE, and ensuring that Guidelines for Salvationists about their inappropriateness, ineffectiveness, and lack of theological foundation or necessity are properly promoted, distributed, and enforced.

It is taken that, despite the history and experience of LGBTQ+ officers, TSA genuinely desires the best for its people. Clearly continuing to assert LGBTQ+ orientations as broken, in the face of scientific evidence, or immoral, despite the clear work of the Holy Spirit in many LGBTQ+ lives and a growing body of current biblical scholarship, cannot continue. If, as the evidence suggests, current and recent practice is doing harm to a group of people within TSA, then that practice needs to change.

---

29. See McConnnaughey, *Trauma in the Pews*, especially chapter 18.

Chapter 10: Writing a Hopeful Queer Theology for The Salvation Army

THE MOST POSITIVE ASPECT of the research participants' stories was expressed in persistent articulations of hope. This was found in two key areas. The first was their expression of authenticity and how this formed part of their Christian experience. The second was through the ways in which they experienced God in the world, leading to unique opportunities for service that they would not have had, should they not have been queer, or "out."

Just focusing on the history of the relationship between TSA and the LGBTQ+ community would be entirely negative. Just focusing on the harms that have been caused to this community, and LGBTQ+ officers in particular, would not be faithful to the stories that they shared or the complexity of their experience. More than 90% of the survey participants stated that they were able faithfully to integrate their sexuality and their faith either to some, or a great extent. Only one felt that they could not do this at all, and it is assumed that this is the person who also said that they had lost their faith altogether. Importantly, the majority had found self-acceptance and affirmation while maintaining and practicing their Christian faith.

As such, it is important to note and celebrate such positive experiences in the overall discourse. Ezzy, Fielder, and McLeay note that it is not only empirically more accurate to understand the positive experiences of LGBTQ+ Christians but also more likely to promote a social justice agenda and advance equality.[1] They also observe the strong dedication of non-heterosexual Christians, noting that there is little discernible

---

1. Ezzy et al., "LGBTQ+ Christians in Australia."

difference between LGB Christians and their heterosexual counterparts in terms of activities such as church attendance.[2]

This chapter continues the discussion of the research findings but with a focus, therefore, on the positivity and theology articulated by the participants. It is noted that personal integration of sexuality and faith is necessarily accompanied by theological reflection and herein takes the form of a positively articulated theological vision drawn from their experience. This gives pre-eminence to the lived experience and testimony of the research participants, but couched in theological terms.

While it is affirmed that TSA should be a place of healing, inclusion, and community that does not discriminate against its own members who identify as LGBTQ+, such activity is unidirectional and presumes that the power and authority to act is entirely within the denomination and its hierarchy. A different approach, as developed here, listens to the voices of LGBTQ+ officers who provide valuable example through how they live out their calling and service at the intersection of sexuality and faith. This is done in the understanding that experiential grace and affective spirituality are authoritative as sources in Wesleyan traditions.

Wesleyan theologians often draw from four authoritative sources: Scripture primarily, then also tradition, reason, and experience. Tradition is understood to be the interpretation of Scripture as handed down by the church, especially the earlier church writers. There are multiple resources that help the Christian see how the law and teaching on sexuality in the Bible has been variably received across history, allowing an inclusive interpretation of these texts based on tradition.[3] In one work, Boswell referenced 60 texts from around the world that assert that there were various forms of Christian marriage rites for same-sex couples up to the eighteenth century.[4] His work is disputed, with some historians interpreting these rites and the related relationships as "brothering" and "sistering" rather than sexually intimate, and others stating that they are more akin to treaties. We cannot be completely sure what these ceremonies were, but importantly they did occur under the auspices of the church, and they did involve enduring commitments by same-sex couples.[5]

2. Ezzy et al., "LGBTQ+ Christians in Australia," Table 3.

3. See as examples: Anderson, *Ancient Laws and Contemporary Controversies*; Mandimore, *A Natural History of Homosexuality*; Boswell, *Christianity, Social Tolerance, and Homosexuality*.

4. Boswell, *Same-Sex Unions in Pre-Modern Europe*.

5. See Harper, *For the Sake of the Bride*, 67.

Looking at the more recent theological tradition of TSA, Wesleyanism demonstrates a long historical pastoral understanding of people with diverse sexualities. While appearing to hold to a theologically conservative belief around homosexual activity, Wesley himself appears to have demonstrated some degree of pastoral leniency toward homosexuals within his sphere. He is recorded as defending Thomas Blair on the occasion he was charged with sodomy and visiting him in prison, as one example.[6] It may well have been that some of his key evangelists, such as George Whitefield were themselves same-sex attracted, based on their demonstrative affection to other men, and their sleeping and bathing arrangements, but this is not necessarily a conclusion that can be certain, as it may confuse the homosociality of another time with homoeroticism.[7] Suffice to say, however, that the Wesleyan tradition is not automatically or definitively anti-LGBTQ+. Unlike TSA, The Methodist Church in Britain supported decriminalization laws in the 1970s and is affirming of LGBTQ+ members now, allowing same-sex marriages in their churches since 2021. The United Methodist Church in the USA is also affirming (since its schism, discussed later).

Reason, as a theological source, is the understanding received from science, learning, and logic.[8] This is the work of theologizing while accepting also the authority of empirical research, then synergizing these with thoughts of God and self in the world, on an informed and evidential basis. While an increasing volume of scientific research into homosexual, intersex, and transgender people is available, it is worth noting Regele's work in specifically tying science to Scripture and same-sex relationships.[9] Specifically, this is because of his work to discuss current scientific findings in biological brain research, psychology, and sociology around LGBTQ+ people in the light of Scripture.

This research has primarily considered the role of experience, as expressed in the lives of the research participants and their service within TSA. Experience in Wesleyan traditions is grounded in the authority of the witness of the Holy Spirit in people's lives as they testify to it, and the outworking of what we learn through the marriage of orthodoxy and orthopraxy. Epistemic certainty for the Christian is more likely due

---

6. Abelove, *The Evangelist of Desire*, 66; O'Brien, "A Divine Attraction Between Your Soul and Mine," 184.

7. O'Brien, "'A Divine Attraction . . . ,'" 179.

8. Rowell, *Thinking, Listening, Being*, 27.

9. Regele, *Science, Scripture and Same-Sex Love*.

to the direct experience of God rather than abstract belief in facts about God. Wesleyanism is phenomenologically grounded, with a theology that is embedded in the world and seeks to engage with and learn from the phenomena that is witnessed and experienced. Such experiences, in turn, lead the Christian to reason with their Scriptures and traditions to test their paradigms. Arguably, all theology is an understanding of God in the crucible of history through people's experiences. A problem with this, for the queer Christian, is that we often anthropomorphize God in this process which historically made God out to be male and therefore reinforces patriarchy. And if God is sexualized, "he" is straight.[10]

Transformative encounters are thoroughly embedded as part of the gospel narrative and the testimonies that followed also transformed communities. On the road to Emmaus (Luke 24) there are two disciples journeying home after the crucifixion of Jesus. They were perplexed, and puzzled over a crucified Messiah and an un-redeemed Israel. But they had an experience with Jesus that was transformational and shifted their paradigm and understanding of Scripture as they knew it. In Acts 10, Peter has an encounter with the Gentile centurion Cornelius and comes to understand that God showed impartiality to all. This encounter transformed his thinking and led to a paradigm shift that changed the trajectory of the church. Transformational encounters such as these are an authoritative source of new thinking in the biblical narrative, and can be so also in contemporary thinking, especially as more Christians come to interact with God-loving and Jesus-following people who identify as LGBTQ+. The research participants overwhelmingly express an assurance of their right relationship with God through knowing Christ. They testify to the change that this has made in their lives and how it is compatible with their sexuality as something God-given.

The participants, therefore, ask the question about how they can be the kind of person that God created them to be, both holy and LGBTQ+. The witness that they offer is that their emotions, instincts, and passions are not just carnal but purified through the transformative work of God in their life. The positive incorporation of the love of God in their lives enlivens their affections to a love *for* God and others. The seeds of holy virtues are awakened through the experience of the divine presence and grow in their lives such that their otherwise human affections are

---

10. Hunt, "Working Together," 4 June 2024.

tempered into holy dispositions.[11] There is no longer a perpetual struggle to change, but a recognition of how they are holy *and gay* at the same time, and live out this holiness in the world.

Considering how their experiences, tradition, and reason dialogue with Scripture is important. In looking to do so, this chapter will not provide extensive exegetical coverage of the biblical texts often cited against LGBTQ+ people, although they come up at points. These are:

- the Genesis 1 & 2 accounts of creation and how humanity is formed;
- the inhospitality of Sodom (Genesis 19) and Gibeah (Judges 19);
- the legal frameworks of Leviticus 18:22 and 20:13;
- Jesus' teaching on marriage in Matthew 19:1-12;
- Paul's observations of the depravity and idolatry in Roman culture in Romans 1:26-27; and,
- Paul's list of vices in 1 Corinthians 6:9 (reflected in 1 Timothy 1:10).

Both the traditionalist and progressive paradigms have been extensively considered by multiple scholars and authors.[12] Rather than repeat their work, I acknowledge the various contributions to this field of study. The traditional readings typically view these verses jointly and severally as condemnations of same-sex sexual behaviors, grounded in the belief that they mandate heterosexual marriage as the only permissible context for sexual intimacy. Progressive interpretations approach these verses through temporal, geographic, linguistic, historical, cultural analysis and contextualization, in the light of contemporary understandings of societal norms and human sexuality, and emphasize

---

11. Maddox, "Wesleyan Theology and Moral Psychology Precedents for Continuing Engagement," 11.

12. Works representing traditional views include: Gagnon, *The Bible and Homosexual Practice*; Wold, *Out of Order*; Hill, "Christ, Scripture and Spiritual Friendship," 124-147; Holmes, "Listening to the Past and Reflecting on the Present," 166-193. Works presenting progressive views include: Loader, *The New Testament on Sexuality*; Bronson, *Bible, Gender, Sexuality*; Martin, *Sex and the Single Savior*; DeFranza, "Journeying from the Bible to Christian Ethics in the Search of Common Ground," 69-101; Vines, *God and the Gay Christian*; Runcorn, *Love Means Love*; Steve Harper, *Holy Love*, 27ff. Those that have changed their position towards an inclusive or progressive reading and include discussion of the biblical texts include: Gushee, *Changing our Mind*; Achtemeier, *The Bible's Yes to Same-Sex Marriage*; and, Hays and Hays, *The Widening of God's Mercy*—this book comes almost 30 years after the elder Hays published a very conservative viewpoint in Hays, *The Moral Vision of the New Testament*.

themes of love, justice, and inclusivity found elsewhere in the Bible.[13] Both traditional and progressive scholars would mostly agree that these texts, together, remind us that there is sexual sin, that people of all sexual orientations sin, and that the Bible opposes excess, abuse, and anything that dehumanizes or objectifies a human person. They disagree on how that applies to people who identify as LGBTQ+.

Having noted these important texts, the remainder of this discussion will focus on other key theological themes in Scripture as prompted by the research participants. It is through such themes that the positive experiences and integration of life expressed by the participants are best heard. They are: The Diverse Creation, Enlivened Grace, Justice in Solidarity, and the Priestly Ministry of all Believers.

The Diverse Creation

In Christian theology, God created the world and called the human part of that creation "very good." This includes gender and sexuality diverse people. When scientists have considered this creation, quantum physicists have taught us that the universe is connected, but also that within that universe is incalculable diversity. This diverse creation reflects the richness and complexity of divine love and community expressed in the variety of identities and experiences within the humanity created in God's image.

Even where there are pairings in the Genesis narrative of creation, such as night and day, they are non-binary—for example, night and day includes first light, dawn, day, dusk, last light, night, and so on. Land and sea are not a binary; there are also tidal shores, deltas, and mangroves. Every pairing in the creation story is a spectrum metaphor, not a binary.[14] Soderblom sees them as "dualistic juxtapositions" emerging from the poetic nature of the text which encompass all that lies between.[15] There is a sense that when God creates "male" and "female," God also creates everything in between. The "and" in the middle represents the continuum across the whole spectrum of gender and sexuality, in the same way the "and" in "Alpha and Omega" (Rev 1:8) represents the whole spectrum

---

13. See Söderblom, *Queer-Affirming Pastoral Care*, 65.
14. Harper, *Holy Love*, 16.
15. Söderblom, *Queer-Affirming Pastoral Care*, 21.

of time between beginning and end.[16] The notion of "male and female" includes humanity made in the pairing of male and female, but also the spectrum of gender and sexuality.

This diversity was affirmed not just ontologically, but also morally. When God affirmed diverse humanity as "very good," God declared it was inherently of worth. While the fall (Gen 3) describes the way in which humanity has become fallen and depraved (in the language of TSA),[17] this relates to unethical or dehumanizing behavior. If we view gender and sexuality in binary terms there is a danger of misinterpreting the fall to become a cause of diverse gender identities or diverse sexual orientations, disregarding that the fall is subsequent to the creation of humanity on the gender and sexuality continuum. Worse, we misinterpret the fall to be the cause of intersex realities that encompass natural diversities and ambiguities in physical and chromosomal sex-binaries.

In the second telling of the creation story, especially, we see that in the first human, the male and female are combined, and the female is made out of the male.[18] The larger story of the Bible identifies fallenness as expressed through abuse and unfaithfulness, not identity.[19] To mistake gender or sexuality as fallen is to distort the diversity of nature in creation and this leads to dehumanizing attitudes toward LGBTQ+ people. When we are able to accept other forms of natural diversity among humans, it is irreconcilable that we cannot accept gender and sexuality variances.

There is a danger that theologians may give the two creation accounts of Genesis a power to essentialize more recent social constructions. Genesis, after all, also provides evidence and some credence to concubinage (Gen 25:6 refers to Abraham's concubines), weaponized sex (mostly condemned—Gen 19—but sometimes redeemed—Gen 34), intra-familial sex (Bilhah and his step-mother, Gen 35:22), and polygamy. There are also strange sexual stories, such as Onan refusing to impregnate his widowed sister-in-law via either coitus interruptus or masturbation (Gen 38), Ham uncovering the nakedness of his father Noah (Gen 9:22), and the women who had sex with angelic Nephilites (Gen 6). Thousands of years of societal constructions of gender and sexuality have passed since the writing of these texts. There is no simple binary in creation and no simple ethic of sexuality in Genesis.

16. Fisk, "God's Creative Diversity," 419-423.
17. Doctrine 5 of TSA.
18. Carden, "Genesis," 7-9.
19. Harper, *Holy Love*, 17.

Genesis does, however, assert that all people are made in the image of God (Gen 1:26). This is not just the first humans, but all people for all time. Also, people made in God's image are made in the image of the trinity, which is another expression of diversity. As God the creating trinity is diverse, so too is God's love, demonstrated in the perichoretic nature of the trinity. To be made in the image of God (Gen 1:27) means we are made to love, and we have the capacity to be in relationship with both God and others. This was expressed in multiple ways by the LGBTQ+ Christians who were interviewed, from their deep, supportive friendships through to their romantic and sexual lives. As they discovered their "suitable partners" to counter the unsuitability of being alone in the world (Gen 2:18-22), they found natural freedom and sustaining support. As observed earlier, one participant expressed absolute confidence in how he was made and how this was to be lived out:

> *I'm a gay man who does not have the gift of celibacy, who does not work well, live well, in isolation. And like many I am designed to be in partnership with another. These two things I know. (John—Interview Participant).*

As all people are made in the image of God, God's love and life are for all and can be experienced by all. This is not for a chosen few, or a chosen nation, or just straight people. Throughout the Scriptures there is an increasingly expansive arc of inclusion from the creation of the proto-human, to Abraham, to the people of Israel (and the refugees and immigrants they needed to care for—Lev 19:33-34; Deut 10:17-19), to first century Gentiles, and to ultimately "every tribe and nation, people and language" (Rev 7:9). This arc of inclusion was set in train from the beginning, for "every living being" (Gen 9:9-10) and "all the families of the earth" (Gen 12:3).

This includes the LGBTQ+ tribe/family. They are signs of God's creativity in the world as people of diversity. They are sacraments that provide a visible expression of God's presence and grace in ways that many heterosexual Christians may not expect—and perhaps not be willing to receive. They are able to articulate and enliven theologies that are in themselves often expressions of intersectionality and liberation.[20] But

---

20. It is interesting to note that this intersectionality often can cause issues within the LGBTQ+ community, as discussed by Cheng who is Asian and Gay, and often felt the curse of racism within the LGBTQ+ community. See Cheng, *Rainbow Theology*, xii.

they also know the truth of Jesus' maxim, that prophets are not without honor except in their own country and in their own house.[21]

The notion of a diverse creation as initiating an expansive arc of inclusion, gives pause to consider the "new creation" towards which humanity is headed. Christians look to this new creation in hope: a place of healing where tears are wiped away, mourning, crying, and pain end and all the injustices and discriminations of the current creation cease (Rev 21:3-4). For sexuality and gender-diverse Christians, the affirmation that the reign of God (the realization of God's sovereignty among people) is among us (Luke 17:21), bolsters this hope with the belief that Jesus' instituted this new creation as something that can be realized now, and not just in eternity.

Enlivened Grace

The diverse creation is not abandoned because it is fallen, but is also subject to God's activity in redeeming and reconciling it to Godself. This is entirely a work of grace that is experienced and enlivened in multiple ways. First, it is God's initiative in the world that is prevenient and drawing people in to relationship with God. Second, it is seen in the acts that provide for justification: holistic salvation and redemption of that which is fallen. And finally, in the sanctification of people such that the loving, living image of God is restored in them.

God's prevenient grace is working in the world and around people such that they are pointed toward the divine in their consciousness and being. It is God's loving inclination to those who were created in God's image.[22] It is suggestive of divine favor on creation in all its diversity, which has already been noted as increasingly inclusive. It underscores the love of God in that God would give such grace.[23] Because of the fallen state of humanity, we cannot initiate our relationship with the holy God, so God must come into our world. God does this in a universal way, bestowing grace and invitation on all humanity.

In this way, grace is queer. It subverts and defies who should be in or out, who is sinner or saint, who is deemed worthy, deserving, or otherwise. No matter how we try to contain it or define it, God's grace is

---

21. Cheng, *Rainbow Theology*, 150.
22. Marquardt, "Christian Conversion," 105.
23. Collins, *The Theology of John Wesley*, Introduction.

always beyond definition or calculation. And if God's grace is queer, then it is no wonder that it may be uniquely experienced by people who defy heteronormative or patriarchal boundaries, nor is it a wonder that they may be vessels and expressions of that grace to the world.

The benefits realized for humanity though God's prevenient grace are many. Grace enables people to discern a sense of the divine despite their otherwise ignorant state. It reminds people that we are not abandoned, rather God desires connection and relationship. This was critical for the research participants who, even in their loneliest and darkest moments, told stories of God's intervention. It provides people with a sense of conscience and understanding of right, a universal principle that requires a source beyond humanity but appears accepted within humanity.

God's ongoing gracious activity and omnipresence were very important to the majority of officers who were surveyed and interviewed. This presence meant that they did not pray, or plead, to a distant God on a remote heavenly throne, but rather they felt that by God's grace, they experienced a sense of presence, imminence, and hope. Only one former officer in the interviews spoke specifically of losing faith in prayer.

They also noted that they were often agents that enlivened this grace for others. Whether it was God's perceived activity in placing them to be the actors supporting other LGBTQ+ people, the ones to counsel and support the families of LGBTQ+ people or the ones who, at times, could intervene to protect members of the LGBTQ+ community—they were especially, it seemed, placed to be the right people, in the right place, at the right time.

Grace looks at the reality of the world, its harms and mysteries, but affirms God's activity. There is an ethical optimism which affirms God's activity despite woundedness, and indeed sin. It is through this grace that the Spirit groans with suffering people, such as the LGBTQ+ religious community, and works to heal, transform, and empower them—turning them into agents of change. It is this form of grace that will not accept the status quo, because God is in the world reconciling it to Godself, so there is always a hope towards fuller experiences and expressions of justice, mercy, and truth in the church and in broader society.[24]

Many queer Christians affirm the way that God's grace moves ahead of them to provide for life and support in the face of adversity. In this research, there was the formation of friendships and supports that

---

24. Field, "The Unrealised Ethical Potential of the Methodist Theology of Prevenient Grace," 6.

seemed to go ahead of the hurts some of the participants experienced. There were stories about leaders changing at critical moments so that more affirming people were in line management to support the officers at key life moments, such as coming out.

The justifying grace of God is the grace that saves people. It is understood primarily in the guise of "forgiveness." God breaks the power of sin in us, and around us, so that there is wholeness and it becomes the point at which right relationship with God is restored, which can then be expressed through restored relationship to ourselves, other humans and the rest of creation.[25] This reset in the order and nature of things is understood by the Salvationist not only to affect the spiritual, but also the social, physical, and psychological areas of life. William Booth understood that salvation was not only personal, but social, and that he had a gospel of deliverance to preach in both spheres.[26] Randy Maddox speaks of this as a "therapeutic focus" of salvation, with a healing that includes a socio-psychological perspective.[27] It moves the focus of salvation from a vulgar notion of escaping eternal hell and going to heaven toward the assumption that the Christian will experience salvation tangibly in their earthly life.[28]

The participants in this research all had accepted, by faith, the saving grace of God at some point in their lives. They, mostly, also confirmed a continuing faith that knew this salvation as available for all, including themselves as people who identify as LGBTQ+. It is notable that the first named convert to Christianity outside of Israel was the Ethiopian eunuch, a foreigner also from a sexual minority (Acts 8:26-39). As O'Brien points out, making sexuality determine the form that the gospel must take is heretical, because the gospel of salvation is grounded in the grace of God alone and is open to all.[29] The research participants articulate and live by this. They assert that God is not arbitrarily determining life for some and damnation for others as a predestined outcome, rather God's grace is universal and "whosoever" believes may be saved in the here and now. This is for all who will receive it, all who believe (John 3:16-17; Rom 10:9; 1 Tim 2:3-6; 2 Pet 3:9), not just those who fit a certain demographic.

25. Marquardt, "Christian Conversion," 99.
26. Cavanagh, "The Wesleyan Roots of The Salvation Army's Holistic Mission," 3.
27. Maddox, *Responsible Grace*, 144.
28. Maddox, "Salvation as Flourishing for the Whole Creation," 9-10.
29. O'Brien, "If we cannot think alike, we may love alike" *ABC Religion and Ethics*, 31 May 2024.

They also affirm the holistic nature of God's salvation. The saving of their psyche through integration of their whole selves was one stated example. The saving experience of coming out and living authentically was another. It was not only a peak performative experience in the lives of many of the research participants, but in many cases also took the form of a salvation testimony: "Once I was lost, but know I am found." Here the church can learn a lot about confession and evangelism from people who identify as LGBTQ+. Professing that which you know to be true, especially in the face of hostility and potential ridicule, takes immense courage. Being "out" in a volatile environment also requires trust in something more important, a higher power, and at times means prioritizing truth over personal safety.

The holistic nature of God's salvation means that it is freedom from anything that dehumanizes people. It is the affirmation of life when facing the threat of death through suicidal ideation, as one example that the participants identified. One problem to be overcome in this conversation, then, is where many Christians see the "queer" part of "queer Christian" as being morally problematic, or even incompatible with the word "Christian" let alone "Salvation Army Officer." While queer people may struggle at times with moral failing, as all people do, people with queer identities can demonstrate a high caliber of moral fiber that is "inspirational and aspirational."[30] Fielder and Ezzy confirm this in their research, saying that LGBTQ+ are inspired by an "ethic of authenticity," one that leads to lives led as their true sexual, gendered and religious selves, something magnified through the paradigm that articulates their sexuality as "God given."[31]

Being authentic and coming out in the church is not only a testimony to salvation but also a political statement. There is a challenge to the heteronormativity of the church culture, and a confrontation to its fear of difference and its established power relationships.[32] Also, while coming out is often considered as a matter regarding personal sexuality, people "come out" for all manner of things, bringing visibility to disability, survival of sexual assault, Indigenous ancestry—anything that discloses an hitherto held truth, but which may bring light and hope to themselves and others, and demonstrate validity to the power structures of the world. The alternative is falsehood, which ironically may not always be

---

30. Edman, *Queer Virtue*, Introduction.
31. Fielder and Ezzy, *Lesbian, Gay, Bisexual, and Transgender Christians*, 2.
32. Oliveto, Our *Hearts Strangely Warmed*, 17.

bad. Jeanne Powers, a United Methodist pastor, noted in 1995 that the phraseology of church law that declared homosexuality incompatible with Christianity and required celibacy in singleness led to a subversive strategy for LGB clergy. In this, she noted, that "perhaps there are times when lying deception and operating under false pretenses is the most life-giving action, the most faithful response for Christians."[33]

The participants in the survey component of this research, with the exception of four, have come out within TSA to some extent. They are making the political statement that they are here, and in doing so, many have found the performative act to be salvific in some form. They are choosing no longer to bifurcate their lives, living openly and finding wholeness and healing as they do.

They also express the way that this healing leads to lives of holiness. Just as grace is inherently queer, so is holiness. Like the grace that enables holiness, it defies boundaries—in fact the irony is that the more that we try to contain it by expressing who is holy and who is not, the less holy we become.[34] The holy life, or the sanctified life, is a life of enlivened love empowered by God's sanctifying grace. As this interaction continues over time, there is a goal for humanity to perfect this love.[35] The indwelling of this love is the power for personal change, the transformation of inclinations and affections such that people flourish in all dimensions of life (not just the spiritual).[36] Herein we see the queerness of holiness described. Whereas philosophical morality is impersonal and often built on certain behavioral constructs and expectations, Christian holiness is based in love.[37]

Notably, this love is a reigning characteristic of God. It is something that is eternal and pre-eminent (1 Cor 13:13), abounding and universal, and distinct from any sentimentality, romanticism, or self-interest as it is pure and only giving.[38] Fixed on God alone, all our energies are focused on living as God wills, and God's will is expressed in the command of

---

33. Oliveto, *Our Hearts Strangely Warmed*, 37.

34. Stone, "Holiness Is Queer," 424-5.

35. Van Buskirk, "The 'Relational Hermeneutic' of Contemporary Wesleyan Moral Theology," 2.

36. Maddox, "Salvation as Flourishing for the Whole Creation," 11, 13, 21.

37. Johnston, "For the Love of God," 115.

38. Collins, *The Theology of John Wesley*, Chapter 1. One of the great hymns of The Salvation Army, *O Boundless Salvation*, by William Booth, refers to this "great ocean love" which is spoken of in words such as: "the whole world redeeming" and "flowing for all men" (sic).

Christ, which is to love. The disciple of Jesus follows his example, which was love. The holy community of people that is the church, is based conceptually and theologically on love. It is the holistic way of living as the people of God, queer and straight together.

Wesley's understanding of grace does not reject nor negate human reason and experience, but rather interrogates it and appeals to it. Humans are increasing understanding how the dimension of sexuality is inherent and important in our lives. We hold this alongside the testimony of queer Christians who articulate faith in God and a transformation of grace through the work of the Holy Spirit. As their identity and orientation are denied and mischaracterized, so is their pursuit of holiness via a denial of their experience, and a refusal to engage in reasoned consideration of the science behind sexuality in discussion with Scripture. Such denial subverts the notion of holiness as if it were a ritual separation from people groups that might "stain" the holy pool, as in the Old Testament, rather than understanding Jesus' example of holiness which drives us into the world to love the disenfranchised, marginalized, and rejected.

Holiness is queer and is about relationship with God realized in love for the other, due to a receptivity toward God's queer grace, not a legalistic behavioral code—a slippery slope for anyone who starts to try and define which behaviors cause one to be "in" or "out." It has been noted that when the first humans were created, the female was made out of the male; they were of the same substance. Adam identified Eve according to that which was the same between them; she was "bone of my bones" and "flesh of my flesh" (Gen 2:23). It was not based on a sexual dynamic, but the suitability of another human for Adam's partner, rather than from among animal kind. He loved her as he loved himself, because she was like him. Holy love is that which loves another as ourselves, because all humanity is human.

The participants in this research, for the most part, are still engaged in the Christian disciplines and pursuing this holy life. They understand the teleological aspects of holiness, knowing that there is often divergence between the espoused theology and the lived reality, that we are in the process of becoming that which we were always intended to be. For them, that means being and becoming a fully integrated queer Christian person. This includes in areas such as the physical expression of their sexuality, affirming that LGBTQ+ Christians often demonstrate lives that conform to Christian standards of mutuality, fidelity, and monogamy.

Ontologically, our nature is said to be transformed in pursuing holiness, but such that God renews our original nature.[39] The intent is for the whole person to be renewed, transformed, and healed in such a way that we reflect the image of God as in our creation. God is not a philosophical abstract, but a life-changing agent at work in the world, and in us. God is experienced as Spirit who is empowering, life-giving, and healing.[40] God-in-us brings wholeness and restoration.

Holiness was meant to be learned and lived in community. The early Methodist societies were the means by which holiness was taught and learned, but also through which holistic, relational community found its expression.[41] They modelled to the larger church, and to the world, a way of doing life with others in loving ways. There were intentionally "in" the world, but so distinct from the ways or values of the world that they stood apart, gaining attention for their mutual support and affection. One of the greatest challenges to TSA is the narrative of the lives of LGBTQ+ people within its ranks that speak of this love and distinctness to the world, but are often treated as divergent from the core of the movement.

People who identify as LGBTQ+ have much to teach the church about life in community. Their concept of "chosen families" that are protective and inclusive often provide an example to the church of how communities could be places of enlivened grace and support. Often, the LGBTQ+ community creates safe and inclusive spaces that put the church to shame—many a gay bar that is full of life, celebration, love, and joy and creates safety for the outcast, would be an example. These places, as such, are holy ground. LGBTQ+ Christians are often very bold and clear demonstrations of discipleship and commitment, and demonstrations of love towards those who would persecute them. LGBTQ+ Christians are people who have a trust in Christ that is expressed in holy love and mercy to their neighbors, even toward those who dehumanize them, attempt their erasure or invalidate their relationships.[42]

They also demonstrate the holy attribute of sacrifice in remaining in service for the sake of others and/or out of the conviction that their dedication makes a real difference in the church. This model of "living sacrifice" (Rom 12:1) examples holy lives that are not conformed to the expectations of the world—although admittedly there are problems when there is still

---

39. LeClerc, *Rediscovering Christian Holiness*, 186.
40. Maddox, *Responsible Grace*, 86.
41. Danker, "Early Methodist Societies as an Embodied Politic," 51.
42. O'Brien, "'If we cannot think alike, we may love alike' . . . "

non-conformity to the expectations of TSA. They live out a holiness that is often refined by patience in the face of exclusion and faithfulness in the face of rejection. They teach God's forgiveness and mercy to those who might otherwise see them as beyond forgiveness.[43]

In living in such ways, queer Christians, including the officers and former officers in this research, have a prophetic role. They are living as a sign and witness of God's new creation—the community of justice, hope, and generosity formed on the teaching of Jesus Christ.[44] They are the enlivenment of God's grace in the world. In undertaking this role, queer Christians tell their story in ways that speak possibility into the lives of others, and as a result save other lives.

They reflect the covenant love of God to the world. They understand that God expects faithfulness in their relationships with people. Relating this to sexuality, most articulate that a holy sexual ethic would be based around the covenantal ideas of faithfulness, fidelity, and permanency. And this sexual ethic could be applied to LGBTQ+ couples in faithful, loving relationships that should be understood to be holy as a result. The TSA soldiers' covenant that requires upholding the sanctity of marriage and family life does not define the gender of the parties to the marriage, and LGBTQ+ soldiers and officers can exemplify this covenantal approach to marriage.

LGBTQ+ Christians also reflect holiness in the mutuality of their relationships which defy gender stereotypes and patriarchal norms. Same-sex desire and eroticism often teach a mutuality that is not always found in patriarchal society. While some homosexuals objectify others, and some heterosexuals manage relationships that defy the patriarchy, sex in patriarchal societies has often been about dominance and dependency because men and women are not treated as societally or politically equal.[45] Homosexual eroticism contains the distinct possibility of holy equality and mutuality.

Any two people can covenant to live together in a sacred relationship that is faithful and intends permanency. These are the key factors in a marriage, meaning that it would be available to and honorable among people who identify as LGBTQ+ as well as those who are heterosexual. On this basis, Harper argues that there is nothing in the biblical

---

43. O'Brien, "'If we cannot think alike, we may love alike' ... "
44. Carder, "What Difference Does Knowing Wesley Make?" 26.
45. Wilson, *Our Tribe*, 44.

covenant that would specifically prohibit same-sex marriage,[46] regardless of whether it was countenanced at the time of the writing of the biblical texts. Even Jesus' affirmation of marriage (Matt 19:1-12) was in response to a question about divorce and must be read in this way, not as an interpretation of marriage according to gender. It is also worth noting that the term Jesus used, "one flesh," is not a term that implies sexual activity. Taken from Genesis 2:24, the term "clave" is used in the Hebrew Bible and refers to kinship, such as in Ruth 1:14 when describing the relationship between Ruth and Naomi (although some writers do cite this as a queer relationship).[47] The Greek term in the New Testament, "sarx," (used by Jesus when quoting Genesis), is used by Paul referring to his "kinsman according to the flesh" (Rom 9:3) and "people of my own race" (Rom 11:14). These terms are not equivalents in a direct sense, and it is recognized that nuanced meaning is determined by the context in which the term is used each time. However, it is observed that primarily it appears to be a term that implies kinship, not intercourse specifically, and could easily apply to same-sex relationships.

The queer officers and former officers in this study are an enlivenment of God's grace. They are witnesses to it in their expression of love, mutuality, and ministry in the world. This leads to their theology of justice.

Justice in Solidarity

Social justice is at the core of many Wesleyan theologies and movements. It is predicated on the understanding, firstly, that God's grace allows everyone in the world some conceptualization of true justice for others.[48] The Salvation Army started its life with some understanding of how this should be expressed in the world. There was, particularly in the earliest days of the movement, an imaginative theo-political response to poverty and hardship, and to gender inequality to an extent.[49] This was in the era where the poor were abandoned by the establishment, including the church, often literally into workhouses and slums.

---

46. Harper, *Holy Love*, 19.
47. For example, Preser, "Things I Learned from the Book of Ruth," 47-65.
48. Thobaben, "Wesleyan Politics at the End of Modernity," 119.
49. Tomlin, "The Politics of Salvation in The Salvation Army," 36.

People who identify as LGBTQ+ are well-versed in, and well-practiced at conceptualizing justice, countering injustice, and acting on the structures of society that need reform. It is noted that queer people disagree among themselves about how such justice is properly defined. On the libertarian right, the reformist scope would be confined to minor legal reform that allows marriage or inclusion in the military. On the left, larger cultural inclusion is the aim of social justice reformers with a view to reform of economic structures and institutions.[50] While the latter is more akin to the work of sanctifying grace transforming society, ironically, for many of the participants in this research, it is the former definition —allowing marriage and inclusion in ongoing service—that would provide a sense of justice.

Wesleyan activism and social justice are based on an understanding that God is a god of mercy and justice. It is an essential aspect of God's character. The biblical accounts, from the earliest times articulate an understanding of a God who knows, sees, hears, understands, and acts for those who suffer, those who are violated, and those who are humiliated or oppressed. In Genesis 4:10 God hears the blood-soaked earth cry out after Abel's murder. In Genesis 16:13 Hagar names God "El Roi," the God who sees her in her distress. In Genesis 18:20-21 God hears the outcry against Sodom and Gomorrah and wants to investigate the veracity of their victims' cries (implying an interesting anthropomorphizing of the divine, but nonetheless an active and merciful God). In Exodus 3:7-9, while calling Moses to action, God states that God has observed, heard, and known the suffering of the people of Israel. The calling to action flows through to one of Jesus' last parables and teachings to his disciples. Matthew 25:31-46, the parable of the sheep and the goats, challenges the church to action for the sick, the poor, and the imprisoned. It is on this basis they will be judged.

A determination to become community with the disinherited is a demonstration of commitment to the truth of the gospel through social justice action.[51] Among people who identify as LGBTQ+ there are those who are privileged by race or class, and who therefore may have few justice-oriented concerns other than preventing discrimination. A biblical view of justice in the LGBTQ+ community would look at the full demographic and experience of the community and see such a narrow view

---

50. Adler, "Distributive Justice for LGBTQ People," Oxford Research Encyclopedias.
51. Maddox, "Introduction," 17.

and scope of reform as insufficient. It would ensure that those who have previously (or currently) been disenfranchised or disinherited are elevated and supported, their voices amplified, while also not being treated as objects of charity. Isaiah 58:6-9 makes it clear that this is the requirement of God: dealing with injustice and enslavement, demonstrating generosity, and hospitality, such that one's light shines in the world and one's own healing is realized. Almost all the prophets contrast this requirement of hospitality with the meaningless religiosity associated with hollow ritualized worship and exclusionary religious feasts.

The participants in this research discussed a number of ways in which they were working toward justice for LGBTQ+ people within and outside of the movement. Within TSA these included advocacy with leaders, education programs for leaders, instigation of support networks, webinars (local and global), the development of research repositories, and the sharing of stories. Outside of TSA they participate in political protest, join Pride marches and events with TSA branding and service information, they network and develop relationships with support agencies, and they provide hope to other LGBTQ+ religious seekers. They often see the work of God in places and communities that the greater church would shun. Pride parades and festivals can, for example, be living examples of Jesus' parable of the wedding banquet. They show how to throw an inclusive party and invite the bystanders to join in, while the religious people stand by thinking that they are too good to even show up. Byas made this observation during Pride month 2019, thanking his "LGBTQ friends and neighbors for being like Jesus & showing me a better way."[52]

There is often discourse around being on the right side of history, even within TSA. Mark Jennings points out that history is not a fence.[53] However, just as there is an arch of increasing inclusion in God's story, there is also an arc of justice over history. For the queer Christian, this arc can feel like a distant dream. It is more likely that they sense symbolic (or actual) violence by those who hold the social capital that can keep others bound, perhaps through a limitation on ministry for LGBTQ+ people, expectations of SOGICE, or denunciation of opposing discourse as "heresy." It can include the monopolization of the goods of salvation and a denial to the individuals who do not fit the expected norm.[54] These

52. Jared Byas (@jbyas), "Pride Parades," Twitter (X), June 19, 2019.
53. Jennings, "Reading Scripture as a Discursive Fight to the Death," Presentation, University of Divinity Research Day, Melbourne, 5 June 2024.
54. Jennings, "Reading Scripture as a Discursive Fight to the Death."

factors can drive much of the activism of queer Christians as they fight to have voice and be recognized as faithful disciples themselves.

The Priestly Ministry of All Believers

As all Christians, heterosexual and non-heterosexual alike, have access to God through the mediation of Christ, so they are called to exercise a priestly ministry on behalf of one another and the world.[55] This research is concentrated on those who, at some point, served as full-time office bearers within the TSA. They were discerned by the church to be people of character suitable for such ministry, regardless of sexuality (albeit mostly undisclosed at the time of acceptance into officership), and commissioned to ministry as such.

Within TSA it is noted that the pre-existing ordination of the Holy Spirit to ministry is recognized in the commissioning ceremony. This recognizes that all believers are empowered and gifted for ministry, rather than the commissioning being seen as a creation of a distinct class of believer. Key in this is that all believers share in the ministry of the Word and its application in service to the world. While this provides a theological affirmation of the various ministries of lay people, it applies here in conversation about the potential diversity of those in ministry and is most clearly demonstrated in the lives of those research participants who have left officership but continue to exercise priestly ministry without an institutional commission. Also, it demonstrates the universality of God's grace that empowers LGBTQ+ believers, in the same way as heterosexual believers, to participate in God's mission to the world as taught by Jesus.

Problematically, it is in the nature of TSA to see ministry in dichotomized categories: male or female, officer or soldier, hierarchy or disorder, and more recently straight—but definitely not gay.[56] The diversity of humanity is not demonstrated in the officer class of the Australian Salvation Army, not just in terms of non-heterosexuals but also through limited people of color or from Indigenous backgrounds. At worst, this dichotomy gives the impression that any form of diversity or equality in service is a threat to unity. Such practices can only be substantiated through the dehumanization or diminishment of a class (or classes) of

---

55. The Salvation Army, *Salvation Story*, 108.

56. Moore notes that this is a problem for the whole church: Moore, "Trinity and Covenantal Ministry," 145.

people, the explicit exclusion of people based on an inherent personal characteristic, an appeal to regulation or tradition to enforce practice, and an expression of fear that the integrity (or size) of the ecclesial community would be threatened by change.

Each of the participants in this research, particularly the interview participants, spoke about their ministry in ways that demonstrated that they had been equipped for service by something beyond themselves. One spoke of a special capacity for caring in the delivery of funerals. One spoke of how they have a special capacity for engaging with community groups. One noted that it was TSA that may have trained them for their ministry, but it was their queerness that gave it authority in the centers and settings where they worked.

Many in the power structures and orthodoxy of the church will not perceive the evidence of the Holy Spirit gifting queer Christians. Others struggle to reconcile the evidence of the Holy Spirit's work in people's lives, when they are known to be gay or lesbian. One participant spoke about how his own mother sees God empowering him for ministry but cannot accept his sexuality and cannot reconcile the two matters. While it is evident in the lives of the research participants that, at some point in their lives (and for many, in ongoing ways), a spiritual empowering and experience of God occurred, their testimony often proves insufficient to be accepted as evidential of salvation or sanctification. Their personal assurance is insufficient to those who form the view that homoerotic activity or gender non-conformity preclude such salvation.[57] Nonetheless, they continue to affirm their calling to ministry and almost all in the survey noted that their calling to ministry remains, albeit for some in more nuanced ways. For those who have left, all bar one, continue to see their lives as a continuation of this service despite not having the office of formal full-time ministry.

LGBTQ+ officers are ministering by demonstrating the love of God and neighbor, and the values taught by Jesus. They take seriously the command of Jesus at the end of his earthly ministry to "tend my sheep" (John 21:16), and often they are the only ones tending to the "rainbow sheep" connected with TSA. Theirs is a calling and ministry that manifests itself both in serendipitous moments of connection with people who need help, support and advice as well as the proactive seeking of opportunities to be present and pastoral for people. Their personal experiences

---

57. This is also noted in Jennings' research in Pentecostal-charismatic churches, see Jennings, *Happy*, 61.

coupled with their relationship with God combine to allow for concrete expressions of ministry that in themselves are announcements of God's redemptive activity—those persons, bodies, and concomitant sexualities that have been derided by the church are appropriating significance and demonstrating love in the world.[58]

The support groups that they are developing could be said to mirror Wesleyan class meetings (small groups). Similar to the class meetings, they have arisen out of pastoral need, out of an understanding that the mission of the church is interpersonal, for support and accountability, for education, to discuss and enhance relationship to God and the church, and (often through moderators on social media, for example) under the oversight of an elder.[59]

There is arguably biblical precedent for the placement of queer people in God's activities in the world. In Mark 14:13 Jesus directs the disciples to make preparations for the Passover meal. He directs them into the city, to find a man carrying a jar of water. They were to follow him to the venue of their celebrations. Carrying water seems innocuous to modern readers. In first-century Jerusalem, however, collecting and carrying water was strictly a female role. For a man to openly carry out a female role and appear in the streets in a female guise would have stood out to the disciples. At the very least this person was undertaking a gender-transgressive task in public.

It appears, one could argue, that Jesus is saying, "Go and find the queer person. Not only will they stand out, they will know what to do."

Implications

There is legitimacy to the notion that someone can be simultaneously, and wholly, queer and Christian. That understanding alone may provide TSA a basis for mutuality in discussions and a recognition of the multiple ways that LGBTQ+ officers have, and continue, to minister within the movement. It may change the manner in which appointments are considered, pastoral care is provided, faithfulness to service is recognized, and may begin a journey toward reconciliation. This has been the intention

---

58. An amazing example of this is also seen in the ways that HIV+ Christian gay men serve despite perceptions of their serostatus, sexuality, and spirituality; see: Goh, "From Polluted to Prophetic Bodies," 133–146.

59. Beck, "Connexion and Koinonia," 133-135.

of presenting this summary and reflection in the theological notions chosen, rather than an apologetic against particular minority texts.

It may also provide a basis on which allies can become advocates. In leaving the Holy Spirit, Jesus did not leave his disciples an "ally", and allyship is insufficient to attain equality for LGBTQ+ officers. A willingness for some, especially key leaders, to be advocates toward equality of service conditions is required. This can be costly. Thomas Oord's efforts to be an effective advocate-ally in the Church of the Nazarene, a sister Wesleyan denomination, led to a denominational trial in July 2024 where he was found guilty of teaching doctrines out of harmony with the doctrinal statements of the church and conduct unbecoming a minister.[60] He was subsequently not only stripped of his ministerial credentials, but also had his membership of the Church of the Nazarene revoked. Oord has maintained his course, however, in the hopes of encouragement for queer people, encouragement for other allies, and potential for using his platform to move the denomination toward an affirming position.[61]

There are some evident challenges. Ongoing work still needs to occur to address theological objections within TSA, understanding that the differences between Christians as they read the Scriptures are not about the authority of the Bible, but rather the interpretation of its contents and their contemporary application. It is not a question of revelation or inspiration, rather one of hermeneutics. Almost all of the research participants were faithful, Bible-believing Christians. Only one said that they had left their faith. Using the Bible to create a sense of superiority over others who also value the Bible makes little sense. Some Salvationist scholars have started this important theological work, including Solevåg and Wood.[62]

An initial step to addressing theological objections to equal service conditions for LGBTQ+ officers is agreement that both "sides" have a high view of Scripture. A second would be to read the whole before exploring the parts; that is to look at the metanarratives of Scripture first to give context and history to the verses that are considered applicable to any debate. Starting with an overarching hermeneutic that sees a metanarrative of humanity created in God's image, love, mercy, and

---

60. Oord, *My Defense*, 11.

61. Oord, "God After Deconstruction," 14 July 2024, The Spiritual Misfits Podcast.

62. Solevåg, "The Salvation Army and Same-Sex Love," Included, Accessed 06 July 2024; Wood, "Whosoever Will," Included, Accessed 22 April 2024;

grace, and then working *down* to specific verses makes a big difference to how they are understood.

Finally, theology must start with God at the center. The Bible is a revelation about God and discussion of humanity's relationship with God. It is not God. If we start with God at the center, understanding God according to the attributes of God discernible in Scripture (and in life through experience and affective spirituality), we start from a place of mercy, grace, faithfulness, forgiveness, and steadfast, or covenant, love. Unfortunately, a theology of human sexuality often starts from a view of God as punitive and retributive and is discussed from our "fallen" anthropology rather than from the point of view of the Creator.[63] Understanding God's character, and viewing others from the point of view of his inclusive love and diverse creativity, changes how we discuss sexuality. God loves all whom God made, without qualification.

If theological barriers can be navigated, then navigating institutional barriers to inclusion still poses difficulties.[64] For many who wish to see significant changes, there is the risk that they will have big appetites but no teeth.[65] While the Holy Spirit may guide the denomination into a new way of being, it is probable that this will be through the continued agency of people like those participating in this research, being signs and witnesses of God's work to The Salvation Army.

Care for non-heterosexual officers needs to consider what may constitute restitution for harms caused. This is not necessarily compensatory, and none of the research participants suggested so. However, funding counselling and treatment, providing voice at the right fora and acknowledging past and ongoing harms would be a valuable start. Supporting peer-support networks is another potential way forward. Understanding the power differentials that exist and providing advocacy toward a point where LGBTQ+ officers share the same conditions of service would be even more meaningful.

Building bridges through fostering dialogue is important. These conversations would require some ground rules, which could include repentance from using the hierarchical structures to avoid personal

---

63. Harper, *Holy Love*, 14.

64. Halliday, "Changing Attitudes, Orders and Regulations" discusses this fully.

65. This phrase is taken from Abraham, "Big Appetites and No Teeth," 31,35. In his essay he discusses the social issues facing the United Methodist Church in the US, who he claims have high aspirations for societal and ecclesial transformation but little energy or capacity to deal with the "plateful of problems" before them.

advocacy and influence, prevention from hiding behind regulations for either personal political protection or expediency, and seeking out engagement with "men of Issachar" who know the times and what should be done (1 Chr 12:32).[66] Then members of TSA may be able to engage in prayerful conversations (perhaps as the aforementioned Faith-Based Facilitation is intended) in order to discern together the work of the Holy Spirit in the lives of people and the church, and seeking a guidance "into all the truth" (John 16:13). However, it must be certain that the dialogue is undertaken as a conversation of equals. As Oliveto points out, the church has historically turned the lives of people who identify as LGBTQ+ into an issue to be resolved, rather than seeing them as children of God whose testimony and spirituality demonstrate grace and sanctification, and who display the fruits of the Spirit in their lives.[67]

Resources

The church has the resources to reconsider its thinking on ethical and theological issues. Slavery was historically affirmed through the use of Scripture (e.g., Col 3:22-25), but was challenged by a more expansive view of the meta-narrative of humanity and God's love in the Bible, along with transformational encounters with slaves, their humanity, suffering, dignity, families, and faith.[68] Nations that used Scripture to justify colonialism, conquest, and egregious harms to indigenous populations have often found, over time, that these views cannot stand in the face of transformation encounters with the suffering people who were impacted. In the last century, a millennia-old contempt of Jews, supported by Scripture, was almost completely rejected within one generation when humanity was confronted by the horror of the holocaust.

Wesleyanism in its earliest days was inextricably linked to the abolition of slavery, justice for the poor and excluded, and enfranchisement of women. Realistically, the legacy is mixed, as there were Methodists on both sides of the abolitionist debate, particularly in America. Also, the initial radical release of women in ministry was later suppressed and controlled by patriarchal systems and structures, including within TSA. But it is perhaps the ordination of women as a concept and issue of justice that

---

66. Rowell, *Thinking, Listening, Being*, 22.
67. Oliveto, *Our Hearts Strangely Warmed*, 49.
68. Gushee, *Changing our Mind*, 107.

can give the church, and specifically TSA, some tools to consider affirming the ministry of LGBTQ+ Christians. The release of women into ministry may have been, at first, pragmatic. However, it recognizes that God works outside the confines of narrow interpretations of ancient texts, most particularly some of Paul's letters. That such a pragmatism (or inclusion) has not also been extended to LGBTQ+ people in ministry could therefore be interpreted as the result of power structures intentionally excluding a class of people by choice rather than theology. Moreover, it is most-often based on anti-queer rhetoric from those who have no idea of what it is to be gender nonconforming or non-heterosexual. Maintaining discriminatory practices defies the perfect love of holiness, the need for more people in ministry, and the grace-filled inclusiveness of the gospel.

Clergy shortages do sometimes bring about change as people are needed to undertake the work.[69] This may lead to some acceptance of LGBTQ+ clergy in congregations where any minister is better than none. However, this is only an evident principle in relation to missional, on the ground, practice and does not immediately lead to institutional policy change. An example is the use of women in pastoral roles with the Roman Catholic Church, particularly in rural parts of the USA.[70]

In the end, denominations are political bodies, and as such represent their constituencies to a greater or lesser extent. Thus, as seen with the ordination of women, we need to keep in mind that equality does not enjoy support across all corners of society. Should LGBTQ+ officers be granted equality by TSA they will not enjoy support across the whole organization, particularly from some conservative congregations or in some conservative geographic regions.

Generally speaking, denominations with centralized command and control structures are slower to adapt to change.[71] TSA has been an exception when it comes to women's ordination. This exception does give some hope to LGBTQ+ officers, as there is precedence for TSA to act against type, however it should be remembered that the move for women's ordination in the movement was at the time of founding and under the guidance of Catherine Booth, the co-founder, acting somewhat in self-interest.

What, then, can LGBTQ+ officers and their allies learn about instituting changes they seek? All social movements have certain strategic

69. Chaves, *Ordaining Women*, 131.
70. Chaves, *Ordaining Women*, 155.
71. Chaves, *Ordaining Women*, 156.

elements and it is no different in churches, as seen in the moves towards women's ordination. Tactics involved in eliciting denominational change have included the full range of activist methodologies: petitioning national bodies, mobilizing congregations, arguments in denominational press and external press, publication of pamphlets and books, research, organizing conferences, establishing networks, gathering mutual support groups, communication, and direct lobbying. Looking at the case of how women's ordination has been advanced, there have also been extra-institutional activities such as the 1974 "irregular ordination" of eleven women to the priesthood of the US Episcopal Church by retired bishops.[72]

Currently, many of these tactics are being utilized by LGBTQ+ officers. Conferences such as the 2021 "Included" conference in Europe (and online) and the 2014 "Thought Matters" conference in New Zealand are examples. Publications such as Kris Halliday's testimony and Christina Tyson's ally articles are achieving circulation.[73] Networks such as secret/closed Facebook groups and broader ally groups (e.g., Salvos for a More Inclusive Church) are providing both mutual support and broader advocacy.

In responding to this advocacy, TSA also has tools in its own history of responses as a justice movement. One of the current stated mission imperatives of TSA in Australia is "working for justice." If TSA is a praxeological incarnation of God's preferential option for the poor and marginalized (as argued by Meeks) this must include those who have been marginalized by its own actions.[74]

There are other Wesleyan traditions that TSA can look to for resources and lessons to be learned. As early as 1962, Glide Memorial (United Methodist) Church in San Francisco facilitated a dialogue between the church and LGB organizations. They shared their findings with the national leaders of The Methodist Church who were willing to fund ongoing consultations. As a result, the Council on Religion and the Homosexual was formed, in order to foster communications and relationships between the church and the gay community. They offered safe spaces for dialogue, orientation to gay and lesbian culture for pastors (including visits to gay bars), listening to the lived experience of LGB people, and education on human sexuality. It is notable that this group of Wesleyans

---

72. Chaves, *Ordaining Women*, 171.
73. Halliday, "A Reflection on Calling"; Tyson, "Rejecting Rejection."
74. Meeks, *The Portion of the Poor*, 87.

is credited with sparking the debate on homosexuality in the American church based on their openness to LGB people and their understanding of reason and experience as sources for theological reflection.[75] The progress that could have been made was stymied by reactionary groups in the 1970s and the AIDS crisis of the 1980s and 1990s. The status and rights of non-heterosexual people have been discussed at each of the General Conferences of the United Methodist Church (UMC) since 1972. From that point in time, various caucus groups formed and politicized within the denomination which initially moved it from a progressive stance on homosexuality to a more conservative one. By 2012, the groups had still only "agreed to disagree."[76] The decision to lift the ban on queer clergy and same-sex marriages in the UMC was only made possible after approximately one quarter of its more traditionally-orientated congregations disaffiliated.[77] While that may be regrettable, a counter-note is that this change was achieved despite the exponential increase in delegates to the General Conference of the UMC from central (overseas) conferences, many of whom hold to more conservative theologies.[78]

The embrace of LGBTQ+ Christians was a major issue for the Uniting Church in Australia (UCA), a successor to the Methodist Church in Australia (following a merge with Presbyterians and Congregationalists). At its 2018 assembly it agreed to two different doctrines of marriage and allowed for local discretion regarding the solemnization of same-sex marriages.[79] It is notable that this form of compromise is not always achievable, as the example of the UMC demonstrates, and the threat of schism does create fear in many in TSA. However, the UMC example also demonstrates that change can be achieved in Wesleyan denominations, including while input is obtained from various national cultures. The ability to accommodate conservative cultures, such as African and South Asian, has often been cited as a restraint to change in TSA.

Ordination has been available to LGBTQ+ Christians, regardless of whether they are celibate, in a range of denominations for some time. The Evangelical Church in America made this decision in 2009, The Presbyterian Church in the United States in 2011, and The Episcopal Church in the USA over a staged process from 2015 (although they had an openly

---

75. Oliveto, *Our Hearts Strangely Warmed*, 23-24.
76. Boggan Dreff, *Entangled*, 205, 260.
77. O'Brien, "'If we cannot think alike, we may love alike' . . ."
78. Oliveto, *Our Hearts Strangely Warmed*, 46.
79. O'Brien, "'If we cannot think alike, we may love alike' . . ."

gay priest in 1977 and bishop in 2003). The Uniting Church in Australia allowed ordination of gay and lesbian people from 2003, and ministers were allowed discretion to bless same-sex relationships prior to the legal introduction of same-sex marriage in 2017. From 2018, as noted, local discretion was allowed in the matter of same-sex marriage.

Conclusion

The twenty-four people who participated in this research bestowed a sacred trust that their stories would be represented well. Faithfully representing these stories has meant that beyond the history and harm, there is clearly also an articulation of hope. Between them they have told of authenticity and holiness that is an example to the rest of the church. They have described ways in which they are being used in ministry, specifically because they are queer, Christian, and available for service. They have jointly articulated a theology that sees how God is eternally inclusive, just, caring, and empowering. They demonstrate God's diversity in creation, enlivened grace, justice in solidarity, and the priestly ministry of all believers.

The grace-filled example of these officers to The Salvation Army and the broader church needs noting. Theirs is a grace that points to the divine, provides comfort to the distressed, has power to respond to challenges, and moves ahead of people to provide support. They act as agents of such grace in the world, testifying to saving grace that is spiritual, social, psychological, and physical, transforming their inward and outward worlds. They are examples of love, community, safety, and faithfulness.

They are people of discipline and spirituality under fire, often despite discrimination. They show love to persecutors, and in places that others fear to tread. At times there may have been some queer blood—but they show that there is also some queer fire.

Appendix 1—Survey

Queer Blood and Fire: The experiences of LGBTQ+ Salvation Army Officers in Australia

I am studying the experiences of LGBTQ+ Salvation Army Officers at The University of Divinity as part of the requirements for the Doctor of Philosophy Degree. This study is being supervised by Associate Professor Glen O'Brien from Eva Burrows College, University of Divinity, and Professor Douglas Ezzy from the University of Tasmania.

The aims of the study are to investigate and document the experience of those members of The Salvation Army Australia Territory called to be officers who identify as LGBTQ+ in order to understand their experiences of serving within the movement. I am also interested in hearing from those officers who are questioning their sexuality. I expect the research to have benefits for both current and former serving LGBTQ+ officers by recording their lived experience and noting areas the denomination could further progress the care and equity for LGBTQ+ officers.

You are being invited to participate in this research because you have self-identified as a current or former LGBTQ+ (or questioning) officer, or candidate for officership, in The Salvation Army in Australia. Please note that participation is entirely voluntary and there are no consequences for you of not participating. Participants will be asked to complete an anonymous online survey. This is likely to take around 15-20 minutes, depending on the depth of answers you provide.

At the end of the survey there will be an option to opt-in for a more in-depth interview. You are under no obligation to participate, but this will provide the opportunity to confidentially expand on your answers and tell your story. If you wish to participate, a separate consent form will be provided to you prior to the interview with more information.

All information gathered from participants will be kept confidentially. The data will be kept for 7 years in password protected files according to the policies of the University of Divinity. The information from this research will be reported in my thesis and in any other articles or publications based on this research but never with any identifiable information.

By continuing with this survey, you are giving your consent to participate. You can withdraw at any stage until you submit the survey on the final page. After this, it will be impossible to withdraw your responses as they will be not be identifiable.

I am happy to provide further information on the research, and you may contact me confidentially at lgbtofficers@gmail.com . The research is approved by the Human Research Ethics Committee at the University of Divinity and any ethical concerns regarding this research may be addressed to secretary_HREC@cra.org.au

Some of the matters covered in this survey may be sensitive for some people as they touch on areas of faith, calling, sexuality and identity. If you need support at any stage, you can leave the survey and contact any of the following:

For current serving or retired officers:

Pastoral Services Team—a confidential in-house service: TSApastoralservices@salvationarmy.org.au

Employee Assistance Program—external support provided by Converge at: 1300 687 327

LGBTQ+ Staff Support Line—external support line for LGBTQ+ TSA staff: 1300 542 874

APPENDIX 1—SURVEY

For all participants:

QLife (counselling and referral service for LGBTQ+ people)—call 1800 184 527 or chat online

Beyond Blue (for anyone feeling depressed or anxious)—call 1300 22 4636 or chat online

The initial questions ask about your identification:

1. Which of the following do you feel most accurately describes your sexuality?
   a. Gay/ Lesbian (same sex/ same gender attracted)
   b. Bisexual (same and other sex/ same and other gender attracted)
   c. Pansexual (sex and gender unimportant in choice of partner)
   d. Queer (any of the above)
   e. Asexual
   f. Questioning
   g. Heterosexual/ Straight (attracted to a different sex/ different gender)—this option will exit the participant from the survey with a note to thank them.
   h. I would rather not say
   i. Something else (Please tell us how you identify)

2. Are you transgender?
   a. Yes
   b. No
   c. Prefer not to say

3. LGBTQ+ and The Salvation Army
   a. What is your current standing as an officer in The Salvation Army?
      i. An applicant or candidate for officership (skip to question 4)
      ii. A current active officer (Skip to question 4)
      iii. A retired officer (Skip to question 4)

iv. A past officer who has left for other employment (Go to questions 3b)

b. If you have concluded your officer service how much of a factor was your sexuality or gender identity in your decision to leave? (Scale 1-10; 1 not very important, 10 very important)

4. Prior to officer training, in which Division was your home Corps?

    a. Western Australia (pre-2018)
    b. Western Australia (post 2018, Australia One amalgamation)
    c. South Australia
    d. Northern Territory Region
    e. South Australia & Northern Territory (post Australia One amalgamation)
    f. Central & North Queensland
    g. South Queensland
    h. Queensland (post Australia One amalgamation)
    i. Tasmania (pre-2018)
    j. Tasmania (post 2018, Australia One amalgamation)
    k. Melbourne Central
    l. Central Victoria
    m. Eastern Victoria
    n. Western Victoria
    o. Northern Victoria
    p. Victoria (post Australia One amalgamation)
    q. ACT & South New South Wales
    r. Greater West (NSW)
    s. Sydney East & Illawarra
    t. Newcastle
    u. Northern New South Wales
    v. New South Wales (post Australia One amalgamation)
    w. Other (not listed, e.g., overseas prior to transfer to Australia)—please name

5. What is your current age?

    a. 18-30

    b. 30-50

    c. 50-65

    d. 65+

6. Year ordained & commissioned as a Salvation Army Officer

7. Years of service as an officer

8. Territory of commissioning

    a. Australia Eastern Territory

    b. Australia Southern Territory

    c. Australia Territory (post 2018)

    d. Other—and if "other," year of move to Australia?

9. Do you still feel the same sense of calling to officership that you did when you first considered application or entered training?

    a. The same sense of calling

    b. My sense of calling has deepened

    c. My sense of calling is now less than it was

    d. My sense of calling is now more complex

    e. Other things in my life are now more important and my sense of calling to officership has changed.

The next questions offer a comparison with The Salvation Army's Workplace Engagement Survey:

10. I would recommend working at The Salvation Army to others: Scale 1-10 (10 highly recommend; 1 not recommend)

11. TSA is genuinely committed to providing a safe working environment: Scale 1-10 (10 most committed; 1 not committed)

12. TSA does not tolerate gender-based harassment or sexual harassment: Scale 1-10 (10 zero toleration)

13. My Salvation Army manager/ supervisor acts (/acted) in accordance with TSA values: Scale 1- 10 (10 always, 1 never)

The following are some questions about being Christian and LGBTQ+. I am interested in your outness with family, friends and people within The Salvation Army. 'Outness' refers to how much of your LGBTQ+ identity you disclose and/or show to your family, friends or people in The Salvation Army.

14. How would you describe your 'outness' with family?

    a. All of my family know

    b. Most of my family know

    c. Some family members know

    d. Prefer not to say

15. How would you describe your 'outness' with friends?

    a. All of my friends know

    b. Most of my friends know

    c. Some of my friends know

    d. Prefer not to say

16. How would you describe your 'outness' within The Salvation Army? Select all that apply

    a. All of the people I work with know

    b. Some or all of my leaders know

    c. Some or all of my colleagues know

    d. Some or all of my congregation know

    e. Some of all of my direct reports know

    f. No one knows

    g. Prefer not to say

17. How would you describe your 'outness' to your line manager/ area officer or officer leader?

    a. I have explicitly told my manager that I am LGBTQ+

APPENDIX 1—SURVEY

   b. I think my manager knows that I am LGBTQ+, but it is not explicit.

   c. My manager does not know.

18. How do you feel about being both LGBTQ+ and Christian?

    a. Very comfortable

    b. More comfortable than conflicted

    c. More conflicted than comfortable

    d. Prefer not to say

19. What are the attitudes toward LGBTQ+ among the majority of people who attend the worship service or event that you most often attend? Check all that apply

    a. Welcoming

    b. Loving

    c. Tolerant

    d. Cautious

    e. Ignorant

    f. Judgmental

    g. Regard as wrong/ sinful

    h. Don't know

    i. Prefer not to say

20. How have you examined your LGTBQ+ identity from the perspective of your faith? Check all that apply:

    a. Read books

    b. Searched the internet

    c. Talked to religious leaders

    d. Talked to family and friends who are also Christian

    e. Participated in online discussions

    f. Attended a seminar or presentation

    g. Formal studies

    h. Talked with other Christians who are LGBTQ+

i. Spiritual Direction

j. Prefer not to say

21. To what extent to do you feel you have been able to assimilate your sexuality with your Christian faith?

    a. To a great extent

    b. To some extent

    c. Very little

    d. Not at all

22. Do you agree that you may find joy or good as someone who is both Christian and LGBTQ+?

    a. Yes, I have found moments of joy or goodness because of both my sexuality and my faith and how they intersect

    b. Sometimes there are moments of joy or goodness because of both my sexuality and faith and how they intersect

    c. No, I don't recall particular moments of joy or goodness where faith and sexuality intersect

23. To what extent do you feel the need to edit your speech, dress or behaviors to be safe within The Salvation Army?

    a. All of the time

    b. Most of the time

    c. Some of the time

    d. I never feel the need to edit my speech, dress or behaviors to feel safe

24. When creating laws to protect religious people's rights, what should be considered? Which statement comes closer to your view?

    a. The rights of religious people need to be balanced against the rights of other groups in society

    b. The primary concern should be to ensure religious people can act with a clear moral conscience as much as possible

    c. Prefer not to say

APPENDIX 1—SURVEY

Would you be prepared to answer some questions regarding conversion therapy? These are practices that are ostensibly intended to change or suppress someone's sexual or gender identity and align it with a heteronormative disposition often celebrated in religious circles.

Yes, I'd be happy to answer some questions about conversion therapy—continue

No, I'd rather not answer questions about conversion therapy—Skip to question 29

25. To what extent have you been subject to conversion therapies/practices?
    a. A great extent
    b. Some extent
    c. Not exposed
    d. I don't know
    e. Prefer not to say

26. During what period did this occur?
    a. Within the last five years
    b. Within the last ten years
    c. Within the last twenty years
    d. More than twenty years ago
    e. I don't know if I've been exposed to conversation therapies or practices

27. What sort of "therapies" or practices have you been exposed to? (click all that apply)
    a. Prayer ministries
    b. Seminars or conferences
    c. Rallies
    d. Counselling sessions
    e. Retreats for intensive 'treatment'
    f. Exorcism

g. Books on how to change or suppress my sexuality/ gender identity

h. Videos on how to change or suppress my sexuality/ gender identity

i. Phone apps

j. Other (Please list)

28. Have you participated in conversion therapies as someone wishing to minister to others of diverse gender or sexuality?

   a. Yes

   b. No

   c. Prefer not to say

The following questions relate to workplace behaviors in the environment where you ministered and/or continue to minister:

29. Sometimes a Salvation Army officer might be expected to act or speak in ways that suggest LGBTQ+ identities or experiences are not acceptable in The Salvation Army. How often do you find yourself required to act or speak in such ways?

   a. Never

   b. Rarely

   c. Occasionally

   d. Sometimes

   e. Often

   f. Regularly

30. Have there been times you have witnessed discrimination in a Salvation Army context against others on the basis of their LGBTQ+ identity?

   a. Never

   b. Rarely

   c. Occasionally

   d. Sometimes

e. Often

f. Regularly

31. If you witness this discrimination, how do you usually respond?

    a. I always remain silent

    b. I am usually silent, but I am sometimes able to intervene

    c. I usually intervene, but sometimes I remain silent

    d. I always intervene

    e. I don't recall witnessing discrimination

32. If you always or sometimes remain silent, why do you think this is?

    a. I'm not sure how to respond

    b. I'm concerned about the consequences of intervening

    c. I've intervened in the past and I experienced discrimination as a result

    d. I don't think it's my responsibility to intervene

    e. I don't always stay silent

33. Do you believe that you have experienced discrimination as a result of the policies or procedures of The Salvation Army, either current policies or past policies?

    a. Yes, often

    b. Yes, sometimes

    c. Yes, but rarely

    d. No, never

34. To what extent do you believe that decisions have been made about you, your calling or your retention on the basis of your gender identity or sexuality?

    a. To a great extent

    b. They have been a consideration

    c. Very little

    d. Not at all

These last few questions help with demography and provide the opportunity for some longer form responses:

35. Demographic questions

    a. Year of birth

    b. Gender Identity—Female/ Male/ Non-Binary/ Other (open field for response)

36. Is there a particular story or other matter that has been formative in your experience as a LGBTQ+ officer that you would like to share, but that you don't feel has been covered so far?

37. Recent LGBTQ+ working groups, Rainbow Tick accreditation processes and the Let's Talk Faith Based Facilitation workshops could all point to a positive shift in the organisation attitude of TSA within Australia. Are these cause for optimism, and, if so, on what grounds?

38. Would you be willing to participate in an individual, confidential interview with the researcher? If so, please send a confidential email to: lgbtofficers@gmail.com with your preferred contact details.

Thank you for taking your time to complete the survey. If there has been anything at all within this survey that you may need support with, please reach out to any of the following providers for their professional and specialised care:

For current serving or retired officers:

Pastoral Services Team—a confidential in-house service: TSApastoralservices@salvationarmy.org.au

Employee Assistance Program—external support provided by Converge at: 1300 687 327

LGBTQ+ Staff Support Line—external support line for LGBTQ+ TSA staff: 1300 542 874

For all participants:

QLife (counselling and referral service for LGBTQ people)
—call 1800 184 527 or chat online

Beyond Blue (for anyone feeling depressed or anxious)
—call 1300 22 4636 or chat online

Appendix 2—Interviews

Interview questions—Queer Blood & Fire

All participants will be asked in the introductory moments to confirm that they have read the information sheet. An opportunity for any questions will be offered. It is expected that the interview will take around one hour.

Questions:

1. What prompted you to participate in an interview for this research?
2. I'm interested in understanding what it is like to be an LGBTQ+ identifying officer for you. Can you tell me about a particular experience or event that you think illustrates this?
3. Can you tell me about what it was like for you when you came out as LGBTQ+?'
4. How did it change the way you felt about yourself?
5. What is your current feeling/ attitude about your sexuality?
6. What is your current feeling/ attitude regarding service in TSA as a LGBTQ+ officer?
7. How would you describe your relationship with God and is that impacted by:
    a. Being LGBTQ+?
    b. Being an officer?

8. What were you taught about being LGBTQ+:

   a. When you were growing up (check to see if this was within a TSA context)?

   b. When you were preparing to become a TSA officer?

   c. When you were in college and training to be a TSA officer?

9. Have you experienced any situations of discomfort as an LGBTQ+ officer?

10. Would you mind if I asked questions relating to conversion practices? If yes, have you been exposed to any particular forms of prayer ministry, conversion practices or other forms of religious ministrations due to your sexuality?

    a. How have you resolved these for yourself, now?

    b. Do you perceive any ongoing difficulties for yourself?

11. Have you experienced or perceived any discrimination because of your sexuality?

12. Do you think there have been times when you believe you have let yourself down, or acted against your true (LGBTQ+) self, as an officer?

13. Do you feel the need to edit your dress or behaviours in any way when performing your duties as an officer?

14. Have there been times when you felt that you were able to act authentically as an LGBTQ+ officer? Can you give an example?

15. Have you had times where you have felt betrayed by others you have trusted regarding your sexuality?

16. We have focused on a lot of the negatives, can you give me an example of something positive or joyful that has come from being LGBTQ+ and an officer?

17. Is there anything that you would like to discuss that you don't think we have covered?

At the end of the interview, I will again remind the participant:

- their responses will be held confidential
- Transcriptions will be sent back to them to confirm their responses
- Their contribution can be withdrawn up to six weeks following the interview, after which time their responses will be aggregated with other participants
- Support services are available if they require them—refer to the information sheet.

Bibliography

Abelove, Henry. *The Evangelist of Desire: John Wesley and the Methodists*. Stanford: Stanford University Press, 1990.

Abraham, William J. "Big Appetites and No Teeth: Theology and Politics in the Wesleyan Tradition." In *Exploring a Wesleyan Political Theology*, edited by Ryan Nicholas Danker, 31-46. Nashville: Wesley's Foundry, 2020.

Achtemeier, Mark. *The Bible's Yes to Same-Sex Marriage: An Evangelical's Change of Heart*. Louisville: Westminster John Knox, 2014.

Adler, Libby. "Distributive Justice for LGBTQ People." Oxford Research Encyclopedias – Politics. Published 28 February 2020, accessed 20 July 2024. https://doi.org/10.1093/acrefore/9780190228637.013.1235

Agnew, Milton. *Manual of Salvationism*, 2nd ed. New York: The Salvation Army, 1974.

Althaus-Reid, Marcella. *Indecent Theology: Perversions in Sex, Gender and Politics*. Milton Park: Routledge, 2000.

Ames, D., Haynes, K., Adamson, S.F., Bruce, L.E., Chacko, B.K., Button, L., and Koenig, H. G. "A Structured Chaplain Intervention for Veterans with Moral Injury in the Setting of PTSD." Durham, NC: Duke University Center for Spirituality, Theology and Health, 2018.

Amos, Natalie, Gene Lim, Pip Buckingham, Ashleigh Lin, Shakara Liddelow-Hunt, Julie Mooney-Somers, and Adam Bourne, *Rainbow Realities: In-depth analyses of large-scale LGBTQA+ health and wellbeing data in Australia*. Melbourne: Australian Research Centre in Sex, Health and Society, La Trobe University, 2023.

Anderson, Cheryl B. *Ancient Laws and Contemporary Controversies: The Need for Inclusive Biblical Interpretation*. Oxford: Oxford University Press, 2009.

Anderson, Joel R., Natasha Darke, Jordan D.X. Hinton, Serena Penlivanidis and Timothy W. Jones. "Moral Injury for LGBTQ+ Individuals and Their Communities." *Current Treatment Options in Psychology* 11 (2024) 279-287.

Aquinas, Thomas. *Summa Theolgiae*. Translated by the Fathers of the English Dominican Province. Milton Keynes: Authentic Media, 2012.

Australian Christian Lobby. "Dear Premier, We Are Not Criminals." Facebook, 1 February 2021, https://www.facebook.com/ACLobby/photos/a.120021108071995/4946127048794686/

Australian Institute of Health and Welfare. "LGBTIQ+ Australians: Suicidal Thoughts and Behaviours and Self-Harm." Suicide and Self-Harm Monitoring. Accessed 20 January 2024. https://www.aihw.gov.au/suicide-self-harm-monitoring/data/populations-age-groups/suicidal-and-self-harming-thoughts-and-behaviours

Australian Psychological Society. "Use of psychological practices that attempt to change or suppress a person's sexual orientation or gender: Position statement." Australian Psychological Society. 2021.https://psychology.org.au/getmedia/7bb91307-14ba-4a24-b10b-750f85b0b729/updated_aps_position_statement_conversion_practices.pdf

Baldock, Kathy. *Forging A Sacred Weapon: How the Bible Became Anti-Gay*. Reno, NV: Canyonwalker Press, 2025.

———. *Walking the Bridgeless Canyon: Repairing the Breach Between the Church and the L.G.B.T. Community*. Reno, NV: Canyonwalker Press, 2014.

Barnes, David M., and Ilan H. Meyer. "Religious Affiliation, Internalised Homophobia, and Mental Health in Lesbians, Gay Men, and Bisexuals." *The American Journal of Orthopsychiatry* 82, no. 4 (2012) 505-515. https://doi.org/10.1111/j.1939-0025.2012.01185.x

Barnes, Haleigh A., Robin A. Hurley, and Katherine H. Taber. "Moral Injury and PTSD: Often Co-Occurring Yet Mechanistically Different." *The Journal of Neuropsychiatry and Clinical Neurosciences* 31, no.2 (2019). https://doi.org/10.1176/appi.neuropsych.19020036

Barns, Greg. *The Rise of the Right: The War on Australia's Liberal Values*. Melbourne: Hardie Grant, 2019.

Bauer, Paul F. "The Homosexual Subculture at Worship: A Participant Observation Study." *Pastoral Psychology* 25, no. 2 (1976) 115-127. https://doi.org/10.1007/BF01759854.

Beard, Matthew. "Conceptual Distinctions." In *Moral Injury: Unseen Wounds in an Age of Barbarism*, edited by Tom R Frame, 112-125. Sydney: University of New South Wales Press, 2015.

Beck, Brian E. "Connexion and Koinonia." In *Rethinking Wesley's Theology for Contemporary Methodism*, edited by Randy L. Maddox, 129-142. Nashville: Kingswood/Abingdon, 1998.

Billboard. "Anita Bryant." *Billboard.com*. Accessed 5 July 2023. https://www.billboard.com/artist/anita-bryant/

Bishop, Meg D., Jessica N. Fish, Phillip L. Hammack and Stephen T. Russell. "Sexual Identity Milestones in Three Generations of Sexual Minority People: A National Probability Sample." *Developmental Psychology* 56, no. 11 (2020) 2177-2193. https://psycnet.apa.org/record/2020-62500-001?doi=1

Blackmore, Neil. *Radical Love*. London: Hutchinson Heinemann, 2023.

Blumberg, Daniel M. "What Should Clinicians Who Care for Police Officers Know About Moral Injury?" *AMA Journal of Ethics* 24, no. 2 (2022) 126-132. https://doi.org/10.1001/amajethics.2022.126

Boggan Dreff, Ashley. *Entangled: A History of American Methodism, Politics and Sexuality*. Nashville: New Room, 2018.

Bolz-Weber, Nadia. *Pastrix: The Cranky, Beautiful Faith of a Sinner & Saint*. New York: Worthy, 2013.

Bongiorno, Frank. *Dreamers and Schemers: A political history of Australia*. Collingwood: La Trobe University Press, 2022.

Booth, William. *In Darkest England and the Way Out*. London: The International Headquarters of The Salvation Army, 1984 [1890].

Boswell, John. *Christianity, Social Tolerance and Homosexuality: Gay People in Western Europe from the Beginning of the Christian Era to the Fourteenth Century*. Chicago: University of Chicago Press, 2009.

———. "Logos and Biography." In *Theology and Sexuality: Classic and Contemporary Readings*, edited by Eugene F. Rogers Jr., 359-361. Malden, MA: Blackwell, 2002.

———. *Same-Sex Unions in Pre-Modern Europe*. New York: Harper Collins, 1994.

Bouma, Gary D. and Anna Halafoff. "Australia's Changing Religious Profile—Rising Nones and Pentecostals, Declining British Protestants in Superdiversity: Views from the 2016 Census." *Journal for the Academic Study of Religion* 20, no. 2 (2017) 127-143. https://journal.equinoxpub.com/JASR/article/view/2089/1974.

Bowean, Lolly and Monica Eng. "Salvation Army Denies Being Anti-Gay." *chicagotribune.com*, 1 December 2012, https://www.chicagotribune.com/news/ct-xpm-2012-12-01-ct-met-salvation-army-20121201-story.html.

Bristow, Joseph. "Remapping the Sites of Modern Gay History: Legal Reform, Medico-Legal Thought, Homosexual Scandal, Erotic Geography." *Journal of British Studies* 46, no.1 (January 2007) 116-142. https://doi-org.divinity.idm.oclc.org/10.1086/508401.

Bronson, James V. *Bible, Gender, Sexuality: Reframing the Church's Debate on Same-Sex Relationships*. Grand Rapids: William B Eerdmans, 2012.

Brumbaugh-Johnson, Stacey M. and Kathleen E. Hull. "Coming Out as Transgender: Navigating the Social Implications of a Transgender Identity." *Journal of Homosexuality* (27 July 2018) 1-30. DOI: 10.1080/00918369.2018.1493253.

Bruni, Frank and Elizabeth Becker. "Charity Is Told It Must Abide by Antidiscrimination Laws." *The New York Times*, 11 July 2001, https://www.nytimes.com/2001/07/11/us/charity-is-told-it-must-abide-by-antidiscrimination-laws.html

Bryan, AnnaBelle O., Craig J. Bryan, Chad E. Morrow, Neysa Etienne and Bobbie Ray-Sannerud. "Moral Injury, Suicidal Ideation, and Suicide Attempts in a Military Sample." *Traumatology* 20, no. 3 (2014) 154-160. https://doi.org/10.1037/h0099852.

Bryman, Alan. *Social Research Methods*. Oxford: Oxford University Press, 2004 (2001).

Budoo-Scholtz, Ashwanee. *Ugandan President Signs Repressive Anti-LGBT Law: New Law Violates Fundamental Rights*. Human Rights Watch, 30 May 2023, accessed 8 July 2023, https://www.hrw.org/news/2023/05/30/ugandas-president-signs-repressive-anti-lgbt-law

Burack, Cynthia. "From Heterosexuality to Holiness: Psychoanalysis and Ex-Gay Ministries." *Journal for the Psychoanalysis, Culture and Society* 20, no. 3 (September 2015) 220-227. https://doi.org/10.1057/pcs.2015.25.

Burger, Ariel. *Witness: Lessons From Elie Wiesel's Classroom*. Boston: Houghton Mufflin Harcourt, 2018.

"Calling, Vocation." In *Dictionary of Biblical Imagery*, edited by Leland Ryken, James C. Wilhoit and Tremper Longman III, 133-134. Downers Grove, IL: Intervarsity, 1998.

Cameron, Helen, Deborah Bhatti, Catherine Duce, James Sweeney, and Clare Watkins. *Talking about God in Practice: Theological Action Research and Practical Theology*. London: SCM, 2010.

Carden, Michael. "Genesis." in *Queer Bible Commentary, Second Edition*, edited by Mona West and Robert E. Shore-Goss, 3-42. London: SCM, 2022.

Carder, Kenneth L. "What Difference Does Knowing Wesley Make?" In *Rethinking Wesley's Theology for Contemporary Methodism*, edited by Randy L. Maddox, 20-34. Nashville: Kingswood/Abingdon, 1998.

Carey, Lindsay B., and Timothy J. Hodgson. "Chaplaincy, Spiritual Care and Moral Injury: Considerations Regarding Screening and Treatment." *Frontiers in Psychiatry* 9, no. 619 (2018). https://doi.org/10.3389/fpsyt.2018.00619.

Carlisle, Erin, and Lou Withers Green. *"There Was Nothing to Fix": LGBT+ Survivors' Experiences of Conversion Practice*. London: Galop, 2022.

Carlström, Charlotta. "Tensions, Power, and Commitment: LGBTQ and Swedish Free Churches." *Lambda Nordica* 27, no. 2 (2022) 17-40. https://doi.org/10.34041/ln.v27.787.

Cavanagh, David. "The Wesleyan Roots of The Salvation Army's Holistic Mission." Academia.edu. Accessed 25 May 2024. https://www.academia.edu/29592932/The_Wesleyan_Roots_of_The_Salvation_Armys_holistic_mission?email_work_card=view-paper

Cenkner, D. P., Yeomans, P. D., Antal, C. J., and Scott, J. C. "A Pilot Study of a Moral Injury Group Intervention Co-Facilitated by a Chaplain and Psychologist." *Journal of Traumatic Stress* 34.2 (2021) 367–374. https://doi.org/10.1002/jts.22642

Chaves, Mark. *Ordaining Women: Culture and Conflict in Religious Organizations*. Cambridge, MA: Harvard University Press, 1997.

Cheng, Patrick S. *From Sin to Amazing Grace*. New York: Seabury, 2012.

———. "Galatians." In *The Queer Bible Commentary*, edited by Deryn Guest, Robert E. Goss, Mona West and Thomas Bohache, 624-629. London: SCM, 2006.

———. *Rainbow Theology: Bridging Race, Sexuality and Spirit*. New York: Seabury, 2013.

Claassens, Julianna. "Resilience in the Book of Jonah: Surviving the Unsurvivable." Presented online, Charles Sturt University Research Seminar, 1 February 2024.

Clark, Timothy R. *The 4 Stages of Psychological Safety: Defining the Path to Inclusion and Innovation*. Oakland, CA: Berrett-Koehler Publishers, 2020.

Clifton, Shaw. "An Ugly Intruder Called Sin." In *The Salvationist Lifestyle*. Edited by John D. Waldron. New York: The Salvation Army USA Eastern Territory, 1989.

Cole, Carolyn and Helen Wilson Harris. "The Lived Experiences of People Who Identify as LGBT Christians: Considerations for Social Work Helping." *Social Work and Christianity* 44, no. 1 (Spring 2017) 31-52. https://www.proquest.com/scholarly-journals/lived-experiences-people-who-identify-as-lgbt/docview/1879491892/se-2.

Collins, Kenneth J. *The Theology of John Wesley: Holy Love and the Shape of Grace*, 2nd edition. Nashville: Abingdon, 2011.

Conley, Garrard. *Boy Erased*. London: William Collins, 2016.

Cook, Jacob Alan. *Worldview Theory, Whiteness, and the Future of Evangelical Faith*. Langham, MD: Lexington, 2021.

Costello, Jacqui. *Primer to Support IGADF Directed Discussions*. Randwick, NSW: Australian Defence Force, 1 Psych Unit, 2020.

Couch, Murray, Hunter Mulcare, Marian Pitts, Anthony Smith and Anne Mitchell. "The Religious Affiliation of Gay, Lesbian, Bisexual, Transgender and Intersex Australians: A Report from the Private Lives Survey." *People and Place* 16, no. 1 (2008) 1-11. https://doi.org/10.4225/03/590bfd60bd261.

Couchman, Adam. ""Not my Will but Yours Be Done": The Use of the Mercy Seat in Theodramatic Perspective." *Studia Liturgica* 51, no. 2 (2021) 217-229.

Cover, Rob, and Rosslyn Prosser. *Queer Memory and Storytelling: Gender and Sexuality-Diverse Identities and Trans-Media Narrative.* New York: Routledge, 2024.

Crowder Noricks, Jennifer. "The Rejected Calling." In *Why the Church of the Nazarene Should be Fully LGBTQ+ Affirming,* edited by Thomas J Oord and Alexa Oord, 29-34. Grassmere, ID: SacraSage, 2023.

D'Almada-Remedios, R. *Inclusion@Work Index 2023-2024: Mapping the State of Inclusion in the Australian Workforce.* Sydney: Diversity Council of Australia, 2024.

Danker, Ryan Nicholas. "Early Methodist Societies as an Embodied Politic: Intentionality and Community as a Wesleyan Political Vision." In *Exploring a Wesleyan Political Theology,* edited by Ryan Nicholas Danker, 47-66. Nashville: Wesley's Foundry, 2020.

Davis, Corwin Malcolm. "Kin/Folk: On Queer Models of Collective Beholding." *Theology and Sexuality* 29, no. 1 (January 2023) 67-81. https://doi.org/10.1080/13558358.2023.2264746.

DeFranza, Megan K. "Journeying from the Bible to Christian Ethics in the Search of Common Ground." In *Two Views on Homosexuality, the Bible and the Church.* Edited by Preston Sprinkle, 69-101. Grand Rapids: Zondervan, 2016.

Del Valle, Gabby. "Chick-Fil-A's Many Controversies, Explained." *Vox,* 19 November 2019, https://www.vox.com/the-goods/2019/5/29/18644354/chick-fil-a-anti-gay-donations-homophobia-dan-cathy.

Downie, Alison. "Christian Shame and Religious Trauma." In *Religions* 13, no. 10 (2022) 1-9. https://doi.org/10.3390/rel13100925.

Downs, Alan. *The Velvet Rage: Overcoming the Pain of Growing Up Gay in a Straight Man's World,* 2nd edition. New York: Hatchett, 2012.

Drescher, Jack, Ariel Shidlo and Michael Schroeder. *Sexual Conversion Therapy: Ethical, Clinical and Research Perspectives.* Boca Raton: CRC, 2002.

Dunlap, Andy. "Changes in Coming Out Milestones Across Five Age Cohorts." *Journal of Gay & Lesbian Social Services* 28, no. 1 (January 2016) 20-38. https://doi.org/10.1080/10538720.2016.1124351.

Duprelle, Pierre, Gabrielle Novacek, Jeff Linquist, Nathan Nicon, Simon Pellas and Glennda Testone. *A New LGBTQ Workforce Has Arrived – Inclusive Cultures Must Follow.* Boston: Boston Consulting Group, 2020.

Dursun, Sanela, and Kimberley Watkins. "Moral Injury: What We Know and What We Need to Know." *Military Behavioural Health* 6 (2018). https://doi.org/10.1080/21635781.2018.1454365.

Edman, Elizabeth M. *Queer Virtue: What LGBTQ People Know About Life and Love and How it Can Revitalize Christianity.* Boston: Beacon, 2016.

Edmondson, Amy, presenter. "Building a Psychologically Safe Workplace," 5 May 2014. TEDxHSGE, TEDx Talks YouTube Channel. https://www.youtube.com/watch?v=LhoLuui9gX8.

———. "Psychological Safety." Amy C. Edmondson, Accessed 4 September 2023. http://www.amycedmonson.com.

———. "Psychological Safety and Learning Behaviour in Work Teams." *Administrative Science Quarterly* 44, no.2 (1999) 350-383. https://doi.org/10.2307/2666999.

BIBLIOGRAPHY

Ellison, Christopher G. and Jinwoo Lee. "Spiritual Struggles and Psychological Distress: Is There a Dark Side of Religion?" *Social Indicators Research* 98, no. 3 (2010) 501-517. https://doi.org/10.1007/s11205-009-9553-3.

Enroth, Ronald M. and Gerald E. Jamieson. *The Gay Church*. Grand Rapids: Eerdmans, 1974.

Evans, W. R., Walser, R. D., Drescher, K. D., and Farnsworth, J. K. *The Moral Injury Workbook: Acceptance and Commitment Therapy Skills for Moving Beyond Shame, Anger, and Trauma to Reclaim Your Values*. New Harbinger Publications, 2020.

Ezzy, Douglas, Bronwyn Fielder and Angus McLeay. "LGBTQ+ Christians in Australia." *Social Compass* (19 June 2024). https://doi.org/10.1177/00377686241255648.

Faragher, Christine. "Challenging History and Telling Herstory: An Interdisciplinary Exploration of the Claims for Equality and Women's Lived Experiences of Officership in The Salvation Army." Doctor of Philosophy Thesis, University of Divinity, 2023.

Fidas, Deena, Liz Cooper and Jenna Raspanti. *The Cost of the Closet and the Rewards of Inclusion: Why the Workplace Environment for LGBT People Matters to Employers*. Washington DC: Humans Rights Campaign Foundation, 2014.

Field, David N. "The Unrealised Ethical Potential of the Methodist Theology of Prevenient Grace," *HTS Teologiese Studies / Theological Studies* 71, no. 1 (October 2015) 1-8. https://doi.org/10.4102/hts.v71i1.2987.

Fielder, Bronwyn and Douglas Ezzy. *Lesbian, Gay, Bisexual and Transgender Christians: Queer Christians, Authentic Selves*. London: Bloomsbury Academic, 2018.

———. "Religious Freedom for Whom? How Conservative Christianity Erodes the Religious Freedom of Those it Seeks to Discriminate Against." In *Australian Journal of Political Science* (2023). https://doi.org/10.1080/10361146.2023.2283005.

Fingerhut, Adam. "Straight Allies: What Predicts Heterosexuals' Alliance With the LGBT Community?" *Journal of Applied Social Psychology* 41, no. 9 (September 2011) 2230-2248. https://doi.org/10.1111/j.1559-1816.2011.00807.x.

Fisk, Forest. "God's Creative Diversity." In *Why the Church of the Nazarene Should Be Fully LGBTQ+ Affirming*. Edited by Thomas Jay and Alexa Oord, 419-423. Grasmere, ID: SacraSage, 2023.

Fize, William. "The Homosexual Exception? The Case of the Labouchere Amendment." *Cahiers Victoriens et Édouardiens* 91 (Spring 2020). https://doi.org/10.4000/cve.7597.

Focus on the Family. "Sexuality." Accessed 5 July 2023. https://www.focusonthefamily.com/topic/get-help/sexuality/.

Forrest, Julie. "A Personal Reflection on the International Symposium on Human Sexuality." *The Officer*, January-March 2023, pp. 20-24.

Fossey, Ellie, Carol Harvey, Fiona McDermott, and Larry Davidson. "Understanding and Evaluating Qualitative Research." *Australian & New Zealand Journal of Psychiatry* 36, no. 6 (2002) 717-732. doi:10.1046/j.1440-1614.2002.01100.x.

Foucault, Michel. *The History of Sexuality – Volume 1*. Translated by Robert Hurley. New York: Pantheon, 1978 [1976].

Frame, Tom R. *Moral Injury: Unseen Wounds in an Age of Barbarism*. Sydney: University of New South Wales Press, 2015.

Fricker, Miranda. *Epistemic Injustice*. Oxford: Clarendon, 2007.

Gagnon, Robert. *The Bible and Homosexual Practice: Texts and Hermeneutics*. Nashville: Abingdon, 2001.

Gandy-Guedes, Mandy, Kirsten Havig, Anthony P. Natale and David A. McLeod. "Trauma Impacts on LGBTQ People: Implications for Lifespan Development." In *Social Work Practice with the LGBTQ Community: the Intersection of History, Health, Mental Health and Policy Factors*, edited by Michael P. Dentato, 118-136. New York: Oxford University Press, 2017.

Garton, Stephen. *Histories of Sexuality*. London: Acumen, 2004.

Gebhard, Paul H. "Incidence of Overt Homosexuality in the United States and Western Europe," In *National Institute of Mental Health Task Force on Homosexuality: Final Report and Background Papers*, edited by J. M. Livingood. Rockville, MD: National Institute of Mental Health, n.d., and quoted by the Kinsey Institute, *Diversity of Sexual Orientation*, Indiana University, 2023, accessed 4 July 2023, https://kinseyinstitute.org/research/publications/historical-report-diversity-of-sexual-orientation.php#Gebhard1972.

Gibbs, Jeremy J., and Jeremy T. Goldbach. "Religious Identity Dissonance: Understanding How Sexual Minority Adolescents Manage Antihomosexual Religious Messages." *Journal of Homosexuality* 68, no. 13 (2021) 2189–2213. https://pubmed.ncbi.nlm.nih.gov/32130085/.

Gibson, Bethany. "Included 2021: Changed Minds with Chick Yuill," 24 July 2021. Included Conference Presentation, Live Stream. https://www.youtube.com/watch?v=G62QokT3re4&list=PLTb2eDP3rt6Uzbght5z-aDsnY5HUM4EK1&t=2s.

Gibson, William, Joanne Bailey, and Joanne Begiato. *Sex and the Church in the Long Eighteenth Century : Religion, Enlightenment and the Sexual Revolution*. London: I.B. Tauris, 2019.

Goh Han Yan. "Parliament repeals Section 377A, endorses amendments protecting definition of marriage." *Straits Times* (Singapore), 29 November 2022. https://www.straitstimes.com/singapore/politics/parliament-repeals-section-377a-endorses-amendments-protecting-marriage-definition.

Goh, Joseph N. "From Polluted to Prophetic Bodies: Theo-Pastoral Lessons from the Lived Experiences of Gay, HIV-Positive Christian Men in Singapore." *Practical Theology* 10, no. 2, 133–146. https://doi.org/10.1080/1756073X.2017.1296240.

Gordon Earle, Carrie. *A Grassroots Guide to Protecting Your Community from Pornography*. Colorado Springs: Focus on the Family, n.d.

Gorman, E. Michael. "A New Light on Zion: A Study of Three Homosexual Religious Congregations in Urban America." Doctor of Philosophy, University of Chicago, 1980.

Goss, Robert E. "Luke." In *The Queer Bible Commentary*, edited by Deryn Guest, Robert E. Goss, Mona West and Thomas Bohache, 527-546. London: SCM, 2006.

Grey, Matt J., Yonit Schorr, William Nash, Leslie Lebowitz, Amy Amidon, Amy Lansing, Melissa Maglione, Ariel J. Lang and Brett T. Litz. "Adaptive Disclosure: An Open Trial of a Novel Exposure-Based Intervention for Service Members with Combat-Related Psychological Stress Injuries." *Behavioural Therapy* 43, no. 2 (June 2012) 407-15. https://doi.org/10.1016/j.beth.2011.09.001.

Grimsley, C. W., and G. Grimsley. *PTSD and Moral Injury: The Journey to Healing Through Forgiveness*. Exulon Press, 2017.

Grow, Kory. "Ellie Goulding, Salvation Army Clash Over Gay Rights and Halftime Performance." *Rolling Stone*, 14 November 2019. https://www.rollingstone.com/music/music-news/ellie-goulding-salvation-army-gay-rights-912521/.

Gruenhage, Jordan. "Internalized Homophobia: Where It Comes From & What You Can Do About It Today." The Centre for Gay Counselling, 2020. https://www.centreforgaycounselling.com/2020/11/21/internalized-homophobia/.

Guidi, Jenny, Marcella Lucente, Nicoletta Sonino, and Giovanni A. Favre. "Allostatic Load and Its Impact on Health: A Systematic Review." *Psychotherapy and psychosomatics* 90, no. 1 (2021) 11-27. doi:10.1159/000510696.

Guinness, Jack. "Introduction." In *The Queer Bible*, edited by Jack Guinness, 8-9. London: Harper Collins, 2021.

Gushee, David P. *After Evangelicalism: The Path to a New Christianity*. Louisville, KY: Westminster John Knox, 2020.

———. *Changing Our Mind: Definitive 3rd Edition of the Landmark Call for Inclusion of LGBTQ Christians with Response to Critics*. Canton, MI: David Crumm, 2017.

Haigt, Wendy, Erin Sugrue, Molly Cahoun and James Black. "'Basically, I Look At It Like Combat': Reflections on Moral Injury by Parents Involved with Child Protection Services." *Children and Youth Services Review* 82 (November 2017) 477-489. https://doi.org/10.1016/j.childyouth.2017.10.009.

Haldeman, Douglas C. "Therapeutic Antidotes: Helping Gay and Bisexual Men Recover from Conversion Therapies." *Journal of Gay & Lesbian Psychotherapy* 5, no. 3 (2002) 117 – 130. https://psycnet.apa.org/doi/10.1300/J236v05n03_08.

———. "When Sexual and Religious Orientations Collide: Considerations in Working with Same-Sex Attracted Male Clients." *The Counselling Psychologist* 32, no.5 (2004) 691-715. https://doi.org/10.1177/0011000004267560.

Halliday, Kristopher J. "A Reflection on Calling: Making Sense of Scripture and The Salvation Army as a Gay Person Called to Officership." Thought Matters Conference 2014, The Salvation Army New Zealand, Fiji and Tonga Territory. Included.page, Accessed 14 September 2024. https://includedpage.com/Testimony—-Reflection.html.

———. "Changing Attitudes, Orders and Regulations: Assessing Grassroots Activism and the Let's Talk Process in The Salvation Army in Regard to Same Sex Relationships." Master of Arts (Leadership) Thesis, Sydney College of Divinity, 2021.

Hanekom, Johannes C. "Internalised Homophobia: Correlations with Depression, Anxiety, Suicidal Ideation and Coming Out Age in the Gay, Lesbian, and Bisexual Community of Aotearoa New Zealand." Master of Health Science in Psychology Dissertation, Auckland University of Technology, 2021.

Hardy, Janet W., and Dossie Easton. *The Ethical Slut: A Practical Guide to Polyamory, Open Relationships and Other Freedoms in Sex and Love*. New York: Clarkson Potter, 2017.

Harper, Steve. *For the Sake of the Bride*. Nashville: Abingdon, 2014.

———. *Holy Love: A Biblical Theology for Human Sexuality*. Nashville: Abingdon, 2019.

Harris, J Irene, Stephen W Cook, and Susan Kashubeck-West. "Religious Attitudes, Internalized Homophobia, and Identity in Gay and Lesbian Adults." *Journal of Gay & Lesbian Mental Health* 12, no.3 (2008) 205-225. https://www.tandfonline.com/doi/pdf/10.1080/19359700802111452.

BIBLIOGRAPHY

Harris, J. I., Erbes, C. R., Engdahl, B. E., Thuras, P., Murray-Swank, N., Grace, D., Ogden, H., Olson, R. H., Winskowski, A. M., Bacon, R., & Malec, C. "The effectiveness of a trauma focused spiritually integrated intervention for veterans exposed to trauma." *Journal of Clinical Psychology* 67.4 (2011) 425–438. https://doi.org/10.1002/jclp.20777.

Harris, J. I., Usset, T., Voecks, C., Thuras, P., Currier, J., & Erbes, C. "Spiritually integrated care for PTSD: A randomized controlled trial of 'Building Spiritual Strength.'" *Psychiatry Research* 267 (2018) 420–428. https://doi.org/10.1016/j.psychres.2018.06.045.

Hayes, S. C., Strosahl, K. D., and Wilson, K. G. *Acceptance and Commitment Therapy: The Process and Practice of Mindful Change*. New York: Guilford, 2011.

Hays, Christopher B. and Richard B. Hays. *The Widening of God's Mercy: Sexuality Within the Biblical Story*. New Haven: Yale University Press, 2024.

Hays, Richard B. *The Moral Vision of the New Testament: Community, Cross, New Creation, A Contemporary Introduction to New Testament Ethics*. New York: Harper One, 1996.

Headstart. "LGBTQ+ in the Workplace: Supporting Authenticity." Headstart. Accessed 28 July 2021. https://www.headstart.io/insights/lgbtq-in-the-workplace/.

Hearon, Holly E. "1 and 2 Corinthians." In *The Queer Bible Commentary*, edited by Deryn Guest, Robert E. Goss, Mona West and Thomas Bohache, 606-623. London: SCM, 2006.

Heasley, Christian and Stacy A. Jacob. "The Experiences of LGBTQ+ Christians in a Support Group and Implications for Practitioners." *Growth: The Journal of the Association for Christians in Student Development* 20, no. 2 (2021) 38-50. https://pillars.taylor.edu/acsd_growth/vol20/iss20/4.

Held, P., Klassen, B. J., Brennan, M. B., and Zalta, A. K. "Using Prolonged Exposure and Cognitive Processing Therapy to Treat Veterans with Moral Injury-Based PTSD: Two Case Examples." *Cognitive and Behavioral Practice* 25.3 (2018) 377–390. https://doi.org/10.1016/j.cbpra.2017.09.003.

Hensman, Savitri. "The Church of England, Same-Sex Love, State and Society." *Ekklesia*, 7 (February 2023). Accessed 24 February 2024. https://www.ekklesia.co.uk/2023/02/07/13570/.

Hentzschel, Garth. "The Army on the Big Screen Part 2." *Pipeline* 20, no. 9 (2016).

Herben, Jeroen. "Working Towards a More Inclusive Salvation Army." Bachelor of Pastoral Care and Psychology Thesis. William Booth College and NCC Havering College, 2021.

Herman, Judith L. *Truth and Repair: How Trauma Survivors Envisage Justice*. London: Basic, 2023.

Higgins, Isabella. "Push to Outlaw Gay Conversion Therapy in the US Should be Mirrored in Australia, Gay Rights Group Says." *The World Today*, ABC, 27 July 2015. https://www.abc.net.au/news/2015-07-27/harmful-gay-conversion-therapy-should-be-banned-rights-group/6651078.

Hill, Harold. *Saved to Save and Saved to Serve: Perspectives on Salvation Army History*. Eugene, OR: Resource, 2017.

Hill, Wesley. "Christ, Scripture and Spiritual Friendship." In *Two Views on Homosexuality, the Bible and the Church*, edited by Preston Sprinkle, 124-147. Grand Rapids: Zondervan, 2016.

Hillier, Lynne, Anne Mitchell, and Hunter Mulcare. "I Couldn't Do Both at the Same Time: Same-Sex Attracted Youth and the Negotiation of Religious Discourse." *Gay and Lesbian Issues and Psychology Review* 4, no. 2 (2008) 81-93. https://www.academia.edu/24836713/I_Couldnt_Do_Both_at_the_Same_Time_Same_Sex_Attracted_Youth_and_the_Negotiation_of_Religious_Discourse.

Hofstien, Anver and Omer Sharvit. "Gay Conversion Therapy to Fix 'Reverse Inclinations' is Alive and Well in Israel." *Times of Israel.* 24 June 2020. https://www.timesofisrael.com/gay-conversion-therapy-to-fix-reverse-inclinations-is-alive-and-well-in-israel/.

Hoge, C. W., and Chard, K. M. "A Window into the Evolution of Trauma Focused Psychotherapies for Posttraumatic Stress Disorder." *Journal of the American Medical Association* 319.4 (2018) 343–345. https://doi.org/10.1001/jama.2017.21880.

Hollier, Joel, Shane Clifton and Jennifer Smith-Merry. "Mechanisms of Religious Trauma Amongst Queer People in Australia's Evangelical Churches." *Clinical Social Work Journal* 50, no. 3 (2022) 275-285. https://doi.org/10.1007/s10615-022-00839-x.

Hollier, Joel. *Religious Trauma, Queer Identities: Mapping the Complexities of Being LGBTQA+ in Evangelical Churches.* Sydney: Palgrave Macmillan, 2023.

Holmes, Stephen R. "Listening to the Past and Reflecting on the Present." In, *Two Views on Homosexuality, the Bible and the Church.* Edited by Preston Sprinkle, 166-193. Grand Rapids: Zondervan, 2016.

Hooker, Evelyn. "The Adjustment of the Male Overt Homosexual." *Journal of Projective Techniques* 21, no. 1 (1957) 18-31. https://doi.org/10.1080/08853126.1957.10380742.

Hoy, Seth. "NYC Commission on Human Rights Charges Four Substance Abuse Centers with Discriminatory Intake Policies for Transgender Patients." New York City Commission on Human Rights, 13 July 2017. https://www1.nyc.gov/assets/cchr/downloads/pdf/press-releases/Press%20Release%20-%20Substance%20Abuse%20Centers%20FINAL.pdf.

Hudson, David. "Salvation Army Commander: Yes, We Are Faith-Based Charity. But We Serve and Love Everyone." *USA Today*, Gannett Satellite Information Network, 22 November 2019. https://www.usatoday.com/story/opinion/voices/2019/11/22/salvation-army-lgbt-backlash-poverty-gay-marriage-column/4269694002/.

Hunt, Mary E., presenter. "Working Together: Feminist and Queer Theologies in Conversation." 4 June 2024, Future Church Pride Series, Online (Zoom).

Hurley, E. C. "Effective Treatment of Veterans with PTSD: Comparison Between Intensive Daily and Weekly EMDR Approaches." *Frontiers in Psychology* 9 (2018) 1458. https://doi.org/10.3389/fpsyg.2018.01458.

Igartua, Karine J., Kathryn Gill and Richard Montoro. "Internalised Homophobia: A Factor in Depression, Anxiety, and Suicide in the Gay and Lesbian Population." *Canadian Journal of Mental Health* 22, no.2 (September 2003) 15-30. https://doi.org/10.7870/cjcmh-2003-0011.

Included. "Included: Connected," 24 July 2021. Webinar. http://www.includedpage.com.

Izard, Carroll E. *Human Emotions.* New York, Plenum: 1977.

Jennings, Mark. *Happy: LGBTQ+ Experiences of Australian Pentecostal-Charismatic Christianity.* Perth: Palgrave Macmillan, 2023.

———. "'My Whole Life Was the Two Suburbs that Surrounded the Church': LGBTQ+ Participation in Australian Pentecostal-Charismatic Churches as 'Greedy Institutions.'" *Sociology of Religion*, srae034 (2024). https://doi.org/10.1093/socrel/srae034.
———. "Reading Scripture as a Discursive Fight to the Death: The Bible and the Battle Over the Truth of Sex and Sexuality." Presentation, University of Divinity Research Day, Melbourne, 5 June 2024.
Johnston, Kenny R. "For the Love of God: Knowing, Certainty, and John Wesley's Vision for Holy Love." *Wesleyan Theology Journal* 57, no. 2 (2022) 108-131.
Jones, Timothy W., Tiffany M. Jones, Jennifer Power, Nathan Despott and Maria Pallotta-Chiarolli. *Healing Spiritual Harms: Supporting Recovery from LGBTQA+ Change and Suppression Practices*. Melbourne: The Australian Research Centre in Sex, Health and Society, La Trobe University, 2021.
Jones, Timothy W., Jennifer Power, Tiffany Jones, Joel Anderson, Nathan Despott, Maria Pallotta-Chiarolli, Percy Gurtler and Christine Migliorini. "Improving Spiritual Health Care for LGBTQA+ Australians: Beyond Conversion Practices." Community Report. Melbourne: La Trobe University, 2024.
Jones, Timothy W., Anna Brown, Lee Carnie, Gillian Fletcher, and William Leonard. *Preventing Harm, Promoting Justice: Responding to LGBT Conversion Therapy in Australia*. Melbourne: La Trobe University and the Human Rights Law Centre, 2018.
Jones, Timothy W., Jennifer Power, and Tiffany M. Jones. "Religious Trauma and Moral Injury from LGBTQA+ Conversion Practices." *Social Science & Medicine* 305 (July 2022) 1-9. https://doi.org/10.1016/j.socscimed.2022.115040.
Jones, Timothy. "The Stained Glass Closet: Celibacy and Homosexuality in the Church of England to 1955." *Journal of the History of Sexuality* 20, no.1 (January 2011). https://link.gale.com/apps/doc/A247037122/PPWH?u=61_ud&sid=bookmark-PPWH&xid=301cd1do.
Jordan, Mark D. *The Invention of Sodomy in Christian Theology*. Chicago: University of Chicago Press, 1997.
Kayrooz, Carole and Chris Trevitt. *Research in Organisations and Communities: Tales from the Read World*. Sydney: Allen & Unwin, 2005.
Keane, Christopher. *What Some of You Were*. Kingsford, NSW: Matthias, 2001.
Kearns, Shannon T. L. *In the Margins: A Transgender Man's Journey with Scripture*. Grand Rapids: William B. Eerdmans, 2022.
Kelly, Michael Bernard. *Christian Mysticism's Queer Flame: Spirituality in the Lives of Gay Men*. New York: Routledge, 2019.
Keltner, Dacher, and Lee Anne Hacker. "The Forms and Functions of the Non-Verbal Function of Shame." In *Shame: Interpersonal Behavior, Psychopathology, and Culture*, edited by Paul Gilbert and Bernice Andrews, 78-98. Oxford: Oxford University Press, 1998.
Killick, David. "Sick Work Environment: Union Survey Slates Government Department." *The Mercury* (Hobart), 17 December 2020: 9.
Kimball, Dan. *They Like Jesus but not the Church: Insights from Emerging Generations*. Grand Rapids, MI: Zondervan, 2007.
Kinsey, Alfred Charles, Wardell Baxter Pomeroy, and Clyde Eugene Martin. *Sexual Behaviour in the Human Male*. Philadelphia: W.B. Saunders, 1948.

Kinsey Institute. *Diversity of Sexual Orientation*. Indiana University. 2023, accessed 4 July 2023. https://kinseyinstitute.org/research/publications/historical-report-diversity-of-sexual-orientation.php#Gebhard1972.

Kleinbaum, Sharon. "A Word to the Bullies." In *Great LGBTQ+ Speeches: Empowering Voices That Engage and Inspire*, edited by Tea Uglow, 102-105. London: White Lion, 2020.

Knott, Kim. "Inside, Outside and the Space In-Between: Territories and Boundaries in the Study of Religion." *Temenos – Nordic Journal of Comparative Religion* 44, no.1 (2008) 41-66. https://www.researchgate.net/publication/290584678_Inside_Outside_and_the_Space_in-between_Territories_and_Boundaries_in_the_Study_of_Religion.

Koenig, Harold and Faten Al Zaben. "Moral Injury: An Increasingly Recognized and Widespread Syndrome." *Journal of Religion and Health* 60, no. 5 (October 2021) 2989-3011. https://doi.org/10.1007/s10943-021-01328-0.

Koenig, Harold, Donna Ames, and Michelle Pearce. *Religion and Recovery from PTSD*. London: Jessica Kingsley, 2019.

Koenig, H. G., Boucher, N. A., Oliver, R. J. P., Youssef, N., Mooney, S. R., Currier, J. M., and Pearce, M. "Rationale for Spiritually Oriented Cognitive Processing Therapy for Moral Injury in Active Duty Military and Veterans with Posttraumatic Stress Disorder." *Journal of Nervous and Mental Disease* 205.2 (2017) 147–153. https://doi.org/10.1097/NMD.0000000000000554.

Koenig, H. G., Pearce, M. J., Nelson, B., Shaw, S. F., Robins, C. J., Daher, N. S., Cohen, H. J., Berk, L. S., Bellinger, D. L., Pargament, K. I., and King, M. B. "Religious vs. Conventional Cognitive Behavioral Therapy for Major Depression in Persons with Chronic Medical Illness: A Pilot Randomized Trial." *Journal of Nervous and Mental Disease* 203.4 (2015) 243–251. https://doi.org/10.1097/NMD.0000000000000273.

Kopacz, M. S., Connery, A. L., Bishop, T. M., Bryan, C. J., Drescher, K. D., Currier, J. M., and Pigeon, W. R. "Moral Injury: A New Challenge for Complementary and Alternative Medicine." *Complementary Therapies in Medicine*, 24 (2016) 29–33. https://doi.org/10.1016/j.ctim.2015.11.003.

Kort, Joe. "How Therapists Often Fail Their LGBTQ Clients: LGBTQ-friendly is not the same as LGBTQ-informed." *Psychology Today*, 30 August 2018. https://www.psychologytoday.com/ca/blog/understanding-the-erotic-code/201808/how-therapists-often-fail-their-lgbtq-clients.

Kosakowski, Jack. "Chick-Fil-A Foundation Announces 2020 Priorities to Address Education, Homelessness, Hunger." *The Chicken Wire*, Chick-Fil-A, 18 November 2019. https://thechickenwire.chick-fil-a.com/news/chick-fil-a-foundation-announces-2020-priorities

Koziol, Michael. "Sydney Anglicans Say Same-Sex Desire 'an Inclination Toward Evil.'" *Sydney Morning Herald*, 17 August 2023. https://www.smh.com.au/national/nsw/sydney-anglicans-say-same-sex-desire-an-inclination-toward-evil-20230816-p5dx10.html.

Kuefler, Matthew. "Homoeroticism in Antiquity and the Middle Ages." *American Historical Review* 123, no. 4 (October 2018) 1246-1266. https://doi.org/10.1093/ahr/rhy023.

Kvale, Steinar and Svend Brinkman. *InterViews: Learning the Craft of Qualitative Research Interviewing*, 2nd edition. Thousand Oaks, CA: Sage, 2009.

LaHaye, Tim. *The Unhappy Gays: What everyone should know about homosexuality*. Carol Stream, IL: Tyndale House, 1978.
LeClerc, Diane. *Rediscovering Christian Holiness: The Heart of Wesleyan-Holiness Theology*. Kansas City: Beacon Hill, 2010.
Lee, Hyemin, Don Operario, Horim Yi, Sungsub Choo and Seung-Sup Kim. "Internalised Homophobia, Depressive Symptoms, and Suicidal Ideation Among Lesbian, Gay, and Bisexual Adults in South Korea: An Age Stratified Analysis." *LGBT Health* 6, no. 8 (November 2019) 393-399. DOI: 10.1089/lgbt.2019.0108.
Lee, Justin. *Torn: Rescuing the Gospel from the Gays-vs.-Christians Debate*. New York: Jericho, 2012.
Lee, L. J. *Moral Injury Reconciliation: A Practitioner's Guide for Treating Moral Injury, PTSD, Grief and Military Sexual Trauma Through Spiritual Formation*. Jessica Kingsley, 2018.
Lee, Raymond M. *Doing Research on Sensitive Topics*. London: Sage, 1995.
Lemmy, Huw and Ben Miller. *Bad Gays: A Homosexual History*. London: Verso, 2022.
LGBTIQ+ Health Australia. *Snapshot of Mental Health and Suicide Prevention Statistics for LGBTIQ+ People*. Sydney: LGBTIQ+ Health Australia, 2021.
Liamputtong, Pranee and Douglas Ezzy. *Qualitative Research Methods*, 2nd edition. South Melbourne: Oxford University Press, 2005.
Litz, Brett T., Ateka A. Contractor, Charla Rhodes, Katherine A. Dondanville, Alexander H. Jordan, Patricia A. Resick, Edna B. Goa, Stacey Young-McCaughan, Jim Mintz, Jeffrey S. Yarvis and Alan L. Peterson. "Distinct Trauma Types in Military Service Members Seeking Treatment for Posttraumatic Stress Disorder." *Journal of Traumatic Stress* 31, no.2 (2018) 286-295. https://doi.org/10.1002/jts.22276.
Litz, B. T., Lebowitz, L., Gray, M. J., & Nash, W. P. *Adaptive disclosure: A New Treatment for Military Trauma, Loss, And Moral Injury*. Guilford Publications, 2017. https://link.springer.com/article/10.1007/s10943-021-01328-0#ref-CR55.
Litz, Brett T., Nathan Stein, Eileen Delaney, Lesley Lebowitz, William P Nash, Caroline Silva and Shira Maguen. "Moral Injury and Moral Repair in War Veterans: A Preliminary Model and Intervention Strategy." *Clinical Psychology Review* 29, no. 8 (December 2009) 695-706. https://doi.org/10.1016/j.cpr.2009.07.003.
Loader, William. *The New Testament on Sexuality*. Grand Rapids: William B Eerdmans, 2012.
Lynch, April and Manny Fernandez. "Salvation Army Cuts S.F. Programs / Charity Spurns City's Domestic Partner Law." *San Francisco Chronicle*, June 4 1998. https://www.sfgate.com/news/article/Salvation-Army-Cuts-S-F-Programs-Charity-3004997.php.
Macquiban, Tim. "Work on Earth and Rest in Heaven: Toward a Theology of Vocation in the Writings of Charles Wesley." In *Our Calling to Fulfill: Wesleyan Views of the Church in Mission*. Edited by M. Douglas Meeks, 47-70. Nashville: Kingswood, 2009.
Maddox, Marion. *God Under Howard*. Sydney: Allen & Unwin, 2005.
Maddox, Randy L. "Introduction." In *Rethinking Wesley's Theology for Contemporary Methodism*, edited by Randy L. Maddox, 13-19. Nashville: Kingswood/Abingdon, 1998.
———. *Responsible Grace: John Wesley's Practical Theology*. Nashville: Abingdon, 1994.

———. "Salvation as Flourishing for the Whole Creation: A Wesleyan Trajectory." In *Wesleyan Perspectives on Human Flourishing*, edited by Dean G. Smith and Rob A. Fringer, 1-23. Eugene, OR: Wipf and Stock, 2021.

———. "Wesleyan Theology and Moral Psychology Precedents for Continuing Engagement." In *Wesleyan Theology and Social Science: The Dance of Practical Divinity and Discovery*, edited by M. Kathryn Armistead, Brad D. Strawn and Ronald W. Wright, 7-19. Newcastle Upon Tyne: Cambridge Scholars Publishing, 2010.

Maguen, S., and K. Burkman. "Combat-Related Killing: Expanding Evidence-Based Treatments for PTSD." *Cognitive and Behavioral Practice* 20.4(2013) 476–479. https://doi.org/10.1016/j.cbpra.2013.05.003.

Maguen, S., Burkman, K., Madden, E., Dinh, J., Bosch, J., Keyser, J., Schmitz, M., and Neylan, T. C. "Impact of Killing in War: A Randomized, Controlled Pilot Trial." *Journal of Clinical Psychology* 73.9 (2017) 997–1012. https://doi.org/10.1002/jclp.22471.

Malyon, Alan K. "Psychotherapeutic Implications of Internalized Homophobia in Gay Men." *Journal of Homosexuality* 7, no. 2-3 (May 1982) 59-69. https://doi.org/10.1300/j082v07n02_08.

Mandimore, Francis M. *A Natural History of Homosexuality*. Baltimore: John Hopkins University Press, 1996.

Mantri, Sneha, Ye Kyung Song, Jennifer M. Lawson, Elizabeth J. Berger, and Harold G. Koenig. "Moral Injury and Burnout in Health Care Professionals During the COVID-19 Pandemic." *Journal of Nervous and Mental Disease* 209, no. 10 (October 2021) 720-726. https://doi.org/10.1097/nmd.0000000000001367.

Marquardt, Manfred. "Christian Conversion: Connecting our Lives with God," in *Rethinking Wesley's Theology for Contemporary Methodism*. Edited by Randy L. Maddox, 99-112. Nashville: Kingswood/Abingdon, 1998.

Marr, David. "The High Price of Heaven" (1999). Republished as "Shame and Forgiveness." In *Growing Up Queer in Australia*, edited by Benjamin Law, 6-9. Collingwood: Black Ink, 2019.

Martin, Dale B. *Sex and the Single Savior*. Louisville: Westminster John Knox, 2006.

Marzetti, Hazel, Lisa McDaid and Rory O'Connor. "'Am I Really Alive?': Understanding the Role of Homophobia, Biphobia and Transphobia in Young LGBT+ People's Suicidal Distress." *Social Science & Medicine* 298 (2022). https://doi.org/10.1016/j.socscimed.2022.114860.

Matthews, Hayley. "Ever, Honestly, Truly Me." In Journeys *in Grace and Truth: Revisiting Scripture and Sexuality*, edited by Jayne Ozanne, 39-46. London: Via Media, 2016.

Matty, Maria R. "Faith and Homosexuality: Grace, Religious Problem-Solving Styles and the Internalized Homophobia of Homosexuals." Honours Thesis, University of Tennessee, 2014. https://scholar.utc.edu/cgi/viewcontent.cgi?article=1003&context=honors-theses.

Mays, Vickie M., Robert-Paul Juster, Timothy J. Williamson, Teresa E. Seeman, and Susan D. Cochran. "Chronic Physiologic Effects of Stress Among Lesbian, Gay, and Bisexual Adults: Results from the National Health and Nutrition Examination Survey." *Psychosomatic medicine* 80, no. 6 (2018) 551-563.

McCarthy, Marjorie M. "An Exploration of Moral Injury as Experienced by Combat Veterans." Doctor of Psychology thesis, Antioch University, 2016.

McConnaughey, Jayne. *Trauma in the Pews: The Impact on Faith and Spiritual Practices.* Glendora, CA: Berry Powell, 2022.

McCormick, K. Steve. "See No-one as Other." In *Why the Church of the Nazarene Should Be Fully LGBTQ+ Affirming.* Edited by Thomas Jay and Alexa Oord, 379-386. Grasmere, ID: SacraSage, 2023.

McCrossin, Julie, host. "Rainbow People Welcome – Interview with Major Jenny Begent and Julie McCrossin," 9 April 2024, Julie McCrossin YouTube recordings. https://www.juliemccrossin.com/rainbow-people-welcome-interview-with-major-jenny-begent/.

McGeorge, Christi R., and Katelyn O. Coburn. "Approaches Mainline Protestant Pastors Use to Work with LGB People and Their Families: Implications for Family Therapists." *Journal of Feminist Family Therapy* 34, no. 3-4 (November 2022) 343-369. https://doi.org/10.1080/08952833.2022.2142410.

McLaren, Brian D. "Foreword." In David P. Gushee, *After Evangelicalism: The Path to a New Christianity,* xi-xiii. Louisville, KY: Westminster John Knox, 2020.

McLeay, Angus, Elenie Poulos, and Louise Richardson-Self. "The Shifting Christian Right Discourse on Religious Freedom in Australia." *Politics and Religion* 16, no. 2 (2023) 197–218. doi:10.1017/S1755048322000414.

McPherson, Timothy. "Not 'Prayed Away.'" *The Latitudinarian,* 05 August 2021 (Accessed 16 March 2024). http://latitudinarismus.blogspot.com/2021/08/.

Meeks, M. Douglas. *The Portion of the Poor: Good News to the Poor in the Wesleyan Tradition.* Nashville: Abingdon, 1995.

Meyer, Ilan H. "Prejudice, Social Stress, and Mental Health in Lesbian, Gay and Bisexual Populations: Conceptual Issues and Research Evidence." *Psychological Bulletin* 129, no. 5 (September 2003) 674-697. https://doi.org/10.1037/0033-2909.129.5.674.

Milar, Katharine. "The Myth Buster: Evelyn Hooker's Groundbreaking Research Exploded the Notion that Homosexuality was a Mental Illness, Ultimately Removing it from the DSM." *Monitor on Psychology (American Psychological Association)* 42, no. 2 (February 2011) 24. https://www.apa.org/monitor/2011/02/myth-buster.

Milne, Glen. "Emboldened Howard Set to Reshape Nation." *Sunday Telegraph* (Sydney), 10 October 2004.

Moon, Dawn, and Theresa Tobin. "Sunsets and Solidarity: Overcoming Sacramental Shame in Conservative Christian Churches to Forge a Queer Vision of Love and Justice." *Hypatia* 33, no. 3 (2018) 451-468. https://doi.org/10.1111/hypa.12413.

Moore, Mary E. M. "Trinity and Covenantal Ministry." In *Rethinking Wesley's Theology for Contemporary Methodism,* edited by Randy L. Maddox, 143-160. Nashville: Kingswood/Abingdon, 1998.

Moorman, Erin. "The Grace of Coming Out." In *Why the Church of the Nazarene Should be Fully LGBTQ+ Affirming.* Edited by Thomas Jay Oord and Alexa Oord, 25-28. Grassmere, ID: SacraSage, 2023.

"Moral Injury." National Centre for PTSD, Department of Veterans Affairs. Accessed 26 November 2020. https://www.ptsd.va.gov/professional/treat/cooccurring/moral_injury.asp.

Morantez, Danielle and John M Becker. "Fired by the Salvation Army for Being Bisexual." *Truth Wins Out,* 25 July 2012. https://truthwinsout.org/opinion/2012/07/27400/.

Nakashima Brock, Rita, and Gabriella Lettini. *Soul Repair: Recovering from Moral Injury After War*. Boston: Beacon, 2012.

Neitz, Mary Jo. "Insiders, Outsiders, Advocates and Apostates and the Religions They Study: Location and the Sociology of Religion." *Critical Research on Religion* 1, no. 20 (2013) 129-140. https://doi.org/10.1177/2050303213490311.

Newman, Alexander, Ross Donohue and Nathan Eva. "Psychological Safety: A Systematic Review of the Literature." *Human Resource Management Review* 27, no. 3 (2017) 521-535. https://doi.org/10.1016/j.hrmr.2017.01.001.

Nieuwsma, J., Walser, R. D., Farnsworth, J. K., Drescher, K. D., Meador, K. G., and Nash, W. "Possibilities Within Acceptance and Commitment Therapy for Approaching Moral Injury." *Current Psychiatry Reviews* 11.3 (2015) 193–206. https://doi.org/10.2174/1573400511666150629105234.

Nixon, David. "Voices Crying in the Wilderness? Theological Reflections on Queer Stories from Trainee Teachers." *Theology and Sexuality* 10, no. 1 (2003) 93-117. https://doi.org/10.1177/135583580301000107.

O'Brien, Glen. "'A Divine Attraction Between Your Soul and Mine': George Whitefield and Same-Sex Affection in 18th Century Methodism," *Pacifica* 30, no. 2 (2017) 177-192. https://doi.org/10.1177/1030570X17736326.

———. "'If We Cannot Think Alike, We May Love Alike': Can the Methodist Schism Over Queer Clergy and Same-Sex Marriage Yet be Healed?" *ABC Religion and Ethics*, 31 May 2024. https://www.abc.net.au/religion/methodist-schism-lgbtqi-sexuality-reality-of-queer-holiness/103920700.

O'Brien, Jodi. "Wrestling the Angel of Contradiction: Queer Christian Identities." *Culture and Religion* 5, no. 2 (February 2004) 179-202. https://doi.org/10.1080/143830042000225420.

Office of the Advocate for Children & Young People. *The Voices of LGBTQIA+ Young People in NSW*. NSW Parliamentary Joint Committee on Children and Young People. Sydney: Government of New South Wales, 2022. https://www.acyp.nsw.gov.au/lgbtqiareport.

Oliveto, Karen P. *Our Hearts Strangely Warmed: Coming Out into God's Call*. Nashville: Abingdon, 2018.

O'Neill George, Jennifer. "Moral Injury, Institutional Betrayal, and Psychological Contract Theory Breach in the Australian Army." Paper presented at the Brown Bag Seminar Series, University of Tasmania, Hobart, Tasmania, 2021.

Oord, Thomas Jay, guest. "God After Deconstruction," 14 July 2024. The Spiritual Misfits Podcast. https://www.buzzsprout.com/1925719/15395684.

———. *My Defense: Responding to Charges that I fully Affirm LGBTQ+ People*. Grassmere, ID: SacraSage, 2024.

Osinski, Keegan. *Queering Wesley: Queering the Church*. Eugene, OR: Cascade, 2021.

Pack, Karen, presenter. "The Future Church is LGBTQIA+ Inclusive." Spiritual Misfits Podcast, 25 January 2024. https://www.buzzsprout.com/1925719/15083653.

Parliament of Australia. *Hansard*. 19 March 2002, accessed 8 July 2023. https://parlinfo.aph.gov.au/parlInfo/search/display/display.w3p;db=CHAMBER;id=chamber%2Fhansards%2F2002-03-19%2F0045;query=Id%3A%22chamber%2Fhansards%2F2002-03-19%2F0024%22.

Parliament of the United Kingdom. "The Labouchere Amendment." 2023, accessed 22 May 2023. https://www.parliament.uk/about/living-heritage/transformingsociety/private-lives/relationships/collections1/sexual-offences-act-1967/1885-labouchere-amendment/#:~:text=This%20changed%20when%20Henry%20Labouchere,of%20%27gross%20indecency%27%20illegal.

Paul, L. A., Gros, D. F., Strachan, M., Worsham, G., Foa, E. B., and Acierno, R. "Prolonged Exposure for Guilt and Shame in a Veteran of Operation Iraqi Freedom." *American Journal of Psychotherapy* 68.3 (2014) 277–286. https://doi.org/10.1176/appi.psychotherapy.2014.68.3.277.

Pearce, M. J., Haynes, K., Rivera, N. R., and Koenig, H. G. "Spiritually-Integrated Cognitive Processing Therapy: A New Treatment for PTSD and Moral Injury." *Global Advances in Health and Medicine* 7 (2018) 1–7. https://doi.org/10.1177/2164956118759939.

Peddle, Brian. "Foreword from the General." In *International Symposium on Human Sexuality 2022: The Story of the Symposium*. Edited by Julie Forrest. London: The Salvation Army, 2022.

———. *Letter to Salvationists*. Available on Includedpage.com. https://includedpage.com/generals_letter.html

Pitt, Richard N. "'Killing the Messenger': Religious Black Gay Men's Neutralization of Anti-Gay Religious Messages." *Journal for the Scientific Study of Religion* 49, no. 1 (March 2010) 56–72. https://doi.org/10.1111/j.1468-5906.2009.01492.x.

Potts, Malcolm and Roger Short. *Ever Since Adam and Eve: The Evolution of Human Sexuality*. Cambridge: Cambridge University Press, 1999.

Preser, Ruth. "Things I Learned from the Book of Ruth: Diasporic Reading of Queer Conversions." In *De/Constituting Wholes: Towards Partiality Without Parts*, edited by Christopher F. E. Holzhey and Manuele Gragnolati, 47–65. Vienna: Turia & Kant, 2017. https://doi.org/10.37050/ci-11_03.

Punch, Julian. *Gay With God: The Life and Times of a Turbulent Priest*. Hobart: Self-Published, 2017.

Purcell, N., Burkman, K., Keyser, J., Fucella, P., and Maguen, S. "Healing from Moral Injury: A Qualitative Evaluation of the Impact of Killing Treatment for Combat Veterans." *Journal of Aggression, Maltreatment & Trauma* 27.6 (2018) 645–673. https://doi.org/10.1080/10926771.2018.1463582.

Rao, Rahul. "Re-Membering Mwanga: Same-Sex Intimacy, Memory and Belonging in Postcolonial Uganda." *Journal of Eastern African Studies* 9, no. 1 (2014) 1–19. doi: 10.1080/17531055.2014.970600.

Regele, Michael B. *Science, Scripture and Same-Sex Love*. Nashville: Abingdon, 2014.

Ring, Trudy. "'Former Gay, Trans Pastor Sy Rogers Dies, Memorialized by Right Wing." *The Advocate*, 22 April 2020. https://www.advocate.com/religion/2020/4/22/former-gay-trans-pastor-sy-young-dies-memorialized-right-wing.

Riseman, Noah. "Australia's History of LGBTI Politics and Rights." In *Oxford Research Encyclopedia of Politics*, ed. William R. Thompson, 1-24. Oxford University Press, 2019. https://doi.org/10.1093/acrefore/9780190228637.013.1260.

Riseman, Noah and Shirleene Robinson. *Pride in Defence: The Australian Military and LGBTI Service Since 1945*. Melbourne: Melbourne University Press, 2020.

Rivera, Bridget Eileen. *Heavy Burdens: Seven Ways LGBTQ Christians Experience Harm in the Church*. Grand Rapids, MI: Brazos, 2021.

Roberts, Campbell. "Rainbow Wellington and The Salvation Army Reach a Rapprochement: A Significant Step Forward." The Salvation Army New Zealand, Fiji, Tonga & Samoa Territory, May 2012. https://www.salvationarmy.org.nz/sites/default/files/uploads/_archive/file/May%202012%20-%20Rainbow%20and%20TSA%20joint%20release.pdf.

Robinson, Jennifer L., and Linda J. Rubin. "Homonegative Microaggressions and Posttraumatic Stress Symptoms." *Journal of Gay & Lesbian Mental Health* 20, no. 1 (2016) 57-69. https://doi.org/10.1080/19359705.2015.1066729.

Rosati, Fausta, Jessica Pistella, Maria Rosaria Nappa and Roberto Baiocco. "The Coming-Out Process in Family, Social and Religious Contexts Among Young, Middle, and Older Italian LGBQ+ Adults." *Frontiers in Psychology* 11 (December 2020). https://doi.org/10.3389/fpsyg.2020.617217.

Rowell, Jeren. *Thinking, Listening, Being: A Wesleyan Pastoral Theology*. Kansas City: Beacon Hill, 2014.

Runcorn, David. *Love Means Love: Same-sex Relationships and the Bible*. London: Society for Promoting Christian Knowledge, 2020.

Ryan, Caitlin. *Supportive Families, Healthy Children*. San Francisco: San Francisco State University, 2009.

Sahoo, Swapnajeet, Velprashanth Venkatesan, and Rahul Chakravarty. "'Coming Out'/Self-Disclosure in LGBTQ+ Adolescents and Youth: International and Indian Scenario - A Narrative Review of Published Studies in the Last Decade (2012-2022)." *Indian Journal of Psychiatry* 65, no. 10 (October 2023) 1012-1024. DOI: 10.4103/indianjpsychiatry.indianjpsychiatry_486_23.

"Same-Sex Attitude Survey." The Salvation Army New Zealand, Fiji, Tonga & Samoa Territory. 2014, republished online 4 June, 2018. https://www.salvationarmy.org.nz/same-sex-attitude-survey.

Satterlee, Allen. "The Mercy Seat." *War Cry* US Edition (May 2018). https://www.thewarcry.org/articles/mercy-seat/.

Schat, Sean, and Cathy Freytag. "What Can Christians Learn from Care Theory." In *How Then Shall We Care? A Christian Educator's Guide to Caring for Self, Learners, Colleagues and Community*, edited by Paul Shotsberger and Cathy Freytag, 1-16. Eugene, OR: Wipf and Stock, 2000.

Schuck, Kelly, and Becky Liddle. "Religious Conflicts Experienced by Lesbian, Gay and Bisexual Individuals." *Journal of Gay and Lesbian Psychotherapy* 5, no.2 (2001) 63-82. https://doi.org/10.1300/J236v05n02_07.

Severson, Eric R. "The Queerness of the Holy." In *Why the Church of the Nazarene Should be Fully LGBTQ+ Affirming*, ed. Thomas J Oord and Alexa Oord, 415-418. Grassmere, ID: SacraSage, 2023.

Shapiro, Francine, and Deany Laliotis. "EMDR Therapy for Trauma-Related Disorders." In *Evidence Based Treatments for Trauma-Related Psychological Disorders*, edited by Ulrich Schnyder and Marylène Cloitre, 205-228. Springer, 2015. https://doi.org/10.1007/978-3-319-07109-1_11.

Shay, Jonathan. "Learning About Combat Stress from Homer's Iliad." *Journal of Traumatic Stress* 4, no. 4 (1991). https://doi.org/10.1002/jts.2490040409.

Shidlo, Ariel and Michael Schroeder. "Changing Sexual Orientation: A Consumers' Report." *Professional Psychology: Research and Practice* 33, no. 3 (June 2002) 249-259. https://www.researchgate.net/publication/232515759_Changing_Sexual_Orientation_A_Consumers'_Report.

Small, Will. "Dr. David Gushee on Christian Humanism After Evangelicalism." Spiritual Misfits Podcast, 1 October 2022. Podtail, https://podtail.com/en/podcast/spiritual-misfits-podcast/dr-david-gushee-on-christian-humanism-after-evange/.

Söderblom, Kersten. *Queer-Affirming Pastoral Care*. Gottingen: Vandenhoeck and Ruprecht, 2024.

Solevåg, A. Rebecca. "The Salvation Army and Same-Sex Love." Included. Accessed 06 July 2024 (published 2020). https://includedpage.com/Research---Same-sex-love.html.

Spencer, J. Louis, Bruce E. Winston, Mihai C. Bocarnea, and Charles A. Wickman. "Validating a Practitioner's Instrument Measuring the Level of Pastors' Risk of Termination/Exit from the Church: Discovering Vision Conflict and Compassion Fatigue as Key Factors." Unpublished manuscript. Virginia Beach: School of Global Leadership and Entrepreneurship, Regent University, 2009. https://web.archive.org/web/20180512080533id_/https://www.regent.edu/acad/global/publications/working/Spencer-Winston-Bocarnea-Wickman%20Pastors%20At%20Risk%20working%20paper.pdf.

Springer, Andrew. "Why Authentic Christianity is Actually Queer." *Medium*, 22 June 2019. Accessed 24 February 2024. https://andrewspringer.medium.com/why-authentic-christianity-is-actually-queer-fac2084e5598.

Stone, Alyson M. "Thou Shalt Not: Treating Religious Trauma and Spiritual Harm with Combined Therapy," *Group* 37, no. 4 (2013) 323-337, https://doi.org/10.13186/group.37.4.0323.

Stone, Bryan P. "Holiness is Queer." In *Why the Church of the Nazarene Should Be Fully LGBTQ+ Affirming*, edited by Thomas Jay and Alexa Oord, 423-426. Grasmere, ID: SacraSage, 2023.

StraightWay Foundation UK. *Statement on Homosexualist Campaign Against Muslim Scholar*, StraightWay.org.uk. 17 November 2004. https://gaymuslims.files.wordpress.com/2006/02/StraightWay%20Statement%2017-11-04.pdf.

Strauss, Anselm L., and Juliet M. Corbin. *Basics of Qualitative Research: Techniques and Procedures for Developing Grounded Theory*, 2nd edition. Thousand Oaks, CA: Sage, 1998.

Street, Andrew. "Why I Won't Be Supporting The Salvation Army This Christmas." *The Sydney Morning Herald*, 7 December 2016. https://www.smh.com.au/national/nsw/why-i-wont-be-supporting-the-salvation-army-this-christmas-20161207-gt5ohs.html.

Strickland, Danielle, and Stephen Court. *Salvationism 101: Soldier Training*. Melbourne: Credo, 2009.

Severson, Eric R. "The Queerness of the Holy." In *Why the Church of the Nazarene Should be Fully LGBTQ+ Affirming*, edited by Thomas J Oord and Alexa Oord, 415-418. Grassmere, ID: SacraSage, 2023.

Talvacchia, Kathleen T. *Embracing Disruptive Coherence: Coming Out as Erotic Ethical Practice*. Eugene, OR: Cascade Books, 2019.

Tan, Rayner, Kay Jin, Timothy Qing Ying Low, Daniel Le, Avin Tan, Adrian Tyler, Calvin Tan, Chronos Kwok, Sumita Banerjee, Alex R. Cook and Mee Lian Wong. "Experienced Homophobia and Suicide Among Young Gay, Bisexual, Transgender and Queer Men in Singapore: Exploring the Mediating Role of Depression Severity, Self-Esteem and Outness in the Pink Carpet Y Cohort Study." *LGBT Health* 8, no. 5 (July 2021) 349-358. doi: 10.1089/lgbt.2020.0323.

Tasmania Law Reform Institute. *Sexual Orientation and Gender Identity Conversion Practices*. Issues Paper No 31, November 2020. https://www.utas.edu.au/__data/assets/pdf_file/0005/1415669/tlri-sexual-orientation-and-gender-identity-conversion-practices-issues-paper-2020.pdf.

Taylor, Charles. *The Ethics of Authenticity*. Cambridge, MA: Harvard University Press, 1991.

Temple, Tracey. "Exploring the Lived Religious Experiences of Gay and Lesbian Ordained Clergy in the United Methodist Church." Doctor of Philosophy thesis, University of Denver, 2019.

The Reformation Project. "An Evening with Rev. David: The Story Behind a Historic Letter About Biblical Translation." YouTube, 8 November 2019. https://www.youtube.com/watch?v=rdfxPDZEO5k.

The Salvation Army. *Building Deeper Relationships Using Faith Based Facilitation*. London: The Salvation Army International Headquarters, 2010.

———. *Called to be a Soldier: Exploring the Soldier's Covenant*. London: The General of The Salvation Army, 2020.

———. *Chosen to be a Soldier: Orders and Regulations for Soldiers of The Salvation Army*. London: The Salvation Army International Headquarters, 1994 (1987).

———. "Clarification Regarding Interview Comments on Homosexuality." The Salvation Army Australia, 23 June 2012. https://www.salvationarmy.org.au/about-us/news-and-stories/media-newsroom/20120623-clarification-sexuality-joyfm/

———. *Exploring Soldiership*. Melbourne: The Salvation Army Australia Territory, 2020.

———. "Faith-Based Facilitation." The Salvation Army International. https://www.salvationarmy.org/fbf.

———. *Guidelines for Salvationists: Conversion Therapies*. Melbourne: The Salvation Army Australia Moral and Social Issues Council, 2024. https://www.salvationarmy.org.au/scribe/sites/masic/files/IPS/Conversion_Therapies_USE_20_MARCH_2024_FINAL_CT.pdf.

———. *Handbook of Doctrine*. London: The Salvation Army, 2010.

———. "Human Sexuality." Position Statements Issued by the Authority of the General. London: The Salvation Army International Headquarters, 1980.

———. "ICL 2022, Limitless God: The Best is Yet to Come." The Salvation Army International, 26 September 2022. https://www.salvationarmy.org/ihq/news/inb260922-limitless-god-the-best-is-yet-to-come.

———. "Inclusion." The Salvation Army Australia. Accessed 20 January 2024. https://www.salvationarmy.org.au/about-us/inclusion/.

———. Letter to the First Minister of Scotland entitled "Re: The Proposed Repeal of Section 2A (28) Local Government Act 1988." 10th February 2000 (accessed 5 March 2025). https://web.archive.org/web/20110131105443/http://www.scottish.parliament.uk/business/committees/historic/x-lg/reports-00/lgr00-06-08.htm#3.

———. "Lost Vegas – The Salvation Army Provides Hope without Discrimination." Youtube, 26 February 2016, https://www.youtube.com/watch?v=W7y7tQla00M&feature=emb_logo.

———. *Marriage and the Recognition of Same Sex Unions*. Submission to the Senate Select Committee on the Exposure Draft of the Marriage Amendment (Same-Sex Marriage) Bill, 2016.

———. "Non-discrimination." The Salvation Army International Headquarters, December 2012. https://www.salvationarmy.org/ihq/nondiscrimination.

———. *Preparation for Soldiership*, 2nd ed. London: The Salvation Army, 1977.

———. *Salvation Army Ceremonies*. London: The Salvation Army, 1986.

———. *Salvation Story: Salvationist Handbook of Doctrine*. London: The General of The Salvation Army, 1998.

———. "The Doctrines of The Salvation Army: As Set Out in Schedule 1 of The Salvation Army Act 1980." The Salvation Army International Theological Council. Accessed 16 March 2024. https://www.salvationarmy.org/doctrine/doctrines.

———. "The Salvation Army Announces National Position on Safe Schools." The Salvation Army. 30 November 2016 (Accessed 3 November 2024). https://www.salvationarmy.org.au/about-us/news-and-stories/media-newsroom/salvation-army-announces-national-position-on-safe-schools/.

———. "The Salvation Army's Response to the Expert Panel on Religious Freedom." Religious Freedom Submissions. Canberra: Department of Prime Minister and Cabinet, 2018. https://www.pmc.gov.au/sites/default/files/religious-freedom-submissions/4830.pdf.

———. *The Salvation Army Year Book 2023*. London: Salvation, 2023.

———. *The Salvation Army Year Book 2024*. London: Salvation, 2024.

The Salvation Army Australia Territory. *Local Mission Delivery Handbook*. Melbourne: The Salvation Army, 2021.

The Salvation Army New Zealand, Fiji, Tonga and Samoa Territory. "Guidelines for Salvationists: Gay Conversion Therapies." The Salvation Army New Zealand, Fiji, Tonga and Samoa Territory. September 2020. https://www.salvationarmy.org.nz/sites/default/files/uploads/2020/Oct/guideline_for_salvationists-gay_conversion_therapies.pdf.

———. "Same-Sex Attitude Survey (2014)." Accessed 8 July 2023. https://www.salvationarmy.org.nz/same-sex-attitude-survey.

The Salvation Army Policy, Research & Social Justice Unit. *Draft Gay Conversion Discussion Paper for Salvationists*. Melbourne: The Salvation Army Australia Territory, 2022.

The Salvation Army United Kingdom and Republic of Ireland Territory. "Conversion Therapy: We Stand Against This Practice." The Salvation Army United Kingdom and Republic of Ireland Territory, 2023. https://www.salvationarmy.org.uk/conversion-therapy.

Thobaben, James. "Wesleyan Politics at the End of Modernity." In *Exploring a Wesleyan Political Theology*, edited by Ryan Nicholas Danker, 97-126. Nashville: Wesley's Foundry, 2020.

Tidd, Floyd. "Salvation Army Responds to Bill C-6." In *Salvationist*. 4 December 2020. https://salvationist.ca/articles/salvation-army-responds-to-bill-c-6/.

Tomlin, Sam. "The Politics of Salvation in The Salvation Army: How Stanley Hauerwas Can Help Develop the Radical Polity of the Corps." Master of Christian Leadership thesis, St Mellitus College, 2017.

Trodden, Christopher. *The Shape of Calling*, 2nd edition. Melbourne: The Salvation Army, 2021.

Tyson, Christina. "Rejecting Rejection: My Journey to Becoming an LGBTI Ally." In *Thought Matters Conference Papers*, 26 Oct 2017. Wellington: The Salvation Army New Zealand, 2017. Accessed 7 July 2023. https://www.salvationarmy.org.nz/sites/default/files/uploads/rejecting_rejection-c_tyson-oct_2017.pdf.

Urban, Rebecca. "Salvation Army Retreat on Safe Schools Program." *The Australian*, 5 December 2016. https://www.theaustralian.com.au/nation/education/salvation-army-in-retreat-on-safe-schools-program/news-story/12b1825e3d842abe5e960a58d304aa93.

Van Buskirk, Gregory P. "The 'Relational Hermeneutic' of Contemporary Wesleyan Moral Theology." Academia.edu, 2013, accessed 25 May 2024. https://www.academia.edu/4066611/The_Relational_Hermeneutic_of_Contemporary_Wesleyan_Moral_Theology.

van der Walt, Charlene. "These are the Days of the Raw Despondence: Finding a Queer Kindred in the Book of Jonah." In *Queering the Prophet: On Jonah, and Other Activists,* edited by L. Julianna M. Claassens, Steed Vernyl Davidson, Charlene van der Walt and Ashwin Shysen. London: SCM, 2023.

Venn-Brown, Anthony. *A Life of Unlearning: A Journey to Find the Truth.* Sydney: New Holland, 2004.

Vines, Matthew. *God and the Gay Christian: The Biblical Case in Support of Same-Sex Relationships.* New York: Convergent, 2014.

Waldron, John D. *The Salvationist Lifestyle.* New York: The Salvation Army USA Eastern Territory, 1989.

Walker, Rebecca E. *Call to Arms: Soldiership Training for The Salvation Army,* ed. Barry Gittins. Melbourne: The Salvation Army Australia Southern Territory Mission Resources Department, 2014.

Walkowitz, Judith R. *City of Dreadful Delight: Narratives of Sexual Danger in Late-Victorian London.* Chicago: Chicago University Press, 1992.

Waters, Chris. "The Homosexual as a Social being in Britain, 1945-1968." *Journal of British Studies* 51, no. 3 (July 2012) 685-710 https://www.jstor.org/stable/23265600.

Wheaton College. "Community Covenant." About Wheaton. Accessed 11 October 2023. https://www.wheaton.edu/about-wheaton/community-covenant/.

Wilcox, Melissa M. *Coming Out in Christianity: Religion, Identity and Community.* Bloomington: Indiana University Press, 2003.

Wilkins, Clara L., Joseph D. Wellman, Negin R. Toosi, Chad A. Miller, Jaclyn A. Linsek and Lerone A. Martin. "Is LGBT Progress Seen as an Attack on Christians?: Examining Christian/ Sexual Orientation Zero-Sum Beliefs." *Journal of Personality and Social Psychology: Interpersonal Relations and Group Processes* 122, no. 1 (July 2021) 73-101. http://dx.doi.org/10.1037/pspi0000363.

Willett, Graham. "Australia: Seven Jurisdictions, One Long Struggle." In *Sexual Orientation, Gender Identity and Human Rights in the Commonwealth: Struggles for Decriminalisation and Change,* Institute of Commonwealth Studies, 207-229. London: University of London, 2013. https://sas-space.sas.ac.uk/4808/.

Williamson, Iain R. "Internalized Homophobia and Health Issues Affecting Lesbians and Gay Men." *Health Education Research* 15, no. 1 (February 2000) 97-107. https://doi.org/10.1093/her/15.1.97.

Wilson, Nancy L. *Our Tribe: Queer Folks, God, Jesus and the Bible.* San Francisco: Harper, 1995.

Windsor, Doug. "Salvation Army Uses Homeless to Fight Gay Benefits." *ChicagoPride.com,* 24 May 2004. https://chicago.gopride.com/news/article.cfm/articleid/1824489.

Wold, Donald J. *Out of Order: Homosexuality in the Bible and the Ancient Near East.* Grand Rapids: Baker, 1998.

Wood, Andrew William, and Abigail Holland Conley. "Loss of Religious or Spiritual Identities Among the LGBT Population." *Counselling and Values* 59, no. 1 (April 2014) 95-111. https://doi.org/10.1002/j.2161-007X.2014.00044.x.

Wood, Karina. "Whosoever Will: The Gap Between Belief and Practice in The Salvation Army's Inclusion of LGBTIQA+ persons." Included. Accessed 22 April 2024 (published 2019). https://includedpage.com/Research—-Whosoever-Will.html.

Yarhouse, Mark A., Janet B. Dean, Stephen P. Stratton, and Michael D. Lastoria. *Listening to Sexual Minorities: A Study of Faith and Sexual Identity on Christian College Campuses.* Downers Grove: IVP Academic, 2018.

Yarhouse, Mark A., Janet B. Dean, Stephen P. Stratton, Heather Keefe, and Michael D. Lastoria. "Listening to Transgender and Gender Diverse Students on Christian College Campuses." *Journal of Religion and Health* 60, no. 6 (September 2021) 4486-4499. doi:10.1007/s10943-021-01425-0.

Yuill, Chick. *Battle Orders: Salvation Army Soldiership.* London: The Salvation Army United Kingdom Territory, 1989.

www.ingramcontent.com/pod-product-compliance
Lightning Source LLC
Chambersburg PA
CBHW051632230426
43669CB00013B/2271